Darwin and Catholicism

Darwin and Catholicism

The Past and Present Dynamics of a Cultural Encounter

Edited by

Louis Caruana

t&t clark

Published by T&T Clark
A Continuum imprint
The Tower Building, 11 York Road, London SE1 7NX
80 Maiden Lane, Suite 704, New York, NY 10038

www.continuumbooks.com

British Library Cataloguing-in-Publication Data
A catalogue record for this book is available from the British Library

Typeset by RefineCatch Limited, Bungay, Suffolk
Printed and bound in Great Britain by Athenaeum Press Ltd,
Gateshead, Tyne and Wear

ISBN: HB: 978-0-567-47631-9
       PB: 978-0-567-25672-0

CONTENTS

NOTES ON CONTRIBUTORS

Albino Barrera, O.P., is a Professor of Economics and Theology at Providence College. His publications include *Globalization and Economic Ethics: Distributive Justice in the Knowledge Economy* (Palgrave MacMillan, 2007), *Economic Compulsion and Christian Ethics* (Cambridge, 2005), *God and the Evil of Scarcity: Moral Foundations of Economic Agency* (Notre Dame, 2005) and *Modern Catholic Social Documents and Political Economy* (Georgetown, 2001).

Frank Budenholzer is a Professor in the Department of Chemistry at Fu Jen Catholic University in Taipei County, Taiwan, and a Catholic priest, member of the Society of the Divine Word. Since 1997 he has shifted his research and teaching to the relationship of religion and science, with publications in both English and Chinese. He is contributing co-editor of: *Religion and Science in the Context of Chinese Culture* (ATF Press, 2006) and *The Cosmos in Becoming: Perspectives of Christianity and Chinese Religions* (forthcoming).

Patrick H. Byrne is a Professor and Chairperson of Philosophy at Boston College. After obtaining a bachelor's degree in physics, he wrote his doctoral dissertation on Einstein's philosophy of science. His recent publications include: *The Dialogue between Science and Religion: What we have learned from one another?* (Scranton, 2005); *Analysis and Science in Aristotle* (SUNY, 1997); 'Lonergan, Evolutionary Science, and Intelligent Design', *Revista Portuguesa de Filosofia* (2007), 'Evolution, Randomness and Divine Purpose: A Reply to Cardinal Schörnborn', *Theological Studies* (2007), and 'The Goodness of Being in Lonergan's Insight', *American Catholic Philosophical Quarterly*, (2007). He is currently working on a book on Bernard Lonergan's ethics.

Louis Caruana, S.J., is Senior Lecturer in Philosophy at Heythrop College, University of London, and Adjunct Scholar at the Vatican Observatory. He did his doctoral studies at Cambridge University, and taught for nine years at the Pontifical Gregorian University, Rome. His research interests and published articles are mainly in the area of explanation, philosophy of mind and philosophy of science. He is the author of *Holism and the Understanding of Science* (Ashgate, 2000); *Science and Virtue: an essay on the impact of the scientific mentality on moral character* (Ashgate, 2006).

Louis Dupré is the Riggs Emeritus Professor in the Philosophy of Religion at Yale University. He wrote and edited a number of books in the fields of Marxism, philosophy of religion and philosophy of culture. Among his principal works are *Passage to Modernity* (Yale, 1993); *The Enlightenment and the Intellectual Foundations of Modern Culture* (Yale, 2004); *The Other Dimension* (Doubleday 1972); *Marx and the Social Critique of Culture* (Yale, 1983); *Religion and the Rise of Modern Culture* (Notre Dame, 2008). He is presently preparing a study on *Romanticism: The Unfinished Revolution*. He has lectured in Belgium, The Netherlands, Italy, Ireland and at many American universities.

François Euvé, S.J., is a Professor of Systematic Theology at the Centre Sèvres-Facultés jésuites de Paris, where he holds the *Chair Teilhard de Chardin*. He is also Dean of the Faculty of Theology. His research interests are in anthropological theology, in the relationship between theology and the natural sciences, and especially in the thought of Pierre Teilhard de Chardin. His books include *Penser la création comme jeu* (Le Cerf, 2000); *Science, foi, sagesse* (L'Atelier, 2004); *Darwin et le Christianism. Vrais et faux problèmes* (Buchet-Chastel, 2009).

Harry J. Gensler, S.J., is Professor of Philosophy at John Carroll University, Cleveland, USA. He has strong interests in logic, ethics, and where these two areas intersect. His ten books include *Ethics: A Contemporary Introduction, Formal Ethics, Historical Dictionary of Ethics, Historical Dictionary of Logic, Introduction to Logic* and *The Sheed & Ward Anthology of Catholic Philosophy*.

John F. Haught (PhD from Catholic University, 1970) is Senior Fellow, Science & Religion, Woodstock Theological Center, Georgetown University. His area of specialization is systematic theology, with a particular interest in issues pertaining to science, cosmology, evolution, ecology and religion. He is the author of seventeen books, most of them on the subject of science and religion. His latest books are: *Is Nature Enough?: Meaning and Truth in the Age of Science* (Cambridge, 2006) and *God and the New Atheism: A Critical Response to Dawkins, Harris, and Hitchens* (WJK Press, 2008).

Pawel Kapusta, S.J., is lecturer in Theology at the Pontifical Gregorian University, Rome. He has doctoral degrees in both physics (London) and theology (Frankfurt). His interests include contemporary challenges to Christian credibility, methodological issues in theology and the natural sciences, and the hermeneutics of Christian doctrine. He is the author of *Articulating Creation, Articulating Kerygma: A*

Theological Interpretation of Evangelisation and Genesis Narrative in the Writings of Augustine of Hippo (Peter Lang, 2005).

Don O'Leary is a Senior Technical Officer in the Department of Anatomy, Biosciences Institute, University College Cork, Ireland. He is professionally qualified in both science and history, and his research is published in both disciplines. Don O'Leary is the author of *Vocationalism and Social Catholicism in Twentieth-Century Ireland* (Irish Academic Press, 2000) and *Roman Catholicism and Modern Science: A History* (Continuum, 2006). He is a co-author of five neuroscience papers published in *Acta Neuropathologica, The Journal of Anatomy* and *Molecular and Cellular Neuroscience.*

Stephen J. Pope is a Professor of Theological Ethics at Boston College, Chestnut Hill, Massachusetts. He received his PhD from the University of Chicago. He is the author of *Human Evolution and Christian Ethics* (Cambridge UP, 2007) and *The Evolution of Altruism and the Ordering of Love* (Georgetown, 1994). He is the editor of *The Ethics of Aquinas* (Georgetown UP, 2003) and *Hope and Solidarity: Jon Sobrino's Challenge to Theology* (Orbis Press, 2008).

Nicholas Rescher is a Distinguished University Professor of Philosophy at the University of Pittsburgh where he is also Chairman of the Center for Philosophy of Science. He has served as a President of the American Philosophical Association, of the American Catholic Philosophy Association, of the American G. W. Leibniz Society, of the C. S. Peirce Society, and the American Metaphysical Society. Author of some hundred books ranging over many areas of philosophy, over a dozen of them translated from English into other languages, he is the recipient of eight honorary degrees from universities on three continents.

Fáinche Ryan was, until recently, Director of Studies at the Margaret Beaufort Institute of Theology, Cambridge, and an associate lecturer at the Divinity Faculty, University of Cambridge. She has now taken up a post as lecturer in Systematic Theology at the Mater Dei Institute, Dublin City University. She is the author of *Formation in Holiness. Thomas Aquinas on Sacra doctrina* (Leuven: Peeters, 2007).

Peter van Inwagen is the John Cardinal O'Hara Professor of Philosophy at the University of Notre Dame. His work has been mainly in the field of analytical metaphysics. He is the author of several books, including *An Essay on Free Will* and *Material Beings*. He has delivered the Wilde Lectures at Oxford University and the Gifford Lectures at St Andrews University. He is a member of the American Academy of Arts and Sciences.

Joseph M. Życiński is a Professor of Philosophy at the Catholic University of Lublin, Poland, Archbishop of Lublin, Grand Chancellor of the Catholic University of Lublin, member of the European Academy of Science and Art in Salzburg, member of the Pontifical Council for Culture, and member of the Russian Academy of Natural Sciences. He is the author of forty-six books on topics in science, philosophy and Christian faith, including *God and Evolution: Fundamental Questions of Christian Evolutionism* (The Catholic University of America, 2006).

PREFACE

Although a lot has been written about the impact of Charles Darwin's intellectual legacy on Christian thought in general, little has focused specifically on his impact on the Catholic tradition, taken as a whole. This volume is meant to fill this gap in the literature. It explores the influence of Darwin's ideas on Catholicism as an interaction between two worldviews, an interaction stretching over a period of, roughly, 150 years. It offers the reader historical insights, it brings the reader to the present state of the various debates, and, in some contributions, explores new ground. It is with great pleasure that I express my profound thanks to the contributing authors. With great generosity and dedication, they applied their expertise in view of the completion of this volume in spite of their many other important commitments. I extend my thanks also to Thomas Kraft, Associate Publisher for Theology at T&T Clark, whose encouragement was very supportive, and also to many others for their help at various stages of this work – in particular, to Dushan Croos, who helped with the translation of Chapter 5 from the original French, to Toon Cavens and Wouter Blesgraaf, who helped with the translation of Chapter 12 from the original Dutch, and to Mary-Ann Webb for help with the bibliography.

Louis Caruana
Heythrop College
University of London

Chapter 1

INTRODUCTION

Louis Caruana

Charles Darwin (1809–82) explained the history and variety of life on earth in terms of evolution. He formulated his ideas for the first time in his book *On the Origin of Species*, published in 1859. His theory brought together under one explanation the innumerable different phenomena observable in the organic world, and suggested moreover that the difference between humans and non-human animals was a difference in degree rather than one of kind.[1] Because of this, philosophical and theological debates soon became inevitable. What had been formulated as a new scientific theory quickly developed into a new philosophical and cultural paradigm with repercussions in ethics, anthropology and theology.

Since then, Darwinism has undergone, and is still undergoing, a kind of evolution in its own right. It is ramifying in various directions, many of which were unforeseeable by Darwin.[2] The original insight, in broad strokes, consisted in the combination of the idea of common ancestors for all living organisms with the idea of natural selection. In the 1850s, around the same time as the appearance of Darwin's *On the Origin of Species*, Gregor Mendel was making biological breakthroughs regarding the role of genes in heredity. Years later, it became clear that a given trait of an organism is often the product of not just one gene but of many genes acting together. This showed researchers how Darwin's idea of natural selection could operate at the genetic level. Eventually, mainly through the work of Theodosius Dobzhansky, natural selection was established on a new foundation of genetics, and the so-called Modern Synthesis emerged as a way of explaining the origin of species in terms of genetics. With the discovery of DNA, scientists can now compare the genetic codes of species, uncovering clear traces of evolution that go back billions of years. Despite all these developments away from what is observable by simple means, the impact of this scientific theory on other disciplines and on culture in general has seen no waning. Nowadays, evolutionary explanation is discussed not only in ethics, anthropology and theology, as in

Darwin's day, but also in economics, social theory, psychology, linguistics, semantics and other disciplines.

This book deals with the impact of Darwin on Catholicism. In the sixteenth and seventeenth centuries, the Copernican revolution had dislodged humanity from the security of the centre of the universe and sent it rushing and spinning through space. Heliocentrism affected Christian teaching in various significant ways, and, once the paradigm took root, there was no turning back.[3] The Darwinian revolution dislodged humanity from the security of a fully law-governed universe and tossed it into the darkness of chance and contingency. The Darwinian paradigm, as the previous one, affects Christian teaching in various ways, and these ways are not all negative. There may very well arise a number of valuable opportunities recognizable only through painstaking research and reflection. A lot has already been written about the impact of evolutionary ideas on how to argue for the existence of God, on how to deal with the problem of evil and on similar particular arguments related to religion. These writings represent the interaction between Darwinism and Christianity in general. What has received less attention is the specific interaction between Darwinism and Catholicism, considered as two major, different and sometimes opposed cultural dimensions in today's world.

Catholicism, of course, is correctly understood only in the light of the Christian Faith, a faith founded on the belief that God revealed himself to human beings through the prophets and finally through Jesus of Nazareth. Since the earliest times, the task of Christian thinkers has been to combine the accepted philosophy of the time with Christian beliefs so as to arrive at a coherent theoretical and practical synthesis. In the course of history, the Catholic Church has emerged as a world-wide religious organization that, apart from other things, emphasizes the importance of doctrinal and liturgical unity. It comprises a hierarchical structure of administration and supervision that ensures the desired degree of unity of faith and of practice across the globe and across the centuries. In spite of the major changes that the Catholic Church has experienced through its long history, the project of retaining such unity has been preserved as an ideal more or less intact from the very beginning. For these last 800 years or so, Catholic thinking has tended to express this unity by referring to the philosophical and theological system known as the Aristotelian–Thomistic tradition. Thomas Aquinas brought together into a coherent synthesis the thought of Aristotle and the Biblical teachings as developed by various Councils and Fathers of the Church. This synthesis formed the structure with respect to which most of the Church's theological output could be checked to guarantee the required degree of unity of doctrine.

The unity the Catholic Church seeks should be distinguished from stagnant uniformity. In fact, any change in doctrine and practice that is recognized as a genuine, continuous development from previous principles and beliefs is considered welcome.[4] The last decades of the twentieth century have seen a significant change on various fronts within the Catholic Church, brought about especially by the Second Vatican Council. One of these involved the acknowledgement of legitimate schools of philosophical thought other than the Aristotelian–Thomistic tradition. In 1998, even though Aquinas was still openly considered a valuable model for theologians, John Paul II announced plainly that 'the Church has no philosophy of her own nor does she canonize any one philosophy in preference to others'.[5] The implication is that just as Aquinas accomplished a useful synthesis between Christian belief and the then newly discovered Aristotelian philosophy of his time, so also scholars nowadays need to do this between Christian belief and new paradigms, such as the evolutionary one.

Interest in Darwinism from the Catholic viewpoint has recently been rekindled in various ways. There have been various significant published debates between academics and publications directed towards the general public. There have also been, moreover, some significant statements from the highest levels of the hierarchy. For instance, in 1996, John Paul II published his important *Message to the Pontifical Academy of Sciences on Evolution*. In 2002, the *International Theological Commission* under the supervision of Cardinal Joseph Ratzinger, the present Pope Benedict XVI, published the document 'Communion and Stewardship: Human Persons Created in the Image of God'. And in 2005, Cardinal Christoph Schönborn was the cause of some concern with his apparent endorsement of Intelligent Design in his *New York Times* article 'Finding Design in Nature'.

One of the basic assumptions underlying the content of this volume is that scientists, philosophers and theologians have something to learn from each other, even though each enjoys full competence in only one of these disciplines. Scientists might learn something about how their conclusions can fit into a wider context that includes the meaning of their life, of human longing, of family values and of moral integrity. Science is not, and cannot be, the source of theological formulations. Such formulations arise from personal religious experience nourished by communities of faith, kept alive by the memory of a tradition of encounter with God. Nevertheless, philosophers and theologians might learn something from scientists. They might learn something about how new knowledge of the physical world could make some parts of the accepted categorical framework more acceptable than others.[6]

This is not a book on evolutionary biology. It does not deal directly with the scientific content of Darwin's ideas and of his intellectual heritage. It is certainly not intended as a scientific justification of the Catholic Faith. And it is neither an attempt at making scientists change their methods and ignore pertinent data, nor an attempt at making theologians discard their characteristic task, which essentially involves interpretation and historical mediation. What this volume offers is different. Taking Darwin's empirical work as the core of a cultural paradigm, it places the accent on philosophy and theology. The book presents a valuable panorama of arguments and reflections from outstanding scholars working in various fields related to Catholicism. The specially commissioned essays offer useful overviews of current debates and carry such debates forward.

There are three parts; they correspond to major characteristic orientations within Catholic scholarship. The first part is historical. It reflects the sensitivity that Catholic scholarship shows towards tradition and towards the precedents and arguments that had determined previous decisions. The second and third parts correspond to the areas of major concern for Catholic intellectual efforts: morals and faith. Darwinism has had a major impact on both these areas.

Part One starts with a comprehensive historical overview. For the purpose of this section of the book, the time-line between Darwin and the present is divided into two periods, with the midpoint being the appearance of Pope Pius XII's encyclical *Humani Generis* in 1950. As regards the first of these periods, Don O'Leary examines a number of arguments that were used as a reaction against Darwinism by prominent Irish Catholic writers, mainly clerics. It must be kept in mind that, towards the end of the nineteenth century and the beginning of the twentieth century, the presence of Irish communities all over the world made the views of the Catholic Church in Ireland very influential. The background for the general anti-modernist reaction within the Church was effectively the *Syllabus of Errors* (1864) and the documents of Vatican Council I (1869–70). One of the major issues causing concern to anti-modernists was precisely Darwinism. O'Leary highlights the importance of Tyndall's Belfast Address of 1874, and explains how Catholic Bishops defended their views by recalling that science and faith are always in harmony. He recalls how the fact that basic evidence was lacking encouraged some Catholic scholars to view popular Darwinism as nothing more than a crude theory on stilts. O'Leary concludes that Irish Catholic apologists continued to express unrelenting opposition to Darwinism. This happened even though there were indications of considerable tolerance for it in the wider church.

Chapter 3 deals with the period including and following *Humani Generis*. Pawel Kapusta focuses on statements made by Popes and dicasteries or commissions of the Holy See, and presents them as a meaningful advance. He divides this chronological development into four stages: from 1950 until the beginning of the Second Vatican Council; from the Council until the beginning of the pontificate of John Paul II; from this event until the Pope's significant 1996 address to the Pontifical Academy of Sciences mentioned above and then from this speech up until today. His reflections converge onto the claim that many current Catholic approaches to this issue need to clarify the relation, and the boundaries, between science, philosophy and theology.

The three chapters that follow offer a detailed study of three eminent Catholic thinkers whose views remain fundamental for most intellectual work in this area. The first one is Thomas Aquinas. Fáinche Ryan argues that the concept of God defended by Aquinas is compatible with the Darwinian explanation of biological life. She first shows that what Darwin rejected was the idea that God is the great designer, understandable on the model of a human designer. For Aquinas, however, God is better understood in terms of first cause, understood in a metaphysical sense. Every existing thing participates in God not only as regards its being, but also as regards its proper action. For Aquinas, the first cause and secondary causation are not to be understood as realized within a temporal sequence. On the contrary, they are to be seen as co-responsible for the observed effect. Ryan recalls here the example of the pen and the scribe: both enable the word to be written, each in a specific way. She draws the conclusion that Aquinas thus seems to have left a door open for a general theory of evolution in nature. Darwin's discovery of descent with modification is not incompatible with Aquinas's concept of the perfectibility of the universe.

Chapter 4 concentrates on Teilhard de Chardin. François Euvé sets off by highlighting the fact that Teilhard is more interested in human beings than in evolution at large. Teilhard, in fact, considers humans to be an indispensable key for the understanding of global evolution. Instead of starting from matter and then building his explanation towards humans, he goes the other way round. For Teilhard, Darwinism remains unfortunately a prisoner of analytic thinking. For a complete understanding of life, one needs to supplant analytic thinking with synthetic thinking. Hence, Teilhard argues that Darwinism explains all there is to explain about life on earth up until the appearance of humans. Euvé summarizes Teilhard's position as follows. Once *Homo sapiens* comes onto the scene, in a sense, Darwinian principles start failing while Lamarckian principles start prevailing. Darwinism emphasizes dispersal and ramification. But Teilhard insists that there is also an opposite movement in life: convergence and synthesis. Traces of this latter dimension are already present in the pre-human history of life, but they become really evident when humans appear. The struggle between convergence and divergence is always present. For its correct interpretation, which depends on the virtue of hope, Teilhard claims that we need to refer to the Christian doctrine of the Paschal Mystery.

The other eminent Catholic thinker who made a contribution regarding Darwin's impact on philosophy and theology was Bernard Lonergan. In Chapter 6, Patrick Byrne and Frank Budenholzer offer a detailed study of Lonergan's originality in this area, namely his concept of 'emergent probability'. This concept is based on the observation that the universe contains what Lonergan calls cycles of change. The term, 'emergent probability' refers to recurrent organized changes that can be explained via laws of nature. Simpler cycles provide the conditions of recurrence of ever more complex cycles, without themselves being dependent on the occurrence of these more complex cycles. From here, Lonergan shows how the emergence of lower and simpler cycles make the emergence of subsequent, more complex schemes more probable. When applied to the organic world, this idea allows him to propose a meta-narrative about the evolving universe, a meta-narrative that neither disregards nor depends upon Darwin's discoveries. Byrne and Budenholzer explain how Lonergan then proceeds into the realm of theology by bringing in the fact that the universe is intelligible. If God is described as the act of unrestricted understanding, what for us look like random mutations are, from God's perspective, in fact not contingent at all. To be able to appreciate this aspect to the full, one needs an element of faith.

At this point, attention is shifted towards more current debates. Part two contains five chapters that explore philosophical topics related to Darwinism, and they address fundamental questions on explanation, ethics, mind, society and economics. The first of these chapters is an original reconsideration of the philosophical presuppositions of intelligent design arguments. Nicholas Rescher argues that the world being intelligently designed does not presuppose its being designed by intelligence. Instead, intelligent design calls for arrangements that favour the prospering of intelligence in the world scheme of things. While evolutionary intelligence-friendly evolutionism, what he calls *noophelia*, does not require assumptions of a theological nature, it certainly is harmoniously compatible not only with traditional theism but indeed even with Catholic doctrine, as suggested for instance by Teilhard de Chardin.

In the next chapter, Peter van Inwagen argues that the major problem with many present day academics who discuss evolutionary theory is that they add on something to what the theory of evolution really entitles them to claim. He shows that some have the tendency to claim that the theory explains all there is to explain, while others from the opposite camp show the tendency to claim that there are certainly other aspects of reality it does not explain. Both these positions, according to van Inwagen, are mistaken. The correct position is one of agnosticism as regards the explanatory power of this theory. He shows the wisdom of his option by referring to three case-studies from the history of science. He then proceeds by arguing that the agnosticism he is advocating does not oblige him to adopt agnosticism with respect to the existence of God. There is no inconsistency between Darwinism and theism.

These two chapters dealing with the explanatory potential and limitations of evolutionary explanations are followed by a chapter on ethics. Harry Gensler argues that the Catholic intellectual tradition, when it is authentic, is open to new ideas that have a rational basis, whether these ideas come from Aristotle or from Darwin or from anyone else. He illustrates how Darwin's approach to ethics needs some expansion in details. To Darwin's natural-history account of how moral thinking evolved in humans, Gensler adds scientific ideas about genetics and sociobiology; he also adds philosophical ideas about moral rationality and the golden rule. He then completes the picture by adding theological ideas about how the evolutionary process could be viewed as a part of a larger divine plan, a plan that goes from the first moment of creation to the fulfilment of the cosmic process. The resulting view, he concludes, is entirely in line with the Catholic tradition.

From the realm of ethics, the reader is invited to move on to the realm of mind and society. My contribution aims at bringing some clarity into the complexity one faces when evolutionary explanation is applied to the realm of moral and social behaviour. The chapter evaluates two perspectives, one related to purely philosophical arguments, and the other to arguments from within the Catholic tradition. The challenges faced by evolutionary ethics discernible from the secular viewpoint turn out to be practically the same as those discernible from the religious viewpoint. Whether we discuss the issues in terms of intentional states or in terms of freedom of human beings created in the image of God, the result seems to be the same: evolutionary explanation turns out to be useful to some extent but not across the board. It leaves out the distinctively moral aspect of individual and social behaviour. When it comes to economic life, as the chapter by Albino Barrera shows, Darwinism and Catholicism diverge from each other on the notion of competitive selection. They partially concur, however, in their views on the evolutionary nature of economic life and on the use of causality as a framework of analysis. Examining and understanding these points of divergence and partial convergence take on even greater importance in the face of contemporary globalization in which ever larger areas of social life are governed by market rules.

Part Three of the volume is dedicated to theological topics. The areas covered deal with God's immanence in creation, moral theology and the problem of evil. Louis Dupré argues that the theory of evolution cannot be legitimately regarded as a full, philosophically complete justification of the nature of biological processes. It assumes certain principles – principles that it does not itself explain, such as the dynamic tendency of matter towards increasing complexity, or the very presence of a DNA code, which regulates the process and is responsible for the changes that occur in it. Opposing naïve ideas about God and about God's relation to creation, Dupré defends the idea of God's total immanence within creation, as advanced by Eckhart and Nicolas of Cusa. Reference to medieval thought is also made by Joseph Życiński in the next chapter. Here, we have an interesting discussion on the use of the principle of ontological parsimony, commonly known as Ockham's razor. This principle is often used as a justification for the elimination of all reference to God in our understanding of the universe. Even at the level of purely scientific research, however, the use of this principle has had a negative heuristic effect. It has often slowed down the process of discovery. Once this principle is thrust aside, the theory of evolution invites theologians to explore models for understanding God other than the one involving determinism and laws of nature. Życiński argues that this theory suggests resorting to aesthetics. It encourages theologians to rediscover how to express the nature of God in terms that are reminiscent of a composer unfolding the possibilities hidden within his composition.

In the following chapter on moral theology, Stephen Pope argues that moral theologians have legitimate concerns about Darwinian, or Darwinian-based, forms of social morality that undercut human dignity. They have legitimate concerns also when such forms of social morality indiscriminately reject all forms of religion, and advance without justification a naturalistic ontology under the guise of natural science. Yet Pope also maintains that a critical appropriation of legitimate scientific methodological reductionism, of the type that recognizes the limits of scientific discourse, is no threat to moral theology. Indeed, a properly interpreted theory of Darwinian evolution, he argues, supports a view of human nature as constituted by capacities that can be incorporated into and trained within the Christian moral life. This reflection is followed by the final chapter concerning the apparently senseless suffering of sentient life over the millennia. John Haught faces this challenge squarely and arrives at the surprising conclusion that Darwinism, far from causing insurmountable theological problems, allows believers to speak of Divine providential care in an authentically biblical way. It allows believers to speak of Divine providence as operating characteristically in the mode of promise, as indicated at various places in the Bible. It allows believers to recall how God's providential activity is, in the first place, that of providing a vision of how the world may become new, and of inviting humans to be free, hopeful and creative. The suffering of all sentient life, dramatically exposed by the Darwinian worldview, gains meaning by the believer's recalling that such suffering is subject, it as well, to God's promise of a new creation. Haught concludes that, to render more meaningful the new picture of the world provided by the theory of evolution, we need to retrieve the idea that providence is not simply guidance, order, design or plan, but, above all else, a promise.

It is hoped that this brief overview of the material covered in this volume provides a taste of the rich, fertile ground that Darwin's legacy has opened up for Catholic scholarship. In the following chapters, numerous areas will be explored, numerous viewpoints will be considered. The reader can rest assured, however, that this volume will certainly not be the last word on the subject.

Notes

1 For the complete works of Charles Darwin, and other related material, see http://darwin-online.org.uk/

2 D.J. Depew and B.H. Weber, *Darwinism Evolving: Systems Dynamics and the Genealogy of Natural Selection* (The MIT Press, 1996).

3 See Louis Caruana, 'The Jesuits and the quiet side of the scientific revolution', in: Thomas Worcester (ed.), *The Cambridge Companion to the Jesuits* (Cambridge: Cambridge University Press, 2008), 243–62.

4 See, for instance, John Henry Newman, *An Essay on the Development of Christian Doctrine* (London: Longmans, Green, 1890). See also *Dogmatic Constitution on Divine Revelation, Dei Verbum* § 8, trans. L. Walsh, in: A. Flannery (ed.), *Vatican Council II, The Conciliar and post Conciliar Documents* (Herefordshire: Gracewing, 1992), 754: 'The Tradition that comes from the apostles makes progress in the Church, with the help of the Holy Spirit. There is a growth in insight into the realities and the words that are being passed on. [. . .] Thus, as the centuries go by, the Church is always advancing towards the plenitude of divine truth, until eventually the words of God are fulfilled in her.'

5 Pope John Paul II, *Faith and reason: Encyclical letter 'Fides et ratio'* (Dublin: Veritas, 1998), § 49.

6 The history of the rich interaction between science, philosophy and theology is well presented and documented in David C. Lindberg & Ronald L. Numbers (eds), *God and Nature* (University of California Press, 1986).

Part One

HISTORICAL STUDIES

Chapter 2

FROM THE *ORIGIN* TO *HUMANI GENERIS*: IRELAND AS A CASE STUDY

Don O'Leary

Social, economic and political conditions have to be taken into account when studying the history of science. The pursuit of scientific knowledge does not occur in a cultural vacuum.[1] There is an obvious international context but national and local circumstances frequently need to be considered. The same points apply to the history of religion. It cannot be understood within the narrow confines of theology and devotional practices without taking cognizance of the cultural milieu in which it is immersed. It too has its international, national and local dimensions. Various responses to developments in modern science have occurred within, as well as between, Christian denominations, and these were influenced by local circumstances.[2] Therefore, in reference to Roman Catholicism, it should not be surprising that, at national level, every community has had its own unique experience of modern science. Cognizance has to be taken of this when studying Catholic attitudes towards Darwinism.

At first glance, the church in Ireland may seem of little consequence in the vastness of international Roman Catholicism. Such an impression would be misleading. Emmet Larkin wrote in his *Historical Dimensions of Irish Catholicism* (1984) that in the nineteenth century Irish Catholicism became:

> a world-wide phenomenon in the English-speaking world. Not only did the Roman Catholic Churches in England and Scotland become essentially Irish, but the Churches in the United States, English-speaking Canada, South Africa, Australia, and New Zealand were all strongly influenced by the developing values and mores of Irish Roman Catholicism.[3]

In view of the above it can be argued that the church in Ireland is eminently suitable as a case study for shedding light on Catholic responses to Darwin in the English-speaking world.

In the late nineteenth century, the Roman Catholic Church in Europe had to contend with a number of adversarial developments such as liberalism, anti-clericalism, anti-Catholicism and the *Risorgimento* which led to the overthrow of the Papal States. Furthermore, like other Christian denominations, it felt threatened by the criticism of Biblical narratives arising from advances in archaeology, history and science. Many Catholics perceived that the church was under attack, which in turn made it more difficult for them to engage positively with a range of contentious issues – social, political and intellectual. The Vatican's response, as indicated by the *Syllabus of Errors* (1864) and the pronouncements of Vatican Council I (1869–70), was reactionary rather than progressive. The Irish Catholic bishops, aware of the difficulties faced by the universal church, adopted a similar attitude. Moreover, they had their own particular difficulties to contend with. They found themselves in a Protestant-dominated state where anti-Catholicism was not uncommon. Their sense of vulnerability was clearly evident in their determination to exert control over that sector of the educational system which was to serve their own community. In addressing the issue of higher education, they demanded a Catholic university for a Catholic people. The Irish Catholic hierarchy did not regard The University of Dublin (Trinity College, Dublin), dominated by Protestants, as suitable for the education of Catholics because they believed it was dangerous to their faith. Neither were the majority of bishops satisfied with the non-denominational Queen's Colleges at Cork, Galway and Belfast. The Catholic University of Ireland was set up in 1854 as an alternative but this educational enterprise eventually ended in failure. Irish Catholic opinions about science, and especially about Darwinism, were influenced considerably by the ongoing controversy about higher education in the late nineteenth century.

There was probably a consensus amongst the Irish Catholic clergy that science could be misused, especially when it seemed to contradict the Bible. Under these circumstances science could 'eclipse the light of faith . . . and be degraded into the accidental tool of infidelity'.[4] There was a tendency to view science as something that was external and threatening, rather than as an instrument of progress and enlightenment. There were a number of reasons for this. In the nineteenth century, Irish scientists were overwhelmingly Protestant and, within that sector of the population, mostly members of the Church of Ireland.[5] Furthermore, the institutions of Irish science came increasingly under the control of the English-based Department of Science and Art from 1853 when the department was founded. Irish science, therefore, was to a large extent, controlled by civil servants in London.[6]

It is likely that Irish Catholics perceived science as an activity strongly linked to Protestantism and foreign influence.[7] Such a perception could only have militated against the acceptance of Darwinism, especially when Darwinism seemed so inimical to the belief that the natural world was divinely created.[8] And yet, in the 1860s, Darwin's theory received very little attention in Catholic Ireland.[9] However, in the early 1870s a number of developments brought Darwin to the attention of those Irish Catholics who were aware of how science could be used to promote irreligious ideas.

In Darwin's *Descent of Man* (1871), humans were seen as highly developed primates, as part of the evolutionary process and subject to natural selection like other species. Furthermore, Darwin had speculated about the origins of moral and religious beliefs, and the social instincts of humans, in purely utilitarian and scientific terms.[10] This led a contributor to *The Irish Ecclesiastical Record* to conclude that:

> the obvious tendency of his doctrines is – if not to eliminate creative action altogether out of the universe of mind and matter, and to reduce the order of harmony of Nature to the results of blind fortuitous forces, which would be to obliterate God altogether – at least to place the Creator at such a distance from His works that His supervision, providence, and justice may be safely ignored.[11]

The promotion of Darwinism in Ireland, and elsewhere, was certainly not helped when eminent supporters of Darwin expressed anti-Catholic opinions. Thomas Henry Huxley believed that the Roman Catholic Church was the 'vigorous and consistent enemy of the highest intellectual, moral, and social life of mankind'. He declared, in controversy with the English Catholic scientist, St George Jackson Mivart, that 'in addition to the truth of the doctrine of evolution, indeed, one of its greatest merits in my eyes, is the fact that it occupies a position of complete and irreconcilable antagonism' to the Catholic Church.[12] At the time, Huxley and a number of other like-minded scientists were actively promoting the professionalization of science and seeking to free it from clerical and other external influences, especially in the educational system. The expression of anti-Catholic sentiments worked to the advantage of professional scientists, enabling them to benefit from anti-papal opinion in Britain.[13] There was probably some awareness of Huxley's anti-Catholicism amongst the clergy of Ireland arising from the sharp differences of opinion published in 1871–72. Huxley's visit to Ireland's leading Catholic seminary, St. Patrick's College, Maynooth, about 1873, could only have intensified such awareness. On that occasion he spoke candidly to the professors of the college about his opposition to Roman Catholicism.[14] His assertion of an inevitable conflict between Roman Catholicism and science received attention in *The Irish Ecclesiastical Record* in 1874.[15] This journal had a considerable influence on the intellectual formation of priests in Ireland and the opinions expressed between its covers can be taken as very much in accordance with the dominant hierarchical outlook.[16]

The strong association between Darwinism and anti-Catholicism was evident in John Tyndall's Belfast Address in August 1874. Tyndall was a close personal friend of Huxley. Speaking at Belfast, as President of the

British Association for the Advancement of Science (B.A.A.S.), Tyndall
anticipated that science would in time enlighten the youth of Ireland and
act as a bulwark against 'any intellectual or spiritual tyranny'. He urged
the expulsion of theological influences from science.[17] In the same speech,
he spoke about natural selection and Darwin. The wonders of nature were
to be explained by natural causes, not by invoking divine intervention.
Tyndall praised Darwin for his analytical and 'synthetic' skills and the
'solidity of his work'.[18]

Tyndall's Belfast Address elicited antagonized responses from both
Catholics and Protestants, not only in Ireland but abroad also.[19] His
provocative opinions received widespread attention largely because of
his status as President of the B.A.A.S.[20] In the polemical atmosphere of
the early 1870s, exacerbated considerably by the publication of Darwin's
Descent of Man (1871), the reaction against the Belfast Address was probably much sharper than it would otherwise have been.[21] The Irish Catholic
bishops responded with a pastoral letter. Tyndall, whose background was
Irish Protestant, had already come to the attention of the Irish Catholic
hierarchy. Protestants were seen as particularly vulnerable to losing their
religious faith when they immersed themselves in scientific studies. Tyndall,
who now embraced a pantheistic variant of scientific naturalism,[22] was
presented as an ideal example.[23]

In their response to Tyndall's Belfast Address, the bishops observed
that threats to the wellbeing of the church emanated from two sources.
The first was of an intellectual nature, epitomized by Tyndall. The second
was political and in this context the bishops referred explicitly to the fall
of the Papal States. Under such hostile circumstances they were in no
mood to engage in intellectual innovation, especially when they saw strong
connections between Protestantism, materialism and Darwinism.

The bishops took the opportunity to make the point that their policy of
insisting on control over university education for Catholics was now even
more justified in the light of Tyndall's explicit expectations that professors
of science would disseminate 'infidelity and irreligion' to the malleable
youth of Ireland.[24] The bishops maintained that science, properly understood, was in perfect harmony with the Catholic faith. Tyndall's views
were judged to be unscientific. He had strayed far beyond the boundaries
of experimental evidence in his attempts to use science against the church.
Fortified by these perceptions, the bishops felt confident in dismissing
natural selection as an ephemeral and unsubstantiated idea in scientific
thinking.[25]

Catholic apologists were concerned about two aspects of biological evolution – natural selection, which seemed to exclude God from nature – and
the inclusion of humans in the evolutionary process. In both cases, scientific arguments could be invoked as a basis for rejection. Although biological evolution was generally accepted by scientists, Darwinism suffered

a sharp decline from the 1870s to about the early 1920s. As alternative theories such as neo-Lamarckism and orthogenesis gained support Darwinists had to contend with a number of valid scientific arguments against natural selection. The extension of evolutionary theory to include humans could also be challenged because of lack of evidence. The fossil record did not yield a single specimen which could be reliably taken as a link between humans and their hypothetical ape ancestors.[26]

Irish Catholic authors took comfort in Darwin's difficulties. For example, the recalculation of the age of the earth by the physicist William Thomson (later Lord Kelvin), left far too little time for natural selection to work in terms of explaining the great diversity of species on earth.[27] In the light of this, it was observed in *The Irish Ecclesiastical Record* that Thomson provided 'some of the best weapons for an assault on Mr. Darwin's position'.[28] Other scientific arguments, such as the scarcity of transitional forms, were also called into service against Darwin's theory.

The highly influential Jesuit, Thomas Finlay (1848–1940), observed that erroneous ideas existed alongside well-established findings based on modern research. It was essential for Catholics to discriminate between 'undeniable scientific truths' and 'crude theories' which were in many instances 'absurd' and 'noxious'. Finlay, writing in *The Irish Monthly* in response to Tyndall's Belfast Address, expressed the opinion that Irish Catholics generally were vulnerable because they lacked the philosophical training to make the distinction between solidly established truths and ideas based on little more than speculation. Darwinism was particularly dangerous because it could be used to explain human origins without recourse to immortal souls.[29] The severest judgment of Darwin's *Descent of Man*, was not that it was unscientific – as it was held to be – but that it was contrary to revelation and was likely to destroy the hopes and faith of many Christians.[30]

The enemies of Christianity were now seen to be in the ascendant in science. Jeremiah Murphy, writing about Darwinism in *The Irish Ecclesiastical Record* (1884) maintained that Protestantism – with its 'cognate broods of heresy' – was now beneath contempt as an adversary, and helpless in the face of scientific naturalism. Revelation could only be defended by the Roman Catholic Church. This, in turn required that Catholics be informed about science so that they would be in a strong position to challenge those who used science to discredit revelation. It was essential to keep scientists 'rigidly' to 'the established facts of science'.[31] Murphy's attitude was not original. Many Catholic scientists, especially in France, had opposed evolution, or Darwin's version of it, on the basis that there was insufficient evidence.[32] Natural selection was especially vulnerable to criticism. Murphy claimed that it was an unfounded assertion and that Darwin himself was 'little better than an average specimen of the Rationalistic school' whose achievements had been grossly exaggerated. Furthermore, Darwinism was not acceptable because its main purpose was to exclude intelligent design from nature.[33] Murphy's hostility towards Darwinism was probably shared by many of his co-religionists, in Ireland and elsewhere, arising from its frequent associations with irreligious tendencies – such as atheism, agnosticism, and free thought. Furthermore, the 'eclipse of Darwinism' made it much more likely that religious apologists would reject it.[34]

Irish Catholicism, as stated earlier, had a profound influence on Catholicism in other English-speaking countries. This influence may have played a role in shaping attitudes towards evolutionary theory. In the 1870s Cardinal Paul Cullen sent 'a steady stream' of his ultramontane protégés to serve in Australian and New Zealand dioceses. It is likely that these men were highly intolerant of Darwinism, especially when many of Darwin's supporters were anti-Catholic.[35] In the *Freeman's Journal* (1898) of New York, Monsignor Michael O'Riordan of Limerick claimed that, not only had Darwinism been abandoned by scientists – the general theory of evolution had also lost credibility. His opinions were vigorously challenged by the American Catholic biologist, William Seton, through the medium of the same journal.[36]

Although the Vatican had not condemned evolutionary theory, its attitude was far from neutral on the matter. It took measures to impede the spread of evolutionary ideas amongst Catholics. But instead of issuing a public condemnation it sought to persuade offending Catholic authors to publish retractions of their works.[37] There was some awareness of the Vatican's adverse attitude towards evolution, especially human evolution, in Irish Catholic circles.[38] There is evidence of some support for evolutionary theory amongst the clergy but it was expressed tentatively. The Augustinian priest, E. A. Selley, acknowledged that God could be regarded as 'the Creator-Evolutionist' working through secondary causes provided that the 'unorthodox phase of Darwinism' was rejected. But he conceded that, even without Darwinism, evolutionary theory in general could still be seen as theologically unacceptable because creationists had pointed to 'grave difficulties' in reconciling it with the Genesis account of creation. Evolution of the human body was seen as 'at least rash, if not proximate to heresy' because it was viewed as inconsistent with the traditional teachings of the church and the consensus of theologians was against it.[39]

Darwinians in Ireland were probably relatively few in number. They were to be found especially amongst the staffs of the anthropometrics laboratory in Trinity College Dublin, the Royal College of Science and the Dublin Natural History Museum. Staff at the Dublin Natural History Museum presented natural history in terms of natural selection but it is highly significant that they did not explicitly mention Darwin because of the frequent association of Darwinism with materialism. Furthermore, no reference was made to human evolution. The cautious presentation of biological exhibits by the museum's staff indicates that there was a strong resistance to Darwinism in Ireland.[40]

When addressing questions concerning university education, Irish Catholic clerical opinion indicated a strong tendency to exercise censorship over scientific theories (such as Darwinism) which impacted on theological issues. There is some evidence to indicate that evolution, as proposed by Darwin, exerted considerable influence over the thinking of Irish scientists.[41] This probably generated considerable tension between traditionalist Catholic and mainstream scientific thinking. A number of eminent Irish scientists – even including those who were probably sceptical of natural selection – were averse to the church's intervention in debates about Darwinism because they saw it as an issue of academic freedom in the universities – in this case the right to teach science free of external interference.[42]

From a traditionalist Catholic perspective, a Darwinian explanation of human origins was untenable in view of the theological difficulties associated with it. Its demise in scientific thinking made it even less acceptable to theologians. Darwinism had been eclipsed to such an extent that it was thought to be in terminal decline as a prominent evolutionary theory.[43] There was some rejoicing in Irish theological circles about the supposed terminal decline of Darwinism in scientific thinking although there was an acknowledgement that this did not apply to evolutionary theory in general.[44]

In the early years of the twentieth century, many Roman Catholic authors grappled with a range of exegetical problems arising from the latest findings in archaeology, history and the natural sciences. A number of Catholic authors attempted to harmonize theology with the latest findings in the natural and social sciences. Their initiatives, in some cases, led them beyond the boundaries prescribed by Catholic dogma. Modernist authors put forward a number of proposals which were at variance with a core doctrine of the Catholic Church concerning the immutability and infallibility of the apostolic deposit of faith. Their outlook in this matter was based on biblical criticism and influenced by an evolutionary philosophy.[45] Two leading figures in the modernist movement, Alfred Loisy and George Tyrrell, argued that the organization and dogmas of the church had developed in response to the social milieu and needs of Catholics throughout history.[46]

The ecclesiastical authorities, during the reign of Pope Pius X (1903–14), took decisive action against the modernists. Professors and lecturers in seminaries who were suspected of holding heterodox ideas suffered censorship and dismissal from their posts. Some of those who were denounced as modernists, such as Loisy and Tyrrell, had strayed far beyond the dogmatic teaching of the church. But many Catholic scholars, although innovative and liberal in their approach to theology and the scriptures, had stayed within the limits prescribed by dogma. Ardent anti-modernists often failed to discriminate between these two categories of Catholic writers. Ireland did not escape the excesses of anti-modernism. This is evident in, for example, Walter McDonald's *Reminiscences of a Maynooth Professor*, originally published in 1926.[47] Expressing support for Darwinism when the excesses of anti-modernism were so rampant would have been dangerous for any priest.

A strong indication of clerical hostility towards Darwinism is clearly evident from Daniel Coghlan's contributions to *The Irish Ecclesiastical Record*. Coghlan, a zealous anti-modernist, had clashed with McDonald on a number of theological issues, and was later appointed bishop of Cork in 1916. He claimed that some Catholic writers had been arguing, implicitly rather than explicitly, that the origins of Catholicism could be explained by recourse to natural selection.[48] He believed that Loisy had led the way in applying Darwin's theory to explanations of the origins and development of Catholic religious beliefs.[49] According to this exposition of Loisy's published works, the Roman Catholic Church, as a social organization, had transformed itself through the centuries in a manner analogous to the adaptive changes in plant and animal species. Morality was a product of natural selection. Its function was to curb anti-social behaviour and to promote social virtues, thus enhancing the survival of humans. The church, like all living organisms, was subject to the law of natural selection and the fundamental tenets of Christian faith were merely ideals with no basis in reality. When the church acknowledged its own evolutionary development then it would be able to make peace with science.[50]

Coghlan's critique of modernism linked heresy with Darwinism which could only have militated against its acceptance in Catholic Ireland. But Darwinism, despite its association with irreligious and anti-Catholic opinions, was a scientific theory and was not necessarily incompatible with Catholic doctrine. The Belgian priest, Canon Henri de Dorlodot, maintained in his *Darwinism and Catholic Thought* (published in French in 1921, and in English in 1925) that Darwinism could not be regarded as synonymous with atheistic evolution, that it was very probable, and that Christians who insisted that Darwinism was incompatible with their faith did a disservice to their religion.[51] Traditionalists in Rome reacted strongly against the opinions of Dorlodot, despite the fact that he had not written about the more sensitive issue of human evolution. Their views were expressed through the Pontifical Biblical Commission under the presidency of Cardinal Willem van Rossum. Attempts were made to intimidate Dorlodot to publish a retraction of his thesis. But the canon enjoyed considerable support from influential figures in the church and he refused to comply. That he was able to resist such pressure, and escape condemnation, indicated that the power of the traditionalists had declined very much since the pontificate of Pope Pius X.[52]

Ernest C. Messenger's *Evolution and Theology* (1931) continued from where Dorlodot had stopped when it examined, at length, the question of human origins. Messenger observed that, from a theological perspective, there was no definite conclusion about whether human evolution was true or not. The church had not pronounced on the issue. From a scientific perspective Messenger accepted that there was strong evidence for the evolution of species. In view of this it was reasonable to believe that human evolution had occurred 'in some way', despite the fact that there was, as yet, no 'convincing scientific evidence' for it. He praised Dorlodot's book as 'a brilliant piece of work.'[53]

The works of Dorlodot, Messenger and other Catholic authors indicate that, generally, Catholic opinions about evolution moved closer to mainstream scientific thinking in the 1920s and 1930s.[54] However, this does not seem to have occurred in Ireland. There was scarcely a mention of Dorlodot and Messenger. Henry V. Gill, a Jesuit priest and scientist, anticipated that Dorlodot's book would exert 'considerable influence' on Catholic philosophy. Despite this anticipation, he was not only sceptical of Darwinism but of the general theory of evolution itself on the basis that it was 'nothing more than a theory'.[55] Messenger's book was reviewed by Professor Michael Browne of Maynooth (later bishop of Galway) in *The Irish Ecclesiastical Record*. Browne praised Messenger's work as one of 'first-rate theological importance' but strongly disagreed with Messenger's reading of evolution into the works of the Church Fathers, such as those of St Gregory of Nyssa.[56]

Irish Catholic scepticism of evolutionary theory was expressed throughout the 1920s, 1930s and 1940s, through the medium of such journals as *The Irish Ecclesiastical Record, Studies, The Irish Monthly*, and through a number of lectures on Radio Éireann.[57] Darwinism was sometimes singled out for particular criticism. Alfred O'Rahilly, professor of mathematical physics, President of University College Cork, and a well known exponent of orthodox Catholic teaching, was so trenchant in his criticism of Darwinism that a journalist with *The Irish Times* observed sarcastically that some listeners to Radio Éireann might assume that it was due to a personal disagreement with the Huxleys and their friends.[58]

Opposition to Darwinism was, of course, not unique to Catholic Ireland and some authors elsewhere continued to claim that natural selection was not a sustainable scientific hypothesis.[59] In Britain the supposed demise of Darwinism in scientific thinking was expressed against the background of an acrimonious debate between H. G. Wells attacking Roman Catholicism, and Hilaire Belloc and G. K. Chesterton defending it. Irish Catholic apologists were probably influenced, to some extent, by Belloc and Chesterton and some comfort was derived from the notion that Darwinism was 'practically dead'.[60] However, Belloc and Chesterton, both of whom believed that mainstream science had abandoned natural selection, had a poor understanding of what was really happening in science.[61] From about 1920 to 1950, Darwinism was revived and transformed (neo-Darwinism) and came to occupy a position of central importance in evolutionary biology. Furthermore, news of its revival was transmitted beyond the environs of the scientific community to a broader readership.

It seems strange that Irish Catholic apologists expressed unrelenting opposition against Darwinism at a time when its position in the life sciences was consolidated and when there were indications of considerable tolerance for it in the wider church. A tendency to associate it with irreligious and unorthodox ideologies, such as materialism, communism, secularism, and the excesses of *laissez faire* capitalism, probably militated considerably against its acceptance.[62] The adverse impact of such a tendency was probably greatly augmented by the very weak position of science in Irish national culture.[63] When Pope Pius issued *Humani Generis* in August 1950 Irish Catholic apologists were still far from coming to terms with neo-Darwinism.

Notes

1 *Science and Society in Ireland: The Social Context of Science and Technology in Ireland, 1800–1950*, edited by Peter J. Bowler and Nicholas Whyte (Belfast: The Institute of Irish Studies, The Queen's University of Belfast, 1997).

2 See, for example, David N. Livingstone, 'Science, region, and religion: the reception of Darwinism in Princeton, Belfast, and Edinburgh', in *Disseminating Darwinism: The Role of Place, Race, Religion and Gender*, edited by Ronald L. Numbers and John Stenhouse (Cambridge: Cambridge University Press, 1999), 7–38.

3 Emmet Larkin, *The Historical Dimensions of Irish Catholicism* (Washington D.C.: The Catholic University of America Press; Dublin: Four Courts Press, 1984), 9. See also Patrick Corish, *The Irish Catholic Experience: a historical survey* (Dublin: Gill and Macmillan, 1985), 215.

4 Jeremiah Molony, 'The Catholic Education Question', *The Irish Ecclesiastical Record*, n.s., 8 (August 1872): 491, quoting Newman's 'Lectures on Education', *Catholic University Gazette*.

5 Gordon L. Herries Davies, 'Irish Thought in Science', in: *The Irish Mind: Exploring Intellectual Traditions*, edited by Richard Kearney (Dublin: Wolfhound Press, 1985), 305–6; James Bennett, 'Science and Social Policy in Ireland in the Mid-nineteenth Century,' in: *Science and Security in Ireland*, edited by Bowler and Whyte, 38; Steven Yearley, 'Colonial science and dependent development: the case of the Irish experience', *Sociological Review* 37 (1989): 312–13.

6 Richard A. Jarrell, 'The Department of Science and Art and control of Irish science, 1853–1905', *Irish Historical Studies* 23, no. 92 (1983): 330–47; and Yearley, 'Colonial science', 316.

7 See John Wilson Foster, 'Nature and Nation in the Nineteenth Century', 417, 424; and Dorinda Outram, 'The History of Natural History: Grand Narrative or Local Lore?' 468; both in *Nature in Ireland: A Scientific and Cultural*

History, edited by John Wilson Foster and Helena C. G. Chesney (Dublin: The Lilliput Press, 1997).

8 See John Hedley Brooke, 'Revisiting Darwin on Order and Design', in: *Design and Disorder: Perspectives from Science and Theology*, edited by Niels Henrik Gregersen and Ulf Görman (Edinburgh: T & T Clark, 2002), 31–2; and Don O'Leary, *Roman Catholicism and Modern Science: A History* (New York: Continuum, 2006), 22; in reference to Emanuel Rádl, *The History of Biological Theories*, trans. E. J. Hatfield (London: Oxford University Press, 1930), 94–5.

9 L. Perry Curtis Jr., *Apes and Angels: The Irishman in Victorian Caricature*, rev. ed. (Washington: Smithsonian Institution Press, 1997), 104; and Nicholas Whyte, *Science, Colonialism and Ireland* (Cork: Cork University Press, 1999), 157.

10 Charles Darwin, *The Descent of Man, and Selection in Relation to Sex* (1871; with an introduction by John Tyler Bonner and Robert M. May, Princeton, NJ: Princeton University Press, 1981), see especially vol. 1, 65–8, 104–6; and vol. 2, 385–405.

11 J. G. C., 'Darwinism', *The Irish Ecclesiastical Record*, n.s., 9 (1873): 361.

12 Jacob W. Gruber, *A Conscience in Conflict: The Life of St George Jackson Mivart* (Westport, CT: Greenwood Press, 1960), 92.

13 Frank M. Turner, *Contesting Cultural Authority: Essays in Victorian Intellectual Life* (Cambridge: Cambridge University Press, 1993), 195. See also Frank M. Turner, 'The Victorian Crisis of Faith and the Faith that was Lost', in: *Victorian Faith in Crisis: Essays on Continuity and Change in Nineteenth-Century Religious Belief*, edited by Richard J. Helmstadter and Bernard Lightman (Stanford, CA: Stanford University Press, 1990), 18–9.

14 Wilfrid Ward, *Problems and Persons* (London: Longmans, Green and Co., 1903), 234–5.

15 'The Church and Modern Thought – IV', *The Irish Ecclesiastical Record*, n.s., 10 (1874): 102, quoting Huxley, *Lay Sermons*, 68.

16 Cardinal Paul Cullen founded *The Irish Ecclesiastical Record* in 1864 for the purpose of creating closer links between the Irish church and Rome. Corish, *Irish Catholic Experience*, 210. The main function of *The Irish Ecclesiastical Record* was to facilitate the discussion of issues 'intimately connected with the professional studies of a priest' but it was also intended to include articles pertaining to literary, scientific, historical and archaeological topics which were the subject of public attention. T. J. C., 'Introductory', *The Irish Ecclesiastical Record*, 3d ser., 1 (1880): 1.

17 John Tyndall, *Fragments of Science: A Series of Detached Essays, Addresses, and Reviews*, vol. 2 (New York: D. Appleton & Co., 1896), 197.

18 Ibid., pp. 177–80.

19 Much has been written about Tyndall's Belfast Address. See David N. Livingstone, 'Darwin in Belfast: The Evolution Debate', in: *Nature in Ireland*, edited by Foster and Chesney, 387–408; John Wilson Foster, *Recoveries: Neglected Episodes in Irish Cultural History 1860–1912* (Dublin: University College Dublin Press, 2002), 14–48; Matthew Brown, 'Darwin at church: John Tyndall's Belfast Address', in: *Evangelicals and Catholics in Nineteenth-Century Ireland*, edited by James H. Murphy (Dublin: Four Courts Press, 2005), 235–46; Thomas Duddy, *A History of Irish Thought* (London: Routledge, 2002), 251–7; W. H. Brock, N. D. McMillan and R. C. Mollan (editors), *John Tyndall: Essays on a Natural Philosopher* (Dublin: Royal Dublin Society, 1981; and O'Leary, *Roman Catholicism and Modern Science*, 31–9.

20 A. S. Eve and C. H. Creasey, *Life and Work of John Tyndall* (London: Macmillan, 1945), 186–7.
21 See Ruth Barton, 'John Tyndall, Pantheist: A Rereading of the Belfast Address', *Osiris*, 2d ser., 3 (1987): 121.
22 Ibid., p. 134.
23 'The Church and Modern Thought – V', *The Irish Ecclesiastical Record*, n.s., 10 (1874): 237–45.
24 'Pastoral Address of the Archbishops and Bishops of Ireland to their Flocks', 14 October 1874, in *Pastoral Letters and Other Writings of Cardinal Cullen*, edited by Patrick Francis Moran, vol. 3 (Dublin: Browne and Nolan, 1882), 606–7.
25 Ibid., pp. 595–6.
26 Peter J. Bowler, *Evolution: The History of an Idea*, 3d ed. (Berkeley, CA: University of California Press, 2003), 208–10.
27 Adrian Desmond and James Moore, *Darwin* (London: Penguin Books, 1992), 547, 566–7.
28 J. G. C., 'Darwinism', 339.
29 T. F., 'Mr. Tyndall at Belfast', *The Irish Monthly* 2 (October 1874): 563–5.
30 T. F., 'The Aggressions of Science', *The Irish Monthly* 4 (December 1875): 16.
31 J. Murphy, 'Darwinism', *The Irish Ecclesiastical Record*, 3d ser., 5 (1884): 586.
32 Robert E. Stebbins, 'France' in: *The Comparative Reception of Darwinism*, edited by Thomas F. Glick (Chicago: The University of Chicago Press, 1988), 156–7; and Harry W. Paul, *The Edge of Contingency: French Catholic Reaction to Scientific Change from Darwin to Duhem* (Gainesville: University Presses of Florida, 1979), 23–4.
33 Murphy, 'Darwinism', 590–1.
34 Mariano Artigas, Thomas F. Glick and Rafael A. Martínez, *Negotiating Darwin: The Vatican Confronts Evolution 1877–1902* (Baltimore, MD: The Johns Hopkins University Press, 2006), 19–21.
35 See John Stenhouse, 'Catholicism, Science and Modernity: The Case of William Miles Maskell', *The Journal of Religious History* 22, no. 1 (February 1998): 65–6.
36 John L. Morrison, 'William Seton – A Catholic Darwinist', *The Review of Politics* 21, no. 3 (1959): 573–5.
37 Artigas, Glick and Martínez, *Negotiating Darwin*.
38 Philip Burton, 'St Augustine and the "Missing Link', *The Irish Ecclesiastical Record*, 4th. ser., 5 (May 1899): n. 3, 455; and n. 1, 457. Burton referred to Marie Dalmace Leroy's retraction of his *L'Évolution Restreinte aux Espèces Organiques* (1891, *Evolution Limited to Organic Species*), published in *The Tablet* (6 March 1897), 379. He also quoted John Cuthbert Hedley, Bishop of Newport, in *The Tablet* (14 January 1899) who accepted, although with some doubt, that the Holy Office regarded the idea of human evolution as 'rash and something more'. See also Alfred J. Rahilly, 'The Meaning of Evolution', *Studies* 1 (March 1912), n. 1, 41, referring to the censorship imposed on Marie Dalmace Leroy, sourced from *Civiltà Cattolica* (7 January 1899): 49.
39 E. A. Selley, 'The Nebular Theory and Divine Revelation: II', *The Irish Ecclesiastical Record*, 4th. ser., 13 (1903): 418–29; see especially 421–2, 428–9. For another expression of cautious acceptance of the idea that God created through the evolutionary process see John Meehan, 'Haeckel and the Existence of God', *The Irish Ecclesiastical Record*, 4th. ser., 14 (1903): 148.

40 Juliana Adelman, 'Evolution on display: promoting Irish natural history and Darwinism at the Dublin Science and Art Museum', *The British Journal for the History of Science* 38, no. 139 (December 2005): 427–8.

41 Greta Jones, 'Scientists against home rule', in: *Defenders of the Union: A survey of British and Irish unionism since 1801*, edited by D. George Boyce and Alan O'Day (London: Routledge, 2001), 192.

42 See Jones, 'Scientists against home rule', 192–3; idem, 'Darwinism in Ireland', in *Science and Irish Culture: Why the History of Science Matters in Ireland*, edited by David Attis and Charles Mollan (Dublin: Royal Dublin Society, 2004), 134–5; and *idem*, 'Catholicism, Nationalism and Science', *The Irish Review*, no. 20 (1997), 50.

43 Peter J. Bowler, *The Eclipse of Darwinism: Anti-Darwinian Evolution Theories in the Decades around 1900* (Baltimore, MD: The Johns Hopkins University Press, 1983).

44 Charles Gelderd, 'Modern Ideas on Darwinism', *The Irish Ecclesiastical Record*, 4th ser., 32 (July 1912): 1–9.

45 Alec R. Vidler, *The Modernist Movement in the Roman Church: Its Origins and Outcome* (London: Cambridge University Press, 1934), 57–8.

46 Kenneth Scott Latourette, *Christianity in a Revolutionary Age: A History of Christianity in the Nineteenth and Twentieth Centuries*, vol. 1: *The Nineteenth Century in Europe: Background and the Roman Catholic Phase* (London: Eyre and Spottiswoode, 1959), 317.

47 Walter McDonald, *Reminiscences of a Maynooth Professor* (Cork: Mercier Press, 1967); 195–6, 201–10. See also Patrick J. Corish, *Maynooth College 1795–1995* (Dublin: Gill and Macmillan, 1995), 247–57.

48 Daniel Coghlan, 'Evolution: Kant and the Loisy Theory of the Evolution of Christianity-II', *The Irish Ecclesiastical Record*, 4th ser., 21 (1907), 62.

49 Daniel Coghlan, 'Evolution: Darwin and the Abbé Loisy-I', *The Irish Ecclesiastical Record*, 4th ser., 19 (June 1906), 481.

50 Ibid., pp. 485–7, pp. 491–5.

51 Canon Dorlodot, *Darwinism and Catholic Thought*, trans. Ernest Messenger (New York: Benziger Brothers, 1925), see 6, 42, 62–3.

52 Raf De Bont, 'Rome and Theistic Evolutionism: The Hidden Strategies behind the "Dorlodot Affair", 1920–26', *Annals of Science* 62, no. 4 (October 2005): 457–78.

53 Ernest C. Messenger, *Evolution and Theology: The Problem of Man's Origin* (London: Burns Oates & Washbourne, 1931). Quotations are from pp. xxiv and 275.

54 O'Leary, *Roman Catholicism and Modern Science*, 133–40.

55 H. V. Gill, 'Catholics and Evolution Theories', *The Irish Ecclesiastical Record*, 5th ser., 19 (June 1922): 614–24; quotations from n. 2, p. 614 and 621.

56 Michael Browne, 'Evolution and Theology: Another Opinion', in: *Theology and Evolution: A Sequel to Evolution and Theology*, edited by E. C. Messenger (London: Sands & Co., 1951), 67–71; quotation from 71. Browne's article was originally published in *The Irish Ecclesiastical Record* (May 1932).

57 Michael Browne, 'Modern Theories of Evolution', parts 1 to 4, *The Irish Ecclesiastical Record* 27–8 (1926); Henry V. Gill, 'Entropy, Life and Evolution', *Studies* 22 (March 1933): 129–38; Alfred O'Rahilly, *Religion and Science: Broadcast Talks* (nine lectures broadcasted by Radio Éireann in early 1944, published in a booklet without amendments by *The Standard* newspaper in 1948), chapter 6; Geoffrey Taylor, 'Evidence and Evolution'; five articles in

The Irish Monthly 76 (March to October 1948) as follows: I, 117–23; II, 157–64; III, 221–7; IV, 407–13; V, 464–71. Taylor's articles were based on broadcasts from Radio Éireann (January, April and May, 1948).

58 'Radio Commentary: A Unique Broadcaster', in newspaper cutting from *The Irish Times*, 28 February 1946, in The O'Rahilly Papers, Scrapbook 5, Archives of Blackrock College, Dublin.

59 See Gordon McOuat, and Mary P. Winsor, 'J. B. S. Haldane's Darwinism in its religious context', *The British Journal for the History of Science* 28, no. 97 (June 1995): 227–31.

60 See P. Sexton, 'Science and Religion', *The Capuchin Annual* (1933): 192.

61 Peter J. Bowler, *Reconciling Science and Religion: The Debate in Early-Twentieth-Century Britain* (Chicago: The University of Chicago Press, 2001), 359–60, 395–8.

62 Alfred O'Rahilly, 'Mr. Wells and Man', *The Standard*, 23 February 1940; vol. 3, 'Reply to Wells 1940', Alfred O'Rahilly Papers, Archives of Blackrock College, Dublin; Liam Brophy, 'In Search of *Homo Perfectus*', *The Irish Ecclesiastical Record*, 5th ser., 68 (December 1946): 398–9; and Geoffrey Taylor, 'Evidence and Evolution 1 – The Evolutionary Setting', *The Irish Monthly* 76 (March 1948): 117, 122.

63 See Herries-Davies, 'Irish Thought in Science', 308–10; and Yearley, 'Colonial science and dependent development', 324–7.

Chapter 3

DARWINISM FROM *HUMANI GENERIS* TO THE PRESENT

PAWEL KAPUSTA

The period from the publication in 1950 of Pius XII's Encyclical Letter *Humani generis* to the present has seen significant changes in Catholic theological and doctrinal approaches towards the question of (neo-) Darwinism, considered both as a purely scientific theory, and as a *Weltanschauung*. Evidently, in a brief, panoramic presentation, it is impossible to present all the developments in Catholic thought on the subject within this period, as – especially after the Second Vatican Council – Catholic theology has witnessed a veritable proliferation of view-points and models that have aimed to integrate evolutionary paradigms. The principal focus of this chapter is on statements made by Popes and dicasteries or commissions of the Holy See. Contributions made by individual Catholic theologians will be mentioned only in a summary manner to indicate changes taking place in Catholic Biblical exegesis and systematic theology, mainly in theological anthropology.[1]

The present chapter covers four periods, articulated respectively by the publication of *Humani generis*, the beginning of the Second Vatican Council, the beginning of the pontificate of John Paul II, and the latter's address to the Pontifical Academy of Sciences from the year 1996. All such divisions are largely subjective and presuppose a decision regarding which developments are more important than others. *Humani generis* marks the first recognition in an official document of the Magisterium of the Catholic Church that some form of evolutionary theory is reconcilable with Catholic doctrine.[2] The Second Vatican Council was obviously a very significant impulse for new approaches in theology, and brought an intensification of the on-going debate on many issues in Fundamental theology (such as: the interpretation of Scripture and its inerrancy; the relationship between the natural sciences, philosophy and theology and the domain of competence of the Teaching Office of the Church) and in dogmatic theology (such as: the nature of original sin; the Catholic understanding of Creation and Providence) which are of direct relevance to the relationship between Catholic thought and the theory of evolution.

The accession of John Paul II to the See of Peter initiated a period of intensive dialogue between the Catholic Church and the natural sciences and exhibits an unprecedented openness on the part of a Pope towards evolutionary theories. I have chosen to end this third period with his well-known, and recently much discussed, address to the Pontifical Academy of Sciences in 1996. The final section covers recent declarations made by the Holy See and some renewed controversies.

1. *From* Humani Generis *to the Second Vatican Council* (1950–62)

Any Christian approach to the theory of evolution will necessarily pre-suppose a kind of hermeneutics for understanding the creation accounts of the Book of Genesis. The Pontificate of Pius XII had already seen the publication in 1943 of the Encyclical *Divino afflante Spiritu* which con-cerned itself with Biblical studies and acknowledged the legitimacy of the historical-critical approach in exegesis. It acknowledged, above all, the necessity of taking into account, when interpreting a given Biblical text, the *Sitz im Leben*, the cross-cultural influences and the literary genre.[3] Of particular interest is the idea that the *literal sense* intended in a text may not be exactly what the modern mentality understands as such. This idea is repeated with respect to *historical sense* in an important letter of the Papal Biblical Commission to the Archbishop of Paris in 1948: the first eleven chapters of the Book of Genesis may indeed not intend to relate 'history' in the modern sense of the term.[4] At least in principle, the way is thus opened for interpretations of the creation accounts of the Book of Genesis which can be more easily reconciled with findings issuing from the natural sciences.

The Encyclical *Humani generis* from the year 1950 reiterates the above points of view with regard to exegesis, but its scope is also more general.[5] It is concerned with 'some false opinions which threaten to undermine the foundations of Catholic doctrine' and contains two passages which refer explicitly to the theory of evolution.[6] The first passage includes three negative observations. First, the doctrine of evolution (*evolutionis systema*) is accepted by many without sufficient evidence being as yet offered by the natural sciences themselves (*nondum invicte probatum in ipso discipli-narum naturalium ambitu*). Secondly, the supporters of evolutionary the-ory claim that it applies to the origin of all things (*ad omnium rerum originem pertinere*). Thirdly, they further harbour a monistic and pan-theistic view of a universe in continuous evolution (*indulgeant opinationi monisticae ac pantheisticae mundi universi continuae evolutioni obnoxii*).[7] The intention of Pius XII is to offer critical comments of a meta-scientific nature; they regard the epistemological status of the theory of evolution, the domain of application of the theory and its possible philosophical generalizations (and their consequences).

The second passage discusses the 'positive' sciences and their relationship to Christian doctrine.[8] Of importance is Pius XII's affirmation that the church does not prohibit serious research or free discussion between Catholic scientists and theologians on the origins of the human body from already existent and living matter.[9] However, there are three provisos that seek to define the proper attitude of Catholics taking part in research and discussion. First, all must be willing to accept the authority of the church in matters of doctrine. Secondly, the human soul cannot be conceived of as evolving from matter (Catholic doctrine requires faith in the immediate creation of human souls by God).[10] And thirdly, the distinction between scientifically demonstrated 'fact' (*de factis demonstratis*) and mere 'hypothesis' (*de hypothesibus*) in matters which are to a greater or lesser extent related to Christian doctrine must be taken into account.[11] In fact, those who prematurely hold evolution to have been demonstrated with certainty abuse their scientific freedom.[12]

As previously indicated, it is important to realize that this passage constitutes the first recognition in a document of the Magisterium addressed to the Bishops of the whole Church that some form of 'evolutionism' may be compatible with Christian faith.[13] At the same time, as far as the biological origins of man are concerned, the Pope sees a grave difficulty in reconciling polygenism – that is, the doctrine that the human race descended independently from more than one individual or primordial couple – with the traditional Christian teaching on original sin. The reason is that, according to *Rom* 5:12–19, as interpreted by the Council of Trent, original sin proceeds from the personal sin of the one Adam and is transmitted to *all* human beings by generation.[14] However, the difficulty is couched in a language that makes clear that the Pope does not intend to make a doctrinal decision with regard to a definitive Catholic option for monogenism.[15]

Although the public allocutions of Pius XII are marked by a clear enthusiasm and appreciation for the natural sciences, this generally regards physics, astronomy or astrophysics, that is, scientific areas of research which only indirectly touch on the origin of human beings.[16] In *Humani generis*, human evolution is discussed in very general terms. There is no mention of Darwin, of natural selection or of mutations.[17] The subject of genetic mutations is, however, considered in an allocution to participants of the First International Symposium of Medical Genetics, delivered at Rome in September, 1953.[18] Here, the Pope is once more keen to stress the merely conjectural nature of many of the affirmations which are entertained in the context of the theory of evolution: descent of all living creatures from a single organism; the exact nature of the passage or 'evolution' from one species to another; the point at which hominids become human; the question of geological dating. Research on human origins is in its infancy but should be encouraged, so that more certain results can be obtained.[19] If there are limits on this research, their aim, according to Pius XII, is to avoid regarding hypotheses as proven facts, to ensure that certain sources of knowledge are complemented by others, to guarantee the correct interpretation of the scale of values and of the degree of certainty afforded by certain sources of knowledge.[20] These limitations reveal once more that Pius XII is concerned not with the biological data as such, or even with their theoretical elaboration, but with an adequate epistemological evaluation of theories of evolution.

Catholic theology in the 1950s and early 60s is still largely hostile to the concept of evolution; the idea of integral transformism (in particular, that the human species has developed continuously and completely naturally from an inferior species) is generally rejected. A mitigated transformism (demanding punctuated, exterior interventions for the initialization of life and of specifically human consciousness) is also treated by many with reserve.[21] Coupled to this is a general tendency to defend monogenism.[22] The exegetes take the lead in breaking new frontiers. Detailed historical and textual studies reveal the 'mythical' character of many aspects of the creation accounts of the Book of Genesis, influenced as they are by ancient oriental themes. Many authors specify, however, that this does not exclude a symbolic communication of religious truth.[23]

2. *The Second Vatican Council and the Pontificate of Paul VI* (1962–78)

Pope John XXIII, elected on October 28, 1958, did not address the relationship between Christian doctrine and evolution.[24] The most significant and far-reaching act of his pontificate was the convocation of the Second Vatican Council.[25] If we are to look for any traces of the evolution debate in the final documents of this Council, we should turn our attention to the Pastoral Constitution on the Church in the World, *Gaudium et spes*. Neither *Humani generis* in its tone, nor indeed ecclesiastical superiors in their actions, had been particularly favourable towards the thought of Teilhard de Chardin. Within a decade of his death (1955), however, we find certain important concepts of an influential conciliar document 'converging' with several of his ideas, among which one can mention: the understanding of the universe and of humanity as dynamic and evolving; the perfection of the world as a task facing humanity; socialization as a process of unification; the close relationship between creation and redemption and the cosmic role of Christ.[26] More generally, the constitution urges theologians to take seriously the new discoveries of science and, indeed, all the faithful should 'incorporate the findings of new sciences and teachings and the understanding of the most recent discoveries with Christian morality and thought'.[27] The Church sees great value in the 'study of the sciences and exact fidelity to truth in scientific investigation'.[28] It 'profits from the progress of the sciences [. . .] through which greater light is thrown on the nature of man and new avenues to truth are opened up'.[29] Of notable significance is the Council's denunciation of 'certain attitudes (not unknown among Christians) deriving from an insufficient perception of the legitimate autonomy of science; they have occasioned conflict and controversy and have misled many into opposing faith and science'.[30]

What of the tenets of *Humani generis* itself? The Second Vatican Council makes no explicit reference to biological evolution or to the monogenism–polygenism debate. However, several months after the final session of the Council, on 11 July 1966, in an allocution to participants of a symposium on original sin, Pope Paul VI takes up both themes.[31] Presupposing the truth of polygenism, some authors, the Pope says, deny that original sin began with Adam's disobedience 'at the beginning of history'. This is irreconcilable with Catholic Doctrine.[32] Moreover, however, the theory of evolution, whenever it is understood to deny the immediate creation of each and every human soul by God, is not acceptable. Paul VI is simply repeating the doctrine of *Humani generis*: apart from the specific question of polygenism, he also seeks to limit the domain of evolution to the corporeal element of the human person. And, indeed, even Pius XII's observation that one should not confuse hypothesis with demonstrated fact is not absent from his allocution.[33] A short time later, the Congregation for the Doctrine of the Faith published a letter sent to the Presidents of the Episcopal Conferences: they are warned against certain errors among which are those that 'obfuscate the question of Adam's original guilt and the transmission of his sin to all mankind'.[34] As far as the monogenism–polygenism debate is concerned, however, Catholic theologians had already been moving towards different horizons.[35] In the post-conciliar period, they are developing conceptions of theological anthropology capable of accommodating polygenism or monophyletism.[36] Karl Rahner, for example, passes from (metaphysical) arguments in favour of monogenism to a certain preference for polygenism, while, in 1967, advising the Magisterium of the Church not to intervene in the matter any more.[37] This question is linked to new interpretations of original sin, particularly – using traditional Catholic theological terminology – of the *peccatum orginale originans*, that is, the sin of origins, whose consequence is the *peccatum originale orignatum*, the tendency to sin which is found in all human beings. Using the convenient typology of B. Pottier, one can say that there are two principal post-conciliar options concerning originating sin.[38] The first views it as structural: it is due to a natural immaturity[39] or is imbedded in the anthropological make-up of the human race.[40] The second, more traditional, is personal and historical: it is really a sin of Adam and Eve, although under the influence of advances in the natural sciences, the supporters of this view tend to think more in terms of a collective Adam (or Eve) or of a type of corporate personality more in the line of monophyletism rather than monogenism.[41]

In the late 1960s and 70s, in large part due to the diffusion of the works of Teilhard de Chardin, systematic theologians in favour of evolutionary approaches constitute the vast majority.[42] Within such frameworks, much ink flows on the subject of God's action in the process of evolution and – more specifically – on the question of the immediate creation of the human soul by God. One distinguishes, for example, principle causality from instrumental causality: God is Principle Cause, just like the (invisible) mind of a sculptor; other physical, finite causes find their analogue in the sculptor's hands and chisel – these are the (visible) instrumental causes.[43] These categories are applied to cases in which the effect 'exceeds' the natural capacities of the (instrumental) cause, as in the case of the creation of the human soul in living matter. The scheme – originally used to account for the co-creation with God of new human individuals by parents – is subsequently invoked to explain God's 'evolutionary concourse' with creation: the generating organism is empowered to exercise a causality which exceeds its own natural capacity, giving rise to a new species. One can still speak of a certain Divine 'intervention' as Principle Cause in the emergence of the human species. Such causality is special and differs from God's ordinary concourse with creatures as Primary Cause (i.e. as the Cause of natural causality).[44] Other ways of envisioning the creation of the soul are perhaps more conducive to the concept of its evolution. Rahner speaks of an absolute, internal ground within every agent which enables its 'becoming', that is, its self-transcendence. In this perspective, even matter has an affinity for spirit.[45]

3. The Pontificate of John Paul II (1978–96)

After Paul VI's address to the symposium on Original Sin, few indeed are the interventions of this Pope in matters related to evolution. After the very brief pontificate of John Paul I, his successor, John Paul II, shows a genuine interest in a dialogue with culture, including the natural sciences. Many and varied are his affirmations concerning the natural sciences, almost exclusively positive in character, and he actively encourages theologians and scientists to work together in search of the truth.[46] For all truth has its source in God and this means that, ultimately, the truths of science and faith cannot be in conflict. When they appear to be, it is due to a confusion of two distinct orders of knowing: that of faith with that of reason. John Paul II readily admits that the Church has in the past not fully respected the legitimate competence and autonomy of the sciences.[47]

Little over a year after his election as Pope, John Paul II addressed the Pontifical Academy of Sciences on the occasion of the 100th anniversary of the birth of Albert Einstein.[48] He reiterates the legitimate autonomy of the sciences and states that the Church has benefited from scientific progress, not least from the fact that the sciences constitute a critical instance which purifies religion from a magical conception of the world and remnants of superstition.[49] The beneficial influence of scientific advances also extends to epistemological questions, for example, to the problem of the interpretation of Scripture. Galileo's own words are quoted to support the view that an adequate interpretation of Scripture requires careful attention to literary genres, in order to get to the true sense of the Biblical text.[50] The mention of Galileo is not insignificant: John Paul II was the Pope who somewhat later – in July, 1981 – commissioned a detailed study of the history and circumstances of his trial and condemnation. The commission presented its results in 1992 and, on this occasion, John Paul II delivered an allocution to the plenary session of the Pontifical Academy of Sciences.[51] Once again it is the relationship between scientific discoveries and Biblical interpretation which is at the centre of attention. In the case of Galileo, new scientific methods forced theologians to re-think their own hermeneutical criteria, a task in which many were found wanting. And, more generally, the Pope notes that such advances oblige various disciplines to re-define their proper domains of competence, their methods and the scope of their conclusions.[52] Thus, the case of Galileo has pedagogical import; one cannot exclude that one day another analogous situation may arise which will demand from all sides a heightened awareness of the limits of one's own competence. And the Pope suggests that the approach taken towards the emergence of complexity in the universe and in life on earth could serve as an illustration.[53]

It is also important, according to the Pontiff, to be aware of the fact that scientific description and formalization necessarily make use of meta-scientific concepts. The role of philosophy is thus of paramount importance, as one must take care to determine the exact nature of such concepts and distinguish the strictly scientific procedure from philosophical (or even ideological) extrapolations.[54] The example of the emergence of the human being and its brain is cited as an example. On a purely scientific level, the respective theories which seek to explain emergence cannot in themselves be taken to prove or disprove the existence of a spiritual soul, nor can they be regarded as a proof or disproof of the doctrine of creation. This is only possible subsequently within an integrated, philosophical framework.[55]

On 1 June 1988, John Paul II addressed a letter to the Director of the Vatican Observatory, George Coyne, S.J., following a study week held the previous September, sponsored by the Holy See and commemorating the Newton Tercentennial.[56] The letter, noting on the one hand, an increasing fragmentation of human knowledge into various specializations, and, on the other, several advances towards a unification of knowledge, especially in physics and in the life sciences, urges mutual dialogue and searching on the part of theology and the sciences.[57] Most notably, the Pope poses the question of the possible integration of the 'evolutionary perspective' to areas of exegesis and theology and repeats the view that religion and science stand in a relationship of mutual correction.[58] Science purifies religion from superstition and error; religion can purify science from idolatry and false absolutes.[59]

The *Catechism of the Catholic Church*, published in English in 1994 during the pontificate of John Paul II, makes little explicit reference to the theory of evolution but states that advances in scientific knowledge concerning the origin of man 'invite us to even greater admiration for the greatness of the Creator'.[60] The *Catechism* stresses the traditional distinction between scientific elaboration and philosophical or theological considerations: it is not simply a question of the 'when and how' of human origins, 'but rather of discovering the meaning of such an origin: is the universe governed by chance, blind fate, anonymous necessity or by a transcendent, intelligent and good Being called 'God'?[61] It is affirmed that the world that God creates freely is 'in a state of journeying' towards its ultimate perfection. An essential part of this journey is the appearance of certain beings and the disappearance of others; nature builds but also destroys.[62]

Important for subsequent discussions is John Paul II's address to the Pontifical Academy of Sciences of 24 October 1996.[63] Once again, the Pope affirms that exegetes and theologians must keep abreast of advances within the natural sciences as this is an aid in demarcating their own proper domains of research.[64] Noting the methodological observations made by Pius XII as far as 'evolutionism' is concerned, namely, that one should not treat this opinion as certain, demonstrated doctrine, and that one cannot totally prescind from Christian Revelation with respect to the questions the theory of evolution raises, the Pope goes on to state that, nevertheless, the current state of knowledge leads to the recognition of the theory of evolution as 'more than a hypothesis'.[65] Very much in the line of Pius XII, however, John Paul II excludes the possibility that the human soul might somehow emerge from the forces innate in living matter or as a mere epiphenomenon of matter.[66] With the human being there is an 'ontological leap'. The natural sciences can observe certain signs of this, but the exact moment of the passage to the spiritual is not observable as such; it is made manifest in the experience of self-consciousness, of freedom, in aesthetic and religious experience, and is an object that properly belongs to the fields of philosophy and theology.[67]

4. The Current Debate

On can say that the recent document of the International Theological Commission, *Communion and Stewardship: Human Persons Created in the*

Image of God (2004) presents the general attitude of Catholic theology towards theories of evolution: there is 'mounting support' for some theory of evolution; Catholic doctrine affirms Divine Creation and Providence and rejects reductionist (materialistic or spiritualistic) interpretations of the theory; Divine providential causality does not exclude contingency; the evidence for design in the universe is a scientific and philosophical question, and cannot be settled by theology; 'the structures of the world can be seen as open to non-disruptive divine action in directly causing events in the world'; the emergence of the first members of the human species (whether as individuals or in populations) 'represents an event that is not susceptible of a purely natural explanation and which can appropriately be attributed to divine intervention'.[68] A question for Catholic theology and for the Church has remained: To what extent can an evolutionary paradigm be extended from biology to encompass other domains such as sociology, psychology, epistemology and even theology itself? As theologian and Prefect of the Congregation for the Doctrine of the Faith, Joseph Ratzinger sought to maintain the distinction between evolution as a scientific theory, and evolutionism as a new form of universal philosophy.[69] Ratzinger himself has criticized transpositions of evolutionary paradigms onto theological questions, notably in the field of Biblical hermeneutics.[70]

As Pope Bendict XVI, Ratzinger has – as yet – made few direct references to current theories of evolution. However, a passage from his 2006 address to the Pontifical Academy of Sciences can be taken to be indicative of some of the current debate within the Catholic Church and beyond it. In relation to the problem of predictability in science, the Pope states:

> Science, cannot, therefore, presume to provide a complete, deterministic representation of our future and of the development of every phenomenon that it studies. Philosophy and theology might make an important contribution to this fundamentally epistemological question by, for example, helping the empirical sciences to recognize a difference between the mathematical inability to predict certain events and the validity of the principle of causality, or between scientific indeterminism or contingency (randomness) and causality on the philosophical level, or, more radically, between evolution as the origin of a succession in space and time, and creation as the ultimate origin of participated being in essential being.[71]

Of particular interest in this passage as far as the debates on evolution are concerned, is the question of the meaning one should ascribe to the 'randomness' and indeterminism of natural processes, and whether such processes exclude Divine action. The Pope clearly wishes to indicate that the question cannot be decided by the natural sciences themselves, but is above all an epistemological problem.

In fact, one could argue that keeping different levels (scientific, philosophical and theological) of knowledge and investigation distinct, as well as determining their respective boundaries, although not always straightforward, is becoming a focus for many contemporary Catholic approaches to the whole question of the relationship between neo-Darwinism and Christian doctrine. Today, the discussion is necessarily ecumenical and even inter-religious, partly due to the rise of the *Intelligent Design* movement. On the one hand, there is an effort to avoid a 'discredited concordism'.[72] On the other hand, it is clear that one should not reject a scientific theory simply because some of its proponents proceed to make claims of a philosophical – sometimes anti-Catholic – nature.[73] That confusions and controversies still arise was illustrated by the discussion following an article in the New York Times on 7 July 2005, by Cardinal Christoph Schönborn of Vienna.[74] The Cardinal claimed that, although evolution in the sense of a common ancestry may be true, 'evolution in the neo-Darwinian sense – an unguided, unplanned process of random variation and natural selection' is not; the 'neo-Darwinian dogma' is not compatible with Catholic teaching.[75] It does indeed seem that the Cardinal has introduced a fundamental ambiguity into the debate as he does not sufficiently differentiate between neo-Darwinism *qua* scientific theory and its philosophical generalization, and between their respective competencies.[76] Such distinctions, however, are essential if Catholics are to develop a coherent, intellectually honest approach to what is becoming the 'Megatheory of Western Thought'.[77] It is this element of *Humani generis* which has certainly lost none of its relevance, even today.

Notes

1 For the period which interests us, see Z. Alszeghy, 'L'evoluzionismo e il magistero ecclesiastico', *Concilium* 3 (1967): 40–7; Carlo Molari, *Darwinismo e teologia cattolica* (Roma : Borla, 1984); Karl Schmitz-Moormann, 'Evolution in the Catholic Theological Tradition,' in: S. Andersen & A. Peacocke (eds), *Evolution and Creation: A European Perspective* (Aarhus: Aarhus University Press, 1987); 121–31; Georges Minois, *L'Église et la science. Histoire d'un malentendu*, vol.2: *De Galilée à Jean-Paul II* (Paris: Fayard, 1991), 364–463; Jacques Arnould, *Darwin, Teilhard de Chardin et Cie. L'Église et l'évolution* (Paris: Desclée de Brouwer, 1996), 43–226; George V. Coyne, 'Evolution and the Human Person: The Pope in Dialogue', in: R. J. Russell, W. R. Stoeger & F. J. Ayala (eds), *Evolutionary and Molecular Biology. Scientific Perspectives on Divine Action* (Vatican City State: Vatican Observatory Publications, 1998), 11–17. For the official text of *Humani Generis*, see *Acta Apostolicae Sedis* (henceforth *AAS*) 42 (1950), 561–78; H. Denzinger & P. Hünermann, *Enchiridion symbolorum definitionum et declarationum de rebus fidei et morum* (Freiburg: Herder, 1999), (38th ed.) (henceforth *DH*), §§ 3875–99.

2 For Pius XII's attitudes to science in general and on the impact of *Humani Generis*, see Minois, 364–70; 378–84.

3 *AAS* 35 (1943), 297–326; particularly 314–16.

4 *AAS* 40 (1948), 45–8.

5 On exegesis, see *AAS* 42 (1950), 576–7. According to Pius XII, the first eleven books of Genesis belong to *genus historiae* in a true sense, but the exact way in which they do so is a matter for exegesis to investigate.

6 Ibid., p. 561. For a concise summary of the main points of the Encyclical, see Molari, 62–4.

7 Ibid., p. 562; *DH* 3877. Pius XII goes on to comment that, apart from being, as a general philosophical concept, a foundation for dialectical materialism, such 'evolutionary fiction' (*evolutionis commenta*) undermines the notion of firm and stable truth within philosophy, and has lead to existentialism and historicism.

8 *AAS* 42 (1950), 575–7; *DH* 3895–9. The 'positive' sciences mentioned include biology, anthropology and history.

9 In an allocution to the Pontifical Academy of Sciences in 1941 (*AAS* 33 (1941), 504–12), referred to in a footnote in the Encyclical, Pius XII had already left open the scientific question of the origin of man. He noted, however, first, the hypothetical character of many of the affirmations of the relevant sciences and, secondly, that further research should be 'illuminated and guided by revelation' (ibid., 506).

10 *DH* 3896: *'animas enim a Deo immediate creari catholica fides nos retinere iubet'*.

11 *DH* 3895.

12 *DH* 3896: *'disceptandi libertatem* [. . .] *temerario ausu transgerdiuntur'*. Pius XII's insistence on the distinction between hypothesis and fact finds an echo several years later in a controversy concerning the publication by Camille Müller of his book *L'encyclique «Humani Generis» et les problèmes scientifiques* (Louvain: E. Nauwelaerts, 1951). In December 1953, the Holy Office – with the approval of Pius XII – condemned the work and placed it on the Index of Prohibited Books (*AAS* 35 (1954), 25). The reasons for doing so are not given in the decree but an article accompanying the reproduction of the decree in the *Osservatore Romano* from 6 January 1954, suggests that the Holy Office took issue with Müller's contention that the theory of evolution is a certain and demonstrated scientific theory. See Arnould, 79–98; R. Kothen, *Documents Pontificaux de sa Sainteté Pie XII: 1953* (Saint Maurice: Editions Saint-Augustin, 1955), 638, footnote 2. Müller himself submitted to the decree; see *AAS* 35 (1954), 64.

13 Kothen, 326, footnote 30.

14 *DH* 1511–41; *DH* 3897.

15 See A. Bea, 'Die Enzyklika «Human generis». Ihre Grundgedanken und ihre Bedeutung', *Scholastik* 26 (1951), 36–56; particularly 50–4. The author notes that most theologians prior to the Encyclical regarded monogenism as an article of faith (*de fide*) or, at least, closely related to the substance of Christian faith (*fidei proxima*). See, for example, R. Garigou-Lagrange, 'La structure de l'Encyclique «Humani generis»' *Angelicum* 28 (1951), 3–17. Bea contends that Pius XII did not wish to decide the scientific issue one way or another. Interestingly, as noted by Alzeghy (*art. cit.*, 44), in contrast to his address to the Pontifical Academy of Sciences in November, 1941 (see *AAS* 33 (1941), 506–7), in which the Pontiff affirmed with a certain insistence that woman had been created from man, *Humani generis* is completely silent on this matter. On this point, see also K. Rahner, 'Peccato originale ed evoluzione', *Concilium* 3 (1967), 73–87; especially 78–9.

16 For a brief review of Pius XII's addresses to representatives of the natural sciences, see Minois, 378–84; Arnould, 91–2.

17 In July 1952, in an address to professors and students of the University of Rome, Pius XII quotes Darwin's words that the idea of God 'often comes over me with overwhelming force' and his admission that the universe cannot be the result of chance, to illustrate that science and religion are not incompatible; *AAS* 34 (1952) 585.

18 *AAS* 35 (1953), 596–607.

19 Ibid., p. 600: 'On croit devoir dire que les recherches sur l'origine de l'homme sont encore à leurs débuts . . .' The Pope goes on to emphasize the distinction between facts (which are always true in themselves) and their scientific interpretation ('élaboration scientifique') which can be premature and prone to error (ibid., p. 602).

20 Ibid., p. 604. Shortly before this passage, the complementary sources are mentioned: they are those sciences which deal with the existence and origin of the spiritual principle of life, the human soul, namely, psychology and metaphysics.

21 See Molari, 65 ff. On variants of transformism, see É. Amman, 'Transformisme', *Dictionnaire de Théologie Catholique*, vol. XV (Paris, 1946); col.1365–96. Works against any form of transformism include: R. Garrigou-Lagrange, *De Deo trino et creatore* (Marietti, Augustae Taurinorum, 1951); J. F. Sagües, *Sacrae Theologiae summa* (B. A. C., Matriti, 1958); C. Boyer, *De Deo creante et elevante* (Rome, 1957); J. Brinktrine, *Die Lehre der Schöpfung* (Paderborn, 1956). Michael Schmaus, in his *Katholische Dogmatik* (München, 1953–1965), affirms that the Bible does not exclude some form of evolution and adopts a reserved 'wait-and-see' attitude.

22 É. Amman, *art. cit.*, col. 1391.

23 J. L. McKenzie, 'Myth and the Old Testament,' *The Catholic Biblical Quarterly* 21 (1959), 265–82; Molari, 74–6.

24 Arnould, 103–90; on evolution, see Minois, 386. It is worth remembering, however, that during his pontificate – 30 June 1962 – a *monitum* of the Holy Office reminds Catholic superiors of religious institutes, seminaries and universities of the 'dangers' of the works of Teilhard de Chardin. See *AAS* 54 (1962), 526; Arnould, 119–20.

25 The Council lasted from 11 October 1962 to 8 December 1965.

26 *Gaudium et spes* (henceforth *GS*) 5. It is not the case that Teilhard's theology was officially recognized by the Council. In the words of Arnould (p. 113): '. . . il vaut mieux parler de l'existence d'une convergence ou même d'une coïncidence de pensée (en particulier de conception du monde) entre *Gaudium et spes* et Teilhard de Chardin'. See also, Henri de Lubac, *Teilhard posthume. Réflexions et souvenirs* (Paris: Fayard, 1977), Chapter 10.

27 *GS* 62; J. Kozhamathadam, 'Vatican II on Science and Technology' in: *Revista Portuguesa de Filosofia* 63 (2007), 609–29.

28 *GS* 57.

29 *GS* 44.

30 *GS* 36; *DH* 4336 [Partly my own translation from the Latin text]. The reference in a footnote to Galileo is significant. According to Minois (388), this is the first time that the Church has officially expressed regret at its treatment of scientists.

31 *AAS* 58 (1966) 2, 649–55. On Paul VI's general attitude of 'extreme prudence' towards the natural sciences, see Minois, 392–9.

32 Ibid., p. 654.

33 Ibid.: 'partendo del presupposto, *che non è stato dimostrato*, del poligenismo' [my emphasis].
34 *AAS* 58 (1966), 659–61.
35 Maurizio Flick of the Pontifical Gregorian University in Rome had presented a more nuanced approach at the very symposium addressed by Paul VI; see 'Peccato originale originato, ricerca di una definizione', *Studia pataviana* 15 (1968), 81–93. P. Grelot prefers to speak in general terms of the unity and solidarity of the human race 'in Adam' which would certainly require some sort of biological basis. But Biblical revelation does not decide the question of exactly how God's creation comes about; see P. Grelot, 'Etudes sur la théologie du Livre Saint', *Nouvelle Revue Théologique* 85 (1963), 897–925.
36 See Francisco José Ayala, 'Man in Evolution', *The Thomist* 31 (1967), 1–20. Among those presenting interpretations of Catholic doctrine compatible with polygenism, the author cites: A.-M. Dubarle, *The Biblical Doctrine of Original Sin* (Herder: 1964); P. Shoonenberg, *Man in Sin* (Notre Dame: 1965); P. Smulders, *La Vision de Teilhard de Chardin* (Brouwer: Desclée, 1964); R. T. Francoeur, *Perspectives in Evolution* (Baltimore: Helicon, 1965).
37 'Peccato originale ed evoluzione', *Concilium* 3 (1967) 6, 73–87. In this article, Rahner argues that the existence of a collective 'originating humanity' from among whom one, several or even all members sinned is not incompatible with the Catholic doctrine of original sin.
38 B. Pottier, 'Interpréter le péché originel sur les traces de G. Fressard', *Nouvelle Revue Théologique* 111 (1989), 801–23.
39 L. Robberechts, *Le mythe d'Adam et le péché originel* (Paris: Ed. Univ., 1967); G. Martelet, *Libre réponse à un scandale. La faute originelle, la souffrance et la mort* (Paris: Cerf, 1986); A. Manaranche, *Je crois en Jésus-Christ aujourd'hui* (Paris: Seuil, 1968); Cl. Tresmontant, *Introduction à la théologie chrétienne* (Paris: Seuil, 1974); 566–84; A. Vanneste, *Het dogma van de erfzonde. Zinloze mythe of openbaring van een grondstructuur von het menselijk bestaan?* (Tielt: Lannoo, 1969).
40 P. Schoonenberg, *op. cit.*, footnote 36. For the questions being considered in the 1960s and 70s concerning the doctrine of original sin, see L. Serenthà, 'Peccato originale', in: Fr. Adrusso, F. Ferretti, *et al.* (eds), *Dizionario Teologico Interdisciplinare* (Torino: Marietti, 1977), 674–90.
41 G. Siewerth, *Die christliche Erbsündelehre. Entwickelt auf Grund der Theologie des heiligen Thomas von Aquin* (Einsiedeln: Johannes Verlag, 1964); G. Fessard, *La dialectique des Exercices spirituels de saint Ignace. I. Temps-Liberté-Grace. II. Fondement-Péché-Orthodoxie* (Paris: Aubier-Montaigne, 1956, 1966); K. Rahner, *art. cit.*, footnote 37; H. Rondet, *Le péché originel dans la tradition patristique et théologique* (Paris: Fayard, 1967); K.-H. Weger, 'Erbsündentheologie heute', *Stimmen der Zeit* 181 (1968), 289–302; M. Flick & Z. Alszeghy, *Il peccato originale* (Brescia: Queriniana, 1972). Today, polygenism is not seen as presenting any great difficulty to the Catholic Doctrine on original sin: see, for example, M. Neusch, 'Le péché originel. Son irréductible vérité', *Nouvelle Revue Théologique* 118 (1996), 237–57; especially 244–5; M. Leclerc, 'Monogénisme/Polygénisme', in: J-Y. Lacoste (ed.), *Dictionnaire critique de Théologie* (Paris: Presses Universitaires de France, 1998), 755.
42 Molari, 68–70. Joseph Ratzinger – the future Prefect of the Congregation for the Doctrine of the Faith and then Pope Benedict XVI – is clearly under Teilhard de Chardin's influence. See, for example, *Introduction to Christianity* (San Francisco: Ignatius Press, 2004), 236–9; 304; 319 ('complexification'). See

also J. Ratzinger, *Eschatologie. Tod und ewiges Leben* (Regensburg, 1977), 158; Schmitz-Moormann, 128; F. Kerr, *Twentieth-Century Catholic Theologians* (Oxford: Blackwell, 2007), 192: 'Remarkably, . . . [Ratzinger] shows considerable enthusiasm for the work of Pierre Teilhard de Chardin'. On the relationship between science and faith seen from the perspective of this period, see Fr. Russo, 'La science et l'incroyance', *Nouvelle Revue Théologique* 96 (1974), 246–65. The author affirms that conflicts had arisen over the previous half-century due to a 'mistaken understanding of God's action in the world' (p. 250) and notes a decidedly more pacific relationship between Catholic faith and science, in large part due to new approaches to Biblical interpretation.

43 The classic example, taken from scholastic text-books, treats of Michelangelo's *Moses*. See Molari, 80.

44 M. Flick & Z. Alszeghy, *Fondamenti di una antropologia teologica* (Firenze: Libreria editrice Fiorentina, 1970), 118–20; 126–8.

45 P. Overhage & K. Rahner, *Das Problem der Hominisation. Über den biologischen Ursprung des Menschen* (Freiburg: Herder, 1961); Schmitz-Moormann, 127–8. Rahner's theory has had its critics. See, for example, Hans-Eduard Hengstenberg, 'Evolutionismus und Schöpfungslehre,' in: R. Spaemann, R. Löw, & P. Koslowski (eds), *Evolutionismus und Christentum* (Weinheim: Acta Humaniora, VCH, 1986), 75–89.

46 A distinct question is how science is applied. Here, John Paul II was far more critical, especially in the area of research on human embryos: cloning, stem cell research and related issues. The same can be said, of course, for his successor, Benedict XVI. For the first decade of the pontificate of John Paul II (1979–88), see the discussion in Minois (404–17) who gives the principal discourses.

47 See, for example, the address to University staff and students in Cologne Cathedral on the 700th anniversary of the death of Albert the Great, November 15, 1980; *AAS* 73 (1981), 49–58; 50–1.

48 *AAS* 71 (1979), 1461–8.

49 Ibid., p. 1463 with reference to the Second Vatican Council, *Gaudium et spes*, 7.

50 Ibid., p. 1466.

51 31 October 1992; for text, see *AAS* 85 (1993), 764–72.

52 Ibid., pp. 766–7.

53 Ibid., pp. 766.

54 One finds a similar observation in the address to the same Academy from 24 October 1996 in *AAS* 89 (1997), 186–90; see page 188.

55 Ibid., p. 765. This approach is in contrast to instances of a certain premature 'concordism' found in statements of previous Popes. Pius XII, for example, claimed that evidence for the Big Bang was a witness to the *Fiat lux* of the first Genesis account of creation. See *AAS* 44 (1952), 41–2; Coyne, 12–13.

56 *AAS* 81 (1989), 274–83.

57 Although theology is not 'to incorporate indifferently each new philosophical or scientific theory', nevertheless, 'the vitality and significance of theology for humanity will in a profound way be reflected in its ability to incorporate these [sc. science's] findings'. ibid., pp. 280–1.

58 Ibid., p. 281: 'If the cosmologies of the ancient Near Eastern world could be purified and assimilated into the first chapter of Genesis, might not contemporary cosmology have something to offer to our reflections upon creation? Does an evolutionary perspective bring any light to bear upon theological anthropology, the meaning of the human person as the *imago Dei*, the problem of Christology – and even upon the development of doctrine itself?' Merely

posing the question already constitutes a significant difference of approach compared to Pius XII's fear of the effects of 'evolutionism' on philosophy and theology. John Paul II, moreover, compares the integration of modern science into theology with that of the reception of Aristotelian natural philosophy by theologians in the Middle Ages, and comments (ibid.): 'Theologians might well ask, with respect to contemporary science, philosophy and the other areas of human knowing, if they have accomplished this extraordinarily difficult process as well as did these medieval masters'.

59 Ibid., p. 282; cfr. above, footnote 49.

60 *Catechism of the Catholic Church* (abbr. *CCC*) (London: Geoffrey Chapman, 1994), § 283. The official Latin text (*Editio typica*) was approved and promulgated by John Paul II on August 15, 1997. See http://www.vatican.va/archive/catechism_lt/lettera-apost_lt.htm

61 Ibid., § 284.

62 Ibid., § 310. It is unlikely that the Catechism text is referring explicitly to the appearance or disappearance of *species*. R. Klaine, in his paper 'Catéchismes et sciences', *Nouvelle Revue Théologique* 117 (1995), 710–23, claims (on page 719, footnote 9) that this passage is the first instance of an official Catholic text acknowledging the extinctions of species which have marked the earth's history. However, the official Latin text – in employing the general term 'beings' – may be talking simply of individuals and not of species as such: 'cum quorumdam *entium* apparitione disparitionem aliorum'.

63 *AAS* 89 (1997), 186–90.

64 Ibid., p. 187; see also the address to the Pontifical Biblical Commission, 23 April 1993 in *AAS* 86 (1994), 232–43.

65 Ibid., p. 188.

66 Ibid., p. 189.

67 Ibid., p. 190.

68 §§ 62–70; quotations from § 70 http://www.vatican.va/roman_curia/congregations/cfaith/cti_documents/rc_con_cfaith_doc_20040723_communion-stewardship_en.html.

69 J. Ratzinger, 'Geleitwort,' in: R. Spaemann, R. Löw, P. Koslowski (eds), *Evolutionismus und Christentum* (Weinheim: Acta Humaniora, VCH, 1986), vii–ix. See also J. Ratzinger, *Glaube, Wahrheit, Toleranz. Das Christentum und die Weltreligionen* (Freiburg: Herder, 2003), 131–47.

70 See, for example, 'Schriftauslegung im Widerstreit: Zur Frage nach Grundlagen und Weg der Exegese heute'. in: J. Ratzinger (ed.), *Schriftauslegung im Widerstreit* (Freiburg: Herder, 1989); 15–44. A central criticism of the modern exegetical approach of Dibelius and Bultmann, for example, is that these authors make an 'evolutionary' presupposition which is not applicable to the history of the human spirit (ibid., p. 22): they claim that, as far as the Biblical message is concerned, the simple message is (chronologically) prior, and the more complex posterior.

71 *AAS* 98 (2006), 889–92; 891.

72 *Communion and Stewardship: Human Persons Created in the Image of God* (2004) warns against 'embracing a discredited concordism' (§ 62). See also B. Michollet, 'Evolution and Anthropology. Human Beings as the 'Image of God', *Concilium* (2000) 1, 79–91.

73 The well-known Darwinian, Richard Dawkins, accuses the Roman Catholic Church of obscurantism and 'disingenuous doublethink' on the question of evolution; quoted from M. Ruse 'Belief in God in a Darwinian age', in:

J. Hodge & G. Radick (eds), *The Cambridge Companion to Darwin* (Cambridge: Cambridge University Press, 2003); 333.

74 The Archbishop's comments are important as he has collaborated closely with Vatican dicasteries and is co-author of the *Catechism of the Catholic Church*.

75 http://www.millerandlevine.com/km/evol/catholic/schonborn-NYTimes.html. The Cardinal goes on to state that John-Paul II's 'vague and unimportant' statement from 1996 that the theory of evolution is 'more that a hypothesis' does not, according to Schönborn, reflect the late Pope's 'robust teaching' on nature, a teaching which affirms that the 'immanent design in nature is real.' In a discussion with his *Schülerkreis* at Castel Gandolfo in September 2006, to a large extent motivated by the New York Times article and its aftermath, Benedict XVI also seems critical of John Paul II's expression. He says: 'quando il Papa [sc. the late John Paul II] disse questo, aveva i suoi buoni motivi. Ma nello stesso tempo è anche vero che la teoria dell'evoluzione non è ancora una teoria completa, scientificamente verificabile'. One can conclude that the current Pontiff would opt for 'incomplete theory' rather than 'more than a hypothesis'. See S. O. Horn & S. Wiedenhofer (eds), *Creazione ed Evoluzione: un convegno con Papa Benedetto XVI a Castel Gandolfo* (Bologna: EDB, 2007), 155.

76 See, particularly, M. Rhonheimer, 'Teoria dell'evoluzione neodarwinista, Intelligent Design e creazione: In dialogo con il Cardinal Christoph Schönborn,' *Acta Philosophica* 17 (2008), 87–132. Rhonheimer is very critical of Schönborn's article. In particular, he makes the important distinction between observing *finality* in natural processes – which is within the competence of the natural sciences – and arguing for *intentional planning* or guidance within natural processes – which is not.

77 Hermann Häring, 'The Theory of Evolution as a Megatheory of Western Thought', *Concilium* (2000) 1, 23–34.

Chapter 4

AQUINAS AND DARWIN

Fáinche Ryan

Charles Darwin (1809–82), and Thomas Aquinas (1225–74), two more
unlikely conversation partners it would be hard to find, or so one might
think. Indeed, an eminent encyclopedia in the English-speaking world,
informs its reader that: 'Darwin did two things: he showed that evolution
was a fact contradicting scriptural legends of creation and that its cause,
natural selection, was automatic with no room for divine guidance or
design.'[1] That this today is a popularly accepted view serves to indicate a
certain lack of knowledge among people regarding both Darwin, and his
theory of natural selection, and what Christians, or more specifically
Catholics, believe as regards God's action in the world. In an attempt to
address this lacuna of knowledge, this paper proposes first to explore
Darwin's theory of 'descent with modification through variation and natural selection',[2] with particular focus on *The Origin of Species*, to see how
he understood natural selection, and to consider whether or not his scientific theory allowed for the active presence of the divine.[3] Then we shall
move to the thought of Thomas Aquinas, one of the most eminent theologians of the Catholic Church, to see to what extent one can see the seeds
of 'evolutionary thought' in his teachings. Aquinas was not, and in his
time, could not have been an evolutionist – this is clear. However, given
that Darwin's theory is not foreign to Catholic thought, as indicated by
John Paul II's official 'recognition of evolution as more than an hypothesis',[4] one can conjecture that, had Aquinas been a contemporary of Darwin,
he would have attended seriously to the writings of Darwin. Throughout
this paper, there is an underlying suggestion that perhaps it might have
been easier for Aquinas, in his day with his concept of God and the world
to accept Darwin's teachings, and maintain faith in a Christian God, than
it was for many of Darwin's Anglican contemporaries whose understanding of natural theology posited a belief in a divine designer. Indeed this
paper intends to show, that the concept of God that Darwin seems to have
rejected was significantly different from the God that Thomas Aquinas
believed in.[5]

1. Charles Darwin

It is difficult today to re-enter the nineteenth-century world of Charles Darwin.[6] He lived in an England which although rapidly changing, was still very much a society where the Church of England was the powerful force. While his time as a student in Edinburgh introduced him to the thoughts of free-thinkers and reformers, most of his life was spent in a country where the 'Anglican Church, fat, complacent, and corrupt, lived luxuriously on its tithes and endowments, as it had for a century'.[7] This was the Church which, for a while, he contemplated becoming a minister in, (hence his years of study at Cambridge); the Church, many members of which were to find in his theory of 'survival of the fittest' a threat to their concept of a Creator God, a divine designer.[8] Darwin was attempting to be a scientist in a world which wished for its science to help prove God. It was the five years of travel on the Beagle (1831–36) that enabled Darwin to move from the natural theology of his years at Cambridge to a more scientific type of approach. Nevertheless, it took more than twenty years before he felt confident enough to publish his *On the Origin of the Species by Means of Natural Selection* (1859).[9] His experience of the society in which he lived led him to fear that the intellectual climate was not suitable for his theory. While he wrote of seeing 'beautiful adaptations everywhere and in every part of the organic world',[10] concepts such as the 'struggle for existence',[11] would surely lead him into controversy. For, what was 'grandeur to him was heresy to geologists and blasphemy to the parsons'.[12] One can just imagine his delight, when after his costly decision to publish, Charles Kingsley, a country rector and renowned novelist, wrote to him in praise of the book: 'It 'awes me', he enthused; 'if you be right I must give up much that I have believed' . . . for it is 'just as noble a conception of the Deity, to believe that He created primal forms capable of self development . . . as to believe that He required a fresh act of intervention to supply the lacunas which He Himself had made'.[13] Not all were so positive, however. A review in the *Athenaeum* (19 November 1859) demanded that Darwin be tried in the 'Divinity Hall, the College, the Lecture Room, and the Museum', indicating that the work had upset many areas of intelligentsia. Not surprisingly, although Darwin had made little reference to the human species and its creation, this theme received much press coverage. People came from monkeys, the press suggested, and hence would die like them. Immortality was in question as was the very existence of God. This was not however what Darwin had written in *Origin*. It now behooves us to return to the text and to see more precisely what Darwin means when he speaks of 'descent with modification through variation and natural selection'.

2. *Descent with Modification*

From the beginning of *Origin* Darwin clarifies his standpoint: 'the view which most naturalists until recently entertained, and which I formerly entertained – namely that each species has been independently created – is erroneous.'[14] Instead, he proposes a theory of descent with modification from a common origin as lying at the core of life. It was the observations made during his time on the Beagle (1831–36) which enabled him to say this, and thus to break away from the natural theology which was a major current of thought in the late eighteenth and early nineteenth-century theology, a natural theology which looked to nature to see how God's work was manifest. 'The study of nature provided the natural theologian with a reasonable foundation independent of biblical revelation for affirming the existence of God'.[15] Today, natural theology, with its desire to present a harmony between science and theology, would not be regarded as meeting scientific criteria; yet it is essential background to a proper understanding of the world in which Darwin operated. As a seminary student at Cambridge, Darwin studied the works of people such as William Paley (1743–1805), whose clear and methodical account for adaptation of species appealed to him.[16] Indeed for the young Darwin 'the logic of this book (*Evidences of Christianity*) and as I may add of his *Natural Theology* gave me as much delight as did Euclid'.[17] However, the experience of his voyage on the Beagle, led to a decisive rejection of Paley's argument of design and to the substitution of the law of natural selection. Darwin was clear:

> We can no longer argue that, for instance, the beautiful hinge of a bivalve shell must have been made by an intelligent being, like the hinge of a door by man. There seems to be no more design in the variability of organic beings and in the action of natural selection, than in the course which the wind blows. Everything in nature is the result of fixed laws.[18]

In a sense there appears to be an internal contradiction in what Darwin writes here – there is no design, but there are fixed laws. What he seeks to reject is the watchmaker Deity of Paley, while seeking to allow space for 'nature'.[19] This attempt to allow for random occurrence, or contingency in Darwin's vision of the world and of nature, is found in a certain sense in the theology of St Thomas Aquinas, as shall be shown. The theory that animals, including humans, come as it were, from the Divine Workshop, and are so evidently designed that there must be a Designer, was no longer tenable to a man who had observed the variation in species found in the Galapagos Islands, islands which are just a few miles apart. These variations, which seemed to result from adaptations to each island's distinctive environment, challenged the idea of a designer God and led Darwin to develop a theory of natural selection. This move from a God of direct intervention was slow, and cautious. Darwin was aware of both the revolutionary nature of what he was exploring as well as the many weaknesses to his theory. Not least was his consciousness of the lack of complete witness to his claim in the geology of the time.

The witness to his development of thought is via the many notebooks he kept in the years following his voyage. He used these notes to pose questions to himself and to strive to find meaningful answers. Conversations with people, such as the bird painter John Gould (1804–81) and the zoologist Thomas Bell (1792–1880), convinced him that what he had observed as variations in species were in fact distinct species.[20] Bell's confirmation that the giant tortoises were native to the Galapagos, and Gould's revelation that Darwin's 'wren' was in fact a finch, provided Darwin with the problem of how to explain species specific to particular islands. Darwin opted for transmutation (what today is termed evolution) – a belief that the alteration which immigrants to the various islands underwent actually produced new species. Life, in a sense, was 'self-made'.[21] This view, as Darwin was well aware, threatened Christian Britain at its core: 'If life was self-made, what became of God's delegated power holding together a precarious paternalist society?'[22]

In mid-July 1837, Darwin began a clandestine notebook ('B') in which to put his musings about transmutation, the change of one species into another. Among his notes, he wrote that 'something must "alter the race to [fit a] *changing* world" ', and that 'species must "become permanently changed". They must pass on and build on their modifications'.[23] In dialogue with thinkers such as Charles Lyell (1797–1875), Thomas Malthus (1766–1834) and Jean-Baptiste de Lamarck, Darwin slowly and with trepidation developed his theory of natural selection. Important to this work was Darwin's observation of the modifications brought about by selective breeding, 'artificial selection', which led him to postulate a type of 'natural selection' at work in the world at large. From Thomas Malthus' 'principle of population', Darwin argued that there was an inevitable struggle for existence. In a world of limited means, this struggle led predictably to the survival of those most suited to their environment, and hence the variation allowing for survival gets passed on to succeeding generations. In this way one can speak of a gradual transmutation of a species, a process whereby the fit will survive. These developments in his thought led to increased awe at nature. If people by artificial selection can bring about modified forms slowly but in a relatively short period of time,

> I can see no limit to the amount of change, to the beauty and complexity of the co-adaptations between all organic beings, one with another and with their physical conditions of life, which may have been affected in the long course of time through nature's power of selection, that is by the survival of the fittest.[24]

Darwin takes care to emphasize the fact that to speak of natural selection does not necessarily imply that development is inevitably progressive. While apes may indeed be the ancestors of humankind, all of creation is not on an escalator towards becoming human, as some of his detractors seemed inclined to think. If it is of no advantage to an intestinal worm, or an earthworm, for example, to be highly organized, their form may be left unimproved or little improved by natural selection. Indeed geology witnesses to the existence of some of the lowest forms for long periods of time in nearly a constant state. However, 'to suppose that most of the many now existing low forms have not in the least advanced since the first dawn of life would be extremely rash; for every naturalist who has dissected some of the beings now ranked as very low in the scale, must have been struck with their really wondrous and beautiful organization'.[25] Species become more complicated as they adapt to changing circumstances, by numerous, successive, slight modifications. Adaptation, and not a designer God directly and deliberately creating all species, is the best way to explain the theory of transmutation, of natural selection. Later in this chapter, it shall be suggested that Thomas Aquinas' theory of secondary causality may be open to accommodating such a view.

3. Darwin and God

In the *Origin*, Darwin is seen to be growing into a different understanding of what God is – his God can no longer be the almost intelligible God of the natural theologians – and this changing concept of God seems to continue throughout his life.[26] Although he does not mention him by name in a very pointed refutation of Paley's argument regarding the complexity of the eye in *Natural Theology*, Darwin places his theory within an uncompromisingly theological vision:

> It is scarcely possible to avoid comparing the eye with a telescope. We know that this instrument has been perfected by the long-continued efforts of the highest human intellects; and we naturally infer that the eye has been formed by a somewhat analogous process. But may not this inference be presumptuous? Have we any right to assume that the Creator works by intellectual powers like those of man?[27]

The eye has not been perfected by a designer God. To suggest this is too simplistic and does not offer a scientific explanation of its complexity. Instead, Darwin suggests what he considers to be a 'real' scientific theory for the development of the complex mechanism of sight – that of 'descent with modification'.[28] He explains how over millions of years, with countless developments and slight alterations, the eye developed, superior to any telescope. Natural selection, he suggests, 'will pick out with unerring skill each improvement'.[29] This process, which takes place over millions of years, he suggests can lead to the formation of a living optical instrument 'as superior to one of glass [i.e. the telescope], as the works of the Creator are to those of man'.[30]

Darwin's principle of preservation and development, descent with modification, 'explains functional adaptation without recourse to an external designer',[31] and in so doing seems to accord a 'higher' place to God in the greater scheme of things. God is not a designer God, nor for Darwin is it helpful to see God as having independently created each species, despite what authors of the highest eminence may have thought at the time. No special intervention of the Creator is necessary to explain the birth or death of an individual:

> To my mind it accords better with what we know of the laws impressed on matter by the Creator, that the production and extinction of the past and present inhabitants of the world should have been due to secondary causes, like those determining the birth and death of the individual. When I view all beings not as special creations, but as the lineal descendants of some few beings which lived long before the first bed of the Cambrian system was deposited, they seem to me to become ennobled.[32]

While Darwin does not explain why this theory ennobles, rather than detracts from, the theory of creation, one might conjecture that it is because he sees the nature he observes as consisting of those things which have been victorious in the struggle for life.

In an essay written in 1842, Darwin's understanding of secondary causes, of 'the laws impressed on matter by the Creator', illustrates how he saw this theory as giving more reverence to the deity than the idea of direct creation of each species.

> There is much grandeur in looking at the existing animals either as the lineal descendants of the forms buried under a thousand feet of matter, or as the coheirs of some still more ancient ancestor. It accords with what we know of the law impressed on matter by the Creator, that the creation and extinction of forms, like the birth and death of individuals should be the effect of secondary [laws] means. It is derogatory that the Creator of countless systems of worlds should have created each of the myriads of creeping parasites and [slimy] worms which have swarmed each day of life on land and water on [this] one globe. [. . .] Doubtless it at first transcends our humble powers, to conceive laws capable of creating individual organisms, each characterised by the most exquisite workmanship and widely-extended adaptations. It accords better with [our modesty] the lowness of our faculties to suppose each must require the fiat of a creator, but in the same proportion the existence of such laws should exalt our notion of the power of the omniscient Creator. There is a simple grandeur in the view of life with its powers of growth, assimilation and reproduction, being originally breathed into matter

under one or a few forms, and that whilst this our planet has gone circling on according to fixed laws, and land and water, in a cycle of change, have gone on replacing each other, that from so simple an origin, through the process of gradual selection of infinitesimal changes, endless forms most beautiful and most wonderful have been evolved.[33]

This passage, quoted at length, shows how Darwin's theory of descent with modification did not lead him away from the Christian God, as many feared such a theory necessarily must, but rather can be seen to 'recover' the idea of secondary causation developed by theologians such as Thomas Aquinas in the thirteenth century. While one cannot call Aquinas an evolutionist, nor Darwin a theologian, the above quote shows many similarities between both men's ways of thinking: study of the world we live in leads to wonder, and enhanced respect, and awe for the 'omniscient Creator', the Creator of the laws of nature. As Aquinas so often teaches, the inability to understand God, and God's work, lies on the side of the human, what Darwin terms 'the lowness of our faculties'.

God has not been rejected by this naturalist, rather the concept of God into which he had been inducted was decisively placed to one side. As Desmond and Moore astutely note, 'he was pulling away from Cambridge theology'.[34] The theory of evolution was for Darwin compatible with a belief in God. His theory of 'natural selection' by descent through modification, simply seeks to affirm that there is a law, a mechanism in nature, which governs species selection. This 'power' 'silently and insensibly working, *whenever and wherever opportunity offers*, at the improvement of each organic being in relation to its organic and inorganic conditions of life', is this not what many Christians call God, he wonders?[35] This power which works from within nature, gifted to nature itself, one might say, is incompatible with the Designing – and interfering – God of Paley. Paley's God must be an intelligent, designing author. 'Secondary causes', the means whereby God brings about God's effects he will admit to, but these causes are like the mechanical functioning of a clock. There will be no room for chance in this system – the world, and the clock, must have a force at their centre accounting for the orderly development in nature.

It is important to note that, despite the strong and influential criticism of scholars such as Paley, Darwin consciously maintained, in six editions, this quasi-divine way of speaking of nature.[36] This speaks not of a man who has lost God, but of one who has found a new way of seeing the outworking of God in the world. Darwin, both during the voyage and at least until the final edition of *The Origin of Species* (1872), was still a believer in God the Creator. Indeed, in a letter written in 1879, Darwin notes that, while in regard to religious matters 'my judgment often fluctuates. [. . .] In my most extreme fluctuations, I have never been an Atheist in the sense of denying the existence of a God. I think that generally (and more and more as I grow older), but not always, that an Agnostic would be the more correct description of my state of mind'.[37] This fluctuation in thought is also evident in his biography. In his biography, in a section where he appears to be struggling with the idea of God, and with what type of 'God' one is speaking of, he notes:

> Another source of conviction in the existence of God, connected with the reason and not with the feelings, impresses me as having much more weight. This follows from the extreme difficulty or rather impossibility of conceiving this immense and wonderful universe, including man with his capacity of looking far backwards and far into futurity, as the result of blind chance or necessity. When thus reflecting I feel compelled to look to a First Cause having an intelligent mind in some degree analogous to that of man; and I deserve to be called a Theist.[38]

This mention of First Cause and Secondary Causes indicates that Darwin is proposing a metaphysical argument for evolution. Although a biologist and not a metaphysician, the language and ideas of metaphysics would have been familiar to him and they find a certain expression in his theory. There are also indications of teleological orientation in his thought – evolution has a direction, although 'natural selection will not necessarily lead to absolute perfection; nor, as far as we can judge by our limited faculties, can absolute perfection be everywhere predicated'.[39] Value words such as 'good', 'progress' and 'perfection' are found throughout the *Origin*, and in many other of his writings. Darwin sees the universe not as either a random state of being or as a tightly controlled automated machine following a strict path – rather it has 'laws' that govern its existence, its life processes. There are laws governing inheritance, laws of embryology and laws of battle. For him, even variability is governed by 'unknown laws'. When he talks of law of nature, by nature he means 'the aggregate action and product of many natural laws, and by laws the sequence of events as ascertained by us'.[40] Darwin was not the first to propose the notion of secondary causes in nature, nor that indeed it was more glorious that the Creator work by means of them rather than producing everything directly, as it were. His unique contribution was to propose the law of selection 'as the secondary cause by which the evolution of the species takes place'.[41] This seems a good point to see what Thomas Aquinas might have had to contribute to the thought of Darwin.

4. Thomas Aquinas

At first glance one might see little in common between Charles Darwin and Thomas Aquinas – the former an English Unitarian come Anglican come agnostic in his thought, the other a Dominican friar from near

Naples, a theologian at heart, who lived 600 years before the time of Darwin – closer inspection suggests they might have made interesting conversation partners. Both men shared a great sense of marvel at the universe, of all that is. Darwin's marveling, as shown above, led him further from a belief in the 'inherited' view of the God of his times, whereas Aquinas' study led him deeper into the mystery of God. This God was not one limited by definition but one who increasingly challenged Aquinas' presuppositions. As with Darwin, the distinction and multitude of things in the universe speak of God:

> For God brought things into being in order that His goodness might be communicated to creatures, and be represented by them; and because God's goodness could not be adequately represented by one creature alone, God produced many and diverse creatures, that what was wanting to one in the representation of the divine goodness might be supplied by another. For goodness, which in God is simple and uniform, in creatures is manifold and divided and hence the whole universe together participates the divine goodness more perfectly, and represents it better than any single creature whatever.[42]

This teaching is not necessarily different to Darwin's, however he would need to explore precisely what is meant by 'God produced many and diverse creatures'. Did Aquinas mean that God created all that is, as it is? This question brings us to a central difference in the scholarship of both men. While Aquinas could not have asked many of the questions that Darwin did, his biological and geographical experience of the 'world' being much more limited, he asked the question Darwin did not – why is there something rather than nothing? What was the beginning of all? From his thoughts and speculations, he developed the theory of *creatio ex nihilo* [creation out of nothing]. This theory is central to Aquinas' thought and addresses the question of *the origin* of the species, while Darwin's starting point comes at a later stage – his questions relate less to what Aquinas terms creation and more to what Aquinas terms Divine providence, causality, necessity and contingency, generation.[43]

An exploration of the concept of *creatio ex nihilo* will be followed by a study of Aquinas' theory of causation in an attempt to see if, within this very precise understanding, Darwin's theory of 'descent with modification through variation and natural selection',[44] might be accommodated to some extent, or if the two ideas are so distant as to necessitate a crisis of faith for either of the thinkers. Could Aquinas, were he living in the time of Darwin or indeed today, remain a committed believer and theologian within a scientific world where so much more can be explained? Might Darwin have been more secure in his faith in a God as Creator had he been influenced by the work of Aquinas? Indeed, might Aquinas's work have helped him to maintain a belief in a merciful God despite the suffering he witnessed in the world, to which he ascribed the term 'survival of the fittest', to continue to believe after the death of his daughter?[45]

5. *Creatio ex nihilo*

While Darwin's concern was with analyzing and considering that which he saw before him, seeking to understand how things developed to be as they are, Creation is the key concept for Aquinas. Creation is a distinct category, patently different from what Aristotle speaks of as a 'becoming', a movement from form to form (ST I q.44 a.2 ad.1). Creation refers to the fact that 'nothing can be, unless it is from God, Who is the universal cause of all being . . . God brings things into being from nothing (ST I q.45 a.2 c). God uniquely is the Creator. 'It is impossible that anything should be created, save by God alone' (ST I q.65 a.3 c), who by His wisdom 'is the cause of diverse things' (ST I q.65 a.3 ad.2). That the world is, is God's doing. In addressing the question of *creatio ex nihilo*, Thomas has gone to a stage before Darwin's musings begin. In ST I q.44 a.2, he makes an interesting, and, from the perspective of this essay, a pertinent point: '[Science] deals only with the particular changes and transformations that matter undergoes, taking its existence for granted; but when we talk of the derivation of things from their universal source of existence, this in-cludes deriving their matter, for the passive basis of things is reasonably to be derived from their primary active source.'[46] The starting point for 'we' the theologians is different from that of the 'scientist'. In this case, the scient-ist is the Philosopher, Aristotle, but the same principle could be applied to the work of Darwin. Where Aristotle speaks of becoming from form to form, Darwin writes of 'the survival of the fittest', of 'natural selection',[47] of progression, transmutation, change. Aquinas' central concern is to show that primary matter is created by God. The fact that God is Creator, that every being in existence is from God, that God is the essentially self-subsisting Being (ST I q.3 a.4), leads Thomas to the belief that 'all beings apart from God are not their own being, but are beings by participation. Therefore it must be that all things which are diversified by the diverse participation of being, so as to be more or less perfect, are caused by one First Being, Who possesses being most perfectly' (ST I q. 44 a.1 c).

This teaching does not necessarily claim that God created all things immediately, but rather that God is involved in creating and in holding all things in being. Before moving further, we must remember that we are now working with a theologian, one who holds by faith a belief in God and one who knows that there are other beliefs that are held by faith alone. Creation, a beginning out of nothing, is one such, as it cannot be proved by demonstration. Thomas is adamant that this must be borne in mind 'lest anyone, presuming to demonstrate what is of faith, should bring forward reasons that are not cogent, so as to give occasion to unbelievers to laugh, thinking that on such grounds we believe things that are of faith' (ST I q.46 a.2 c).

Aquinas' God is a Creator God, and hence also First Cause. The idea of change happening within God's good creation remains a definite possibility from what has been said thus far. This thirteenth-century Catholic belief in a First Cause, a *creatio ex nihilo*, a universal cause of all things who creates primary matter, may be congruous with a theory of 'descent with modification through variation and natural selection', what today is commonly termed evolution. And so, the next part of this paper will explore the type of change that the theology of St Thomas Aquinas permits in creation.

6. Causality and Change

A recent document from the *Congregation of the Doctrine of the Faith* advises that the 'current scientific debate about the mechanisms at work in evolution requires theological comment insofar as it sometimes implies a misunderstanding of the nature of divine causality'.[48] This seems to have been no less true at the time of Darwin. Can a belief in a God as First Cause, a Creator God, who creates matter from nothing, be congruent with the probability of evolution? In an attempt to address this question, focus will now turn to the theme of divine and secondary causality in the theology of Aquinas. The aim is to show that the theory of descent with modification, together with an acknowledgement of contingency and chance, is not necessarily incompatible with divine providence.[49]

In talking of change Aquinas is clear – 'God alone is altogether immutable' (ST I q.9 a.2 c), while in every creature there is a potentiality to change. Change is understood in a twofold sense, it can occur by another's power, that is to say God's, or a thing is changeable by its own potentiality. Hence, although God is the Creator of primary matter, and is that which holds all that is in existence, primary matter is not static. This idea seems clear in a close examination of ST I q.44 a.2. Here, as Thomas asserts that God has made primary matter, he also takes note of the transmutations which the ancient philosophers noted taking place in bodies as regards their essential forms. Thomas' concern is to establish God as creator of primary matter, and yet it is notable that matter is created always with form, and with what Thomas terms 'potential'. This potential is also a gift from God and it is this concept which allows for change.

Like many scholars of his time, Aquinas had a conception of primary and secondary causes that was strongly influenced by his study of *The Book of Causes* (*Liber de causis*). God is first cause, and as such is pure being (*esse tantum*). God, as first and universal cause, causes things to be, bringing things into being from nothing, for God is the Creator of all that is. God is the source of all *esse* and thus Aquinas taught that all beings apart from God are beings by participation (ST I q.44 a.1). Furthermore, when an agent acts as a secondary cause, it acts by the power of the first agent, God. Secondary causes for Aquinas are true causes. Moreover, they give their effects limited being, always bearing in mind that 'whatever gives being, does so in so far as it acts by the power of God'.[50] The primary cause gives being; the secondary agents 'particularize and determine the action of the first agent, produce the other perfections, as their proper effects, which are particular kinds of being' (ScG III, 66). Every thing acts by God's power. To allow, as Darwin does, for 'laws of nature' would not for Aquinas in any way lessen the activity of a First Cause. For it is not absurd that the same effect be produced by the inferior agent and by God, and by both immediately, though in a different way. It is also clear that the same effect is ascribed to a natural cause and to God, not as though part were effected by God and part by the natural agent: but the whole effect proceeds from each, yet in different ways: just as the whole of the one same effect is ascribed to the instrument, and again the whole is ascribed to the principal agent.[51] This is the case with a pen and a scribe: both enable the word to be written, each in their own way.[52]

To ascribe a true causality to creatures does not take anything away from God. In so far as God bestowed God's likeness on creation with respect to its being, it follows that God will also bestow God's likeness on creation with respect to its acting, so that creatures also should have their proper actions. To believe otherwise is to detract from the power, perfection and goodness of God:

> Perfection of effect indicates perfection of cause: since greater power produces a more perfect effect. Now God is the most perfect agent. Therefore things created by him must needs receive perfection from him. Consequently to detract from the creature's perfection is to detract from the perfection of the divine power.[53]

The creature is inextricably related to God. It is due to the abundance of its perfection, itself a gift of God, that a thing can communicate this perfection to another. That the good be shared is God's will and benefits all creation. 'Accordingly God communicated His goodness to His creatures in such wise that one thing can communicate to another the good it has received. Therefore it is derogatory to the divine goodness to deny things their proper operations'.[54] In asserting the natural efficacy of secondary causes, Thomas contended that 'created beings by their own powers – presupposing the action of the first cause – do produce new substances'.[55]

What is remarkable about Aquinas is his trust in God and his respect for creation. Etienne Gilson puts it well: 'in St. Thomas God delegates His gifts through the mediacy of a stable nature which contains in itself-divine subsistence being taken for granted – the sufficient reason of all its operations.'[56] Aquinas will always opt for the solution which gives greater glory to God, in this way he believes he also gives greater glory to God's creation. Thus it is his teaching that it is better for God to create by secondary causes although God might have produced the same effect as a First Cause.

7. A Theory of Evolution?

Here, an opening appears for a certain accommodation of a theory of evolution.[57] Before proceeding further, it is necessary to repeat that Thomas did not know of, nor could he have countenanced, any theory akin to the modern idea of the 'evolution of species'. In *De Potentia* he writes that 'The universe in its beginning was perfect as regards the species of things, [*quantum ad species*]'.[58] This teaching, which speaks of perfection, does not necessarily preclude the addition of new species through the agency of secondary causes. Indeed how exactly Thomas understood the 'beginning' of the universe is a question which he seems to have been happy to leave open, although he does teach that temporal succession seems to better demonstrate the order of divine wisdom.[59] Interestingly, St Thomas 'did not think that the world was created from the start as it was actually in his day'.[60] Some things were created 'only *originaliter* or *causaliter* or *potentialiter* at the beginning, which would include not only the succession of individuals that were to follow in the different species, but also most of the intermediate species that were produced actually as time went on, from the elements and through the influence of heavenly bodies'.[61] In an interesting exegesis of Thomas' work, Oliva Blanchette invites a 'rather broad interpretation' to statements such as ST I q.118 a.3 ad 2: 'Something can be added every day to the perfection of the universe, as to the number of individuals, but not as to the number of species.' Blanchette suggests that this can be read as meaning that the appearance of a new species is not strictly contrary to the perfection of the universe but rather that the 'appearance of new species concerns the perfection of the universe more than the appearance of new individuals'.[62] The appearance of new species is not an everyday occurrence as it affects the *per se* order of the universe, but it is not an impossibility. In the *Summa theologiae*, Thomas does seem to allow for Blanchette's interpretation:

> Species, also, that are new, if any such appear, existed beforehand in various active powers; so that animals, and perhaps even new species of animals, are produced by putrefaction by the power which the stars and elements received at the beginning. Again, animals of new kinds arise occasionally from the connection of individuals belonging to different species, as the mule is the offspring of an ass and a mare;

but even these existed previously in their causes, in the works of the six days.[63]

Thus while it cannot be said that Thomas advanced a theory akin to Darwin's 'descent with modification through variation and natural selection',[64] he does seem to have left a door open to allow for a general theory of evolution in nature.

Notes

1 Gavin de Beer, 'Evolution', *The New Encyclopedia Britannica*, 15th edition (1973–74).

2 Charles Darwin, *The Origin of Species by means of Natural Selection or the Preservation of Favored Races in the Struggle of Life* (First edition 1859, sixth edition 1872), 404; henceforth *Origin*. Unless indicated otherwise, all texts of Charles Darwin have been accessed at http://darwin-online.org.uk/index.html

3 It is interesting to note that Darwin did not use the term 'evolution'. Anne M. Clifford suggests that this may have been a deliberate choice to avoid confusion, as the notion of biological evolution was being debated at this time. See Anne M. Clifford, 'Darwin's Revolution in *The Origin of Species*: A Hermeneutical Study of the Movement from Natural Theology to Natural Selection', in: Robert John Russell, William R. Stoeger, Francisco J. Ayala (eds), *Evolutionary and Molecular Biology. Scientific Perspectives on Divine Action*. Vatican Observatory Publications (Vatican City State/ Center for Theology and the Natural Sciences, Berkeley, California, 1998), 281–302.

4 John Paul II, *Truth Cannot Contradict Truth: Address to the Pontifical Academy of Sciences* (22 October 1996) (English version in: *L'Osservatore Romano*, English edition, Oct. 1996), § 4.

5 Darwin's writings indicate that it was life, and suffering, that led him towards atheism. Most influential was the death of his eldest daughter Annie, on Wednesday 23rd April 1851, at the age of nine. With her death it seems that Charles's fragile belief in Christianity was destroyed.

6 For an excellent biography of the life of Charles Darwin see Andrew Desmond and James Moore, *Darwin. The Life of a Tormented Evolutionist* (New York/ London: W. H. Norton & Company, 1994 [1991 Warner books Ltd]).

7 Ibid., p. 47. This vision of life was challenged during Darwin's lifetime, a period of great political reform in England and of growing uncertainty for the established Church.

8 Frederick Temple, who became Archbishop of Canterbury in 1896, found Darwin's theory of species transformation acceptable as it presupposed an original Creator while Bishop Samuel Wilberforce argued against Darwinian evolution due to the lack of sufficient fossil evidence and to his personal 'commitment to harmony between science and theology which natural theology strongly affirmed', a harmony threatened by Darwin's theory. See Ann Clifford, 'Darwin's Revolution in *The Origin of Species*', 281–302.

9 '*Of course* Darwin could not publish . . . He had no illusions about how he would be treated . . . he risked being identified with atheistic low-life . . . Ultimately he was frightened for his respectability'. See Desmond and Moore, *Darwin. The Life of a Tormented Evolutionist*, 296.

10 *Origin*, 48.
11 *Origin*, Chapter 3.
12 Desmond and Moore, *Darwin. The Life of a Tormented Evolutionist*, 294.
13 Desmond and Moore, *Darwin. The Life of a Tormented Evolutionist*, 477.
14 *Origin*, 4.
15 Ann Clifford, 'Darwin's Revolution in *The Origin of Species*', 283.
16 In Darwin's time, many already regarded Paley's writings as dated belonging to an era when Christianity was regarded as the faith of reasonable men, and reasonable men ruled the world. His own reading of Paley became more critical due to the influence of Rev. Prof John Stevens Henslow, Regius Professor of Botany at Cambridge, a man who was to be most influential in Darwin's life.
17 *The Autobiography of Charles Darwin 1809–1882*. With original omissions restored. Edited with Appendix and Notes by his grand-daughter Nora Barlow (St James's Place, London: Collins, 1958), 59. Accessed at http://darwin-online.org.uk/index.html
18 Desmond and Moore, *Darwin. The Life of a Tormented Evolutionist*, 87.
19 Paley argues: 'The marks of design are too strong to be got over. Design must have had a designer. That designer must have been a person. That person is God'. William Paley, *Natural Theology: or, Evidences of the Existence and Attributes of the Deity, Collected from the Appearances of Nature* (1802).
20 Desmond and Moore, *Darwin. The Life of a Tormented Evolutionist*, 220.
21 The distinction between 'creation' and 'change' is central here.
22 Desmond and Moore, *Darwin. The Life of a Tormented Evolutionist*, 221.
23 Desmond and Moore, *Darwin. The Life of a Tormented Evolutionist*, 229.
24 *Origin*, 85.
25 *Origin*, 99.
26 See *The Autobiography*, 92, 93.
27 *Origin*, 146.
28 As noted above (note 3) Darwin seems to prefer this term to that of Evolution.
29 *Origin*, 146.
30 *Origin*, 146.
31 Ann Clifford, 'Darwin's Revolution in *The Origin of Species*', 292.
32 *Origin*, 428.
33 *The Foundations of the Origin of the Species. Two Essays Written in 1842 and 1844 by Charles Darwin*. ed. Francis Darwin (Cambridge: Cambridge University Press, 1909), 51, 52. Accessed at http://darwin-online.org.uk/index.html.
34 Desmond and Moore, *Darwin. The Life of a Tormented Evolutionist*, 241.
35 *Origin*, 66.
36 Not all Christians were opposed to the idea of natural selection. Asa Gray, America's leading botanist in the mid-nineteenth century, and an early supporter of Darwin, believed that 'mediate production of species by natural selection may indeed be completely theistic'. Asa Gray, *Natural Science and Religion* (New York: Scribners, 1880), 68.
37 Francis Darwin (ed.), *The Life and Letters of Charles Darwin* (London: Murray, Albemarle Street, 1887), vol. 1, p. 304. Available at http://darwin-online.org.uk/
38 *The Autobiography of Charles Darwin*, 92, 93.
39 *Origin*, 166. Later he writes, 'As natural selection works solely by and for the good of each being, all corporeal and mental endowments will tend to progress towards perfection'. *Origin*, 428.
40 *Origin*, 63.

41 Armand Maurer, 'Darwin, Thomists, and Secondary Causality', *The Review of Metaphysics*, 57 (March 2004): 491–514: 503.

42 Thomas Aquinas, *Summa theologiae*. English translation: The Leonine edition by the Dominican Fathers of the English Province. Cincinnati, Chicago: Benziger Brothers, 1947 edition. Ia *Questio* 47, article 1 *corpus*, henceforth ST I q.47 a.1 c.

43 'Unlike the atheists, seeking an alternative to Anglican Creationism in a chemical soup, Darwin kept ultimate origins out of the picture. Life's initial appearance on the earth was unscrutable . . . All that should concern the naturalist was its subsequent change'. Desmond and Moore, *Darwin. The Life of a Tormented Evolutionist*, 412.

44 *Origin*, 404.

45 See note 5.

46 Timothy McDermott (ed.), *Summa theologiae. A concise translation* (Allen, Texas: Christian Classics, 1989), 84.

47 *Origin*, 103.

48 Congregation of the Doctrine of the Faith, *Communion and Stewardship: Human Persons Created in the Image of God* (2004), § 69.

49 'True contingency in the created order is not incompatible with a purposeful divine providence', *Communion and Stewardship*, § 69.

50 *Summa Contra Gentiles* Book III, Chapter 66; henceforth: ScG III, 66. English translation: The Leonine edition by the Dominican Fathers of the English Province. Cincinnati, Chicago: Benziger Brothers, 1924 edition.

51 Cf.: 'Ita non est inconveniens quod producatur idem effectus ab inferiori agente et deo: ab utroque immediate, licet alio et alio modo . . .' (*ScG* III, 70).

52 This ascribing of a true active power and causality to creatures was not universally acceptable. See: Maurer, 'Darwin, Thomists, and Secondary Causality', 508.

53 *ScG* III, 69. See also Etienne Gilson, *The Christian Philosophy of St. Thomas Aquinas*, trans. L.K. Shook (New York: Random House, 1966), 182: 'to deprive things of actions of their own is to belittle God's goodness'.

54 *ScG* III, 69.

55 Maurer, 'Darwin, Thomists, and Secondary Causality,' 509. See also: Thomas Aquinas, *De veritate*, q.11 a.1.

56 Etienne Gilson, *Notes for a Seminar in École Practique des Hautes Études, the University of Paris in 1921*, printed as an Appendix in: Laurence K. Shook, *Etienne Gilson* (Toronto: Pontifical Institute of Mediaeval Studies, 1984), 397. Cited in Maurer, 'Darwin, Thomists, and Secondary Causality', 510.

57 See: Norman Kretzmann, The Metaphysics of Creation. Aquinas's Natural Theology in Summa Contra Gentiles II (Oxford: Clarendon Press, 1999). In Chapter 6, entitled 'The Origin of Species', he claims that 'Aquinas's natural theology is of more than historical interest, that intelligent, educated, late twentieth-century people can take it seriously as a theistic account of what there is' (184–5). This is directly in line with my argument.

58 *De Potentia* Bk.I q.3 a.10 ad 2.

59 In a very interesting treatise in *De Potentia* Bk.II q.4 a.2, he presents the arguments in favour of both the formation of the universe in an instant or according to a temporal succession. See also ST I q.66 a.1; q.74 a. 2.

60 Oliva Blanchette, *The Perfection of the Universe According to Aquinas. A Teleological Cosmology* (Pennsylvania: The Pennsylvania State University Press, 1992), 149. In *De Potentia*, Thomas argues that, in the beginning, the

world was perfect only 'with regard to the causes of natural things, from which afterward other things can be propagated, but not with regard to all the effects' (q.3 a.10 ad. 2).

61 Blanchette 149, 150.
62 Blanchette 150.
63 ST I q.73 a.1 ad.3.
64 *Origin*, 404.

Chapter 5

TEILHARD DE CHARDIN: EVOLUTION FOR A BELIEVING SCIENTIST

FRANÇOIS EUVÉ

Pierre Teilhard de Chardin (1881–1955) is a major figure in the history of relations between Christian Churches, particularly the Catholic Church, and an evolutionary vision of the world. Having been educated in a traditional Catholic family, he entered the novitiate of the Society of Jesus in 1899. He then studied philosophy, theology and natural sciences, in which he obtained a doctorate in 1921. From these modest beginnings, he proceeded to become the person who contributed most to drawing together the scientific world and the religious world during the twentieth century. His influence largely overflows the borders of his country of origin: his work has been translated into numerous languages and still generates a large number of commentaries. All sorts of thinkers are interested in his thought, but it is clear that in general he has been better received by the general public than by specialized scientists or theologians.

The difficulty of interpreting his thought arises because Teilhard is neither a professional philosopher nor theologian. He never claimed to be one; instead, he sought to 'make one see' (*faire voir*), to return to a sort of elementary level of experience from which thinking and reflection could be developed.[1] As a result, his concepts do not always have the precision that one could rightly expect from an expert philosopher. His concepts are most often evocative and suggestive images capable of provoking reflection. The Dominican theologian Olivier Rabut speaks of 'very accurate "mother-intuitions" (*intuitions-mères*), which are capable of providing new-blood to Christian thinking'.[2] The absence of rigor in the concepts which he uses (often invented by himself) must not preclude appreciation of the relevance of his fundamental intuitions. Could such an innovative way of thinking flow as easily from the mould of older notions?

In addition, his reflection is underpinned by a desire for a *global vision* of the world. Against the tendency of modern science towards greater specialization, he tries to draw out an overview through a multitude of images. For him, the world is 'one', or at least it tends towards unity: 'to be more is to be more united.'[3] This unity is the truth of being more than distinctions or definitions. It does not seek to classify organisms in various categories, but to perceive what they have in common, what brings them together. However, for him, this unity is yet to come. It does not yet exist in the current state of the world. But, there does exist in every being a 'tendency', an 'aspiration', a 'desire' towards unity: humanity experiences a characteristic of all being. The evolutionary process is nothing other than this tendency, stretched out to the whole of the cosmos.

It is first necessary to look again at Teilhard's relationship with the scientific approach in general. After that, I will enter into his way of thinking, by reconstructing its movement: a search for the absolute, which motivates his interest in life and above all in the 'human phenomenon'. This allows us to see where he situates scientific enquiry in the search for the meaning of life. I will then examine his complex relationship with Darwinism, and proceed by examining the central place of the figure of Christ, who reconciles the advance of the world with the growth of the Kingdom of God.

It is certain that, in the work of Teilhard, theological reflection is not only an appendix, as it seems to be the case in *Le Phénomène Humain* where the 'Christian phenomenon' comes at the end as an epilogue. David Grummett helpfully recalls that 'Teilhard's theology provides the hermeneutic for the whole of his thought'.[4] Nevertheless, Teilhard aims to dialogue with the scientific world. This dialogue is not lacking in consequences for the representation of God.[5]

1. Teilhard and the Scientific World

Teilhard's work was received in the scientific world in very different ways. As an example, shortly after the appearance of the English translation of Teilhard's principle work, *Le Phénomène Humain*, Sir Peter Medawar, winner of the Nobel Prize for Medicine, delivered a systematic attack on the work, in an article in the journal *Mind*, which had a great impact in the English-speaking world.[6] On the other hand, the historian of science, Joseph Needham, judged the *Le Phénomène Humain* 'the work of a first-rate evolutionary biologist who knew his facts'.[7]

Because of this, there has been a tendency to neglect his scientific work and reflection and concentrate rather on his more spiritual writings. George Murray wrote in 1967: 'Discussion of his evolutionary theory from a more scientific point of view is relatively rare.'[8] This diagnosis was confirmed in 1992 by Ludovico Galleni, who considers the analysis of his scientific works 'a largely neglected perspective'.[9] We must recall some basic facts.[10] His abilities as a researcher are undeniable. He was much appreciated by his first professor, the great French paleontologist

Marcellin Boule, who wanted to make him one of his disciples. Teilhard's scientific works are numerous.[11] These received recognition by his being elected to the *Académie des sciences*. His rejection by part of the scientific community is not due to his specialized publications but to texts in which he tried to conduct a fundamental reflection that he also intended as scientific.

It has to be recognized that a large part of Teilhard's texts are disconcerting for minds rigorously formed in the scientific approach. It is particularly true of *Le Phénomène Humain*, which moreover, according to its author, 'must not be read as a metaphysical work, still less as some kind of theological essay, but solely and exclusively as a scientific study'.[12] This first phrase of the work can be understood as a kind of protection against the sensitivities of Church authorities who had forbidden Teilhard to publish philosophical or theological texts. It can also be understood as the desire to reach a wider public than believers alone. By situating himself on the terrain of the universally shared 'phenomenon', the author can speak to all people capable of reason.

What is problematic, therefore, is Teilhard's style. Christian de Duve explains why biologists rejected Teilhard by referring to his 'grandiloquent style and his lack of scientific rigor'.[13] He notes however that Teilhard is better received by cosmologists. De Duve refers to John Barrow and Frank Tipler, who affirm that 'the fundamental structure of his theory is truly the only structure in which the cosmos in evolution as presented by modern science can be associated with an ultimate meaning of reality'.[14]

Another difficulty, in my opinion, seems to be linked to the importance which Teilhard gives to the 'human phenomenon'. For him, scientific research has no other sense than to help humanity reflect on its presence in the Universe. There exists an intimate connection between humanity and the rest of the cosmos, just as there is a connection between all the components of the cosmos. That is the point and purpose of Teilhardian research. One can understand why this central idea enters into conflict with that of Jacques Monod, who aims at denouncing the 'Old Alliance' between humanity and nature by showing that 'man knows at last that he is alone in the universe's unfeeling immensity, out of which he emerged only by chance. His destiny is nowhere spelled out, nor is his duty'.[15] Monod rejects the entire idea of an evolutionary direction. In contrast to this, the thought of Teilhard is in line with the doctrine of those who defend the idea of the progress of humanity. It is in line, for instance, with the thought of his agnostic friend Julian Huxley, who wrote the preface of the English edition of *Le Phénomène Humain*. One must recall, however, that the idea of evolutionary progress, allegedly demonstrated particularly by the development of self-regulation, by the growth of the complexity of organisms or by their autonomy with respect to their external environment, is frequently contested by the majority of paleontologists.

George Murray proposes four reasons why Teilhard is convinced of a directed evolution, of an orthogenesis: first, because 'he was not a trained biologist'; secondly, because Lamarckism was dominant during his early studies; thirdly, because his fundamental mentality was 'continental' and fourthly and 'perhaps more decisively, his philosophical and theological presuppositions and beliefs were active in his cross-disciplinary judgments'.[16] The first point is fairly widely confirmed. The second one, however, is contested by Ludovico Galleni, especially as regards Teilhard's Chinese period. The scientific environment in Peking was more notably Darwinian, and Teilhard was influenced by it.[17] As for the fourth point, the accent placed on the interdisciplinary dimension seems correct. It is this dimension that is often snubbed by the 'specialists'.

Those who think that no communication can exist between disciplines as apparently diverse as the natural sciences, philosophy and theology, or that the knowledge of the world and the meaning of life are two domains that should remain radically separate, will, by necessity, be offended by the Teilhardian style. However, those who judge that the gulf separating the world of science from the world of life causes detriment to humanity are on the contrary attracted by the ambition of his approach. Thus, Georges Gusdorf criticizes the 'technical anthropologists', who enclose themselves within their discipline 'without ever taking into consideration the cosmic scale of the human phenomenon in its totality'. So, the 'visionary genius' of Teilhard opens the way for a renewal of anthropology.[18]

If Teilhard's scientific reflection remains relevant it remains so because of its global vision of the world. I already referred to the support he enjoys from cosmologists. One can also think of the ecological sensibility, as expressed in the works of Vladimir Vernadsky or in those of James Lovelock, this latter being another author criticized by many a biologist. In this regard, as suggested by Galleni, Teilhard's idea of a geo-biology could be considered a sort of anticipation of the Gaia hypothesis.[19] This discipline, which Teilhard tried to launch in the 1940s, consists in taking into account the totality of phenomena constituting the living world: 'to study living beings in their totality as a single closed system.'[20]

2. A Search for the Absolute in a World in Genesis

Since his youth, Teilhard had been interested in natural history. His father introduced him to the discovery of nature. He felt particularly drawn to rocks, because in his eyes the mineral world reflected the consistency of existence. In his autobiography, *Le cœur de la matière*, written towards the end of his life, he insisted on the search for consistency, for the absolute, for the 'sense of plenitude'.[21] Straight away, his scientific interest became combined with a *mystical aspiration*: contact with nature leads him towards the 'Spirit'. It was not simple curiosity that made him collect rocks or fossils, but the face that these different objects reflect something common from the same world.

An important discovery, which he himself qualified as an upheaval (*renversement*), is that the true consistency he had been seeking is not in the minerals as such. It lies within the development of being, within its evolution. At the outset of his reflection, the living organism has no great value: it is too fragile. Nevertheless, he perceives that this fragility is a strength, because the living organism can be transformed. What interests him is neither stability nor the permanence of being, but *its capacity to become something else*, on condition that the change indicates a *direction*, a goal. Later on, in the 1920s, he will reflect on the central importance of the human organism, the organism that pushes to the extreme this capacity of self-transformation and of transformation of the world.

It is during his years of theological formation that he discovers the great book of Henri Bergson, *L'évolution créatrice* (1908). This work confirms his intuition of the profoundly dynamic nature of being. In his *Note on Progress*, a text of 1920, Teilhard assumes it is obvious that the world in its present state is the 'outcome of movement'. He adds: 'Nothing is comprehensible except through its history. "Nature" is the equivalent of "becoming" or self-creation: this is the view to which experience irresistibly leads us.'[22] Here, one needs to note the two fundamental elements in his thought: history and experience.[23] In spite of all his admiration, Teilhard thinks nevertheless that Bergson did not go far enough. He appreciates Bergson's capacity to highlight the importance of evolution as such, but he criticizes him for thinking that evolution has no defined goal. For Bergson, it is a pure movement. For Teilhard, the movement 'tends towards'. What interests Teilhard is not the process as such, but the purpose that this process manifests.

This research leads him to want to unearth the laws behind the observed phenomena. The most famous – and most controversial – law is the law of 'complexity–conscience', which he describes in *Le Phénomène humain* in the following terms: 'Spiritual perfection (or conscious "centricity") and material synthesis (or complexity) are merely the two connected faces or parts of a single phenomenon.'[24]

3. The Human Phenomenon

Up to now, we have restricted ourselves to the observation of phenomena in an objective way. For Teilhard, this approach alone is not enough, because the key to what is real lies in the 'human phenomenon'. His book, *Le Phénomène humain*, demonstrates the value of the human organism, which is that particular living system that is the most complex of all the different organisms in the biosphere.

The first aspect he highlights is the continuity between the human organism, the other living things and the world of matter. The human world constitutes a *noosphere* that is inscribed within the *biosphere*, above the *lithosphere*. Within the entire universe, and particularly on Earth, everything is interconnected. His second aspect marks more clearly how the nature of human beings differs from that of other beings. With the emergence of human beings, a threshold is crossed in the history of life. Before that threshold is breeched, one can take the evolutionary process to be mechanical, with individual organisms adapting themselves to their surrounding environment. With the emergence of humanity, we have the eruption of consciousness, in other words, of *freedom*. It is true that some animals can indeed transform their environment. Hence, the tool, in the broad sense of the word, is not a characteristic of the human species. With the advent of *Homo sapiens*, however, we see something else happening in the history of the cosmos. Moreover, the specific human transformative capacity is not static but increases with the development of humanity.

The importance given to human freedom brought together Teilhard and the philosopher Edouard Le Roy, successor of Henri Bergson at the Collège de France. From 1921 onwards, their relationship developed steadily. Le Roy's lectures at the Collège de France were greatly inspired by Teilhard, but Le Roy made Teilhard aware of the importance of freedom.[25] A central notion is that of *invention*, which Le Roy defines as 'a becoming, a progress, a perpetual springing up, an incessant genesis, a bursting out of an ever ascending creative tendency'.[26] He contrasts it to habit. It has three characteristic elements. First, it is *the orientation towards the future* which remains, in part, *unforeseeable*: the goal itself has to be created, out of a call, a desire, or the lack of something. The goal attained may prove itself different from the representation of it previously formed. A second trait is the *tentative character of research*, 'the struggle for adaptation between the ideas coming to birth and the body of acquired habits'. A third trait links the individual effort (creation is an irreducibly personal process) with the ambient milieu which conditions and amplifies research, a 'system of circumstances which prepares, orients or sometimes even launches it; and in every case supports, nourishes, strengthens and generates it'.[27] For Teilhard, invention is defined as 'everything in human activity that in one way or another contributes to the socio-organic construction of the Noosphere and to the development within it of new powers of "arrangements of Matter" '.[28]

Teilhard willingly celebrates the role and the importance of *technology*. A significant event for him was the domestication of nuclear energy, which the world discovered with the explosion of the first atomic bomb in 1945. It is regrettable that this first manifestation should have been so destructive.

What interests Teilhard, however, is that such an event demonstrates the human capacity to transform the world. '[Humanity] has succeeded in seizing and manipulating the sources that govern the very origins of matter'.[29] Here is an example: '[humanity] not only can, but also must, for the future, collaborate in its own genesis.'[30] One can understand the serious *moral questions* this raises. The issue is all the more crucial since, in an evolutionary world, a natural determination of human action does not exist. There is no permanent nature to conserve: 'biological realities no longer provide a fixed set of conditions within which humanity makes moral decisions.'[31] Humanity becomes capable of self-transformation; but not all transformative action is in itself good. It is profoundly ambivalent. For Teilhard, transformative action manifests either of two spirits. The first he calls a Promethean or a Faustian spirit; the second he calls the Christian spirit. When transformative action is done according to the first spirit, it highlights the force of individuals acting for their own benefit without taking into account that they act with others and in relation with the world. When transformative action is done according to the second spirit, it reflects 'the spirit of service and of gift'. Humanity has to decide between these two spirits.[32]

4. Analysis and Synthesis

Teilhard is aware that the classical scientific enquiry cannot lead to the understanding of the human phenomenon as such, insofar as it is an analytic approach that breaks down its object into smaller parts, preventing the understanding of it as a whole. During his 1921 lecture 'Science and Christ', he proposes his own contrasting approach.[33]

In the first section, he highlights the importance of knowledge for humanity. Humanity seeks knowledge more than material well-being. It is this longing for knowledge that motivates humanity to go out exploring the world. This exploration of the surface of things is insufficient. One needs to add exploration of the deep side, so as to penetrate the 'inside' of things. The scientist takes over from the explorer. The first kind of research pushes the analysis forward: it breaks down the complex system into simple elements to understand their function. But this quest is indefinite. It never reaches its goal. The more it plunges on towards the simple element, the more it loses sight of the phenomenon which it was supposed to understand. This is why Teilhard suggests doing an about-turn (*faire volte-face*), passing from analysis to synthesis: 'the only consistency beings have comes to them from their synthetic element.'[34] We have followed the direction of analysis, which breaks down its object, 'whereas the absolute, the intelligible, lies at the centre, in the direction in which everything is heightened to the point of being but one'.[35] While the analytic path leads us towards the past, the synthetic path unlocks the future. For Teilhard, the two are linked together: 'to the informed observer, analysis of matter reveals the priority and primacy of Spirit.'[36] Analysis necessarily leads to synthesis.

5. Teilhard and Darwin

Teilhard's taste for a synthetic vision and his valorizing of the 'human phenomenon' as the key for the understanding of evolution situate him in a delicate relationship with Darwinian orthodoxy. While he has no problem with the idea of the evolution of living things, he shows little interest in the mechanisms of evolution. During his scientific formation, the dominant paradigm in France was Lamarckian. It is, therefore, not surprising to find him leaning more in this direction, even if his meetings with English-speaking researchers in China led him to be more interested in the Darwin's theory.[37] In 1926, he wrote: 'The specificity of Transformism is not the introduction of some mechanism or other into our explanation of life's developments. It just is rather the vision of a universe, and especially of an organized world, whose parts are physically linked together in both their appearance and their destiny.'[38] The point which interests him is therefore above all the *interconnection* between elements. In the same article, which raises the question of the morality of an evolutionary vision of the world, he denounces the danger of identifying Transformism with 'its mechanistic or materialist forms, and more especially with Darwinism'.[39]

It has been seen above that the central point in his reflection was the *question of the human being*. At various points, he recalls how the old anthropocentrism has been dismantled first by Galileo's rejection of geocentrism and then by Darwin. Modern science has definitely rejected this naïve form of anthropocentrism. Having avoided one danger, however, one needs to take care not to succumb to the opposite danger. For, after all these efforts, humans could be left thinking of themselves as 'definitely submerged and flattened by the "temporal" flow' their intelligence has managed to discover.[40] It is because of this that the Darwinian vision must be, not rejected, but *completed*. The reason for this is that today, in Teilhard's view, the human being 'now seems to be emerging in the forefront of Nature'. Teilhard further explains: 'Far from being swallowed up by Evolution, Man is now engaged in transforming our earlier idea of Evolution in terms of himself, and thereafter plotting its new outline.'[41]

Thus, the novelty of humanity is this 'transformation of transformism'. It is no longer nature which rules this process, but humanity. The human being is no longer 'a simple branch of evolution'. On the contrary, we should say that 'the principal shoot of the tree of earthly life passes through him'. Life 'shows an absolute direction of progress towards the value of growing consciousness'.[42]

The rejection of anthropocentrism by modern thought has been excessive: 'In the space of a few generations man saw, or at least believed, himself reduced to nothing in a universe in which [. . .] the thinking being now seemed no more than one poor little leaf among tens of thousands on the huge tree of life.'[43] Between the psyche of humans and the psyche of non-human primates, there is more than a simple 'difference of degree'.[44] In the course of evolution, a split is being created: 'We are gradually coming to see that anthropogenesis is specifically distinct from the rest of biogenesis,'[45] Humanity is a 'life of the second species', no longer at the centre of a static cosmos, but at the forefront of a dynamic cosmos, 'that has acquired the faculty of foresight, of invention, and, by deliberate skill, of associating in an ever more marked process of planetary co-adjustment and co-reflection'.[46] In contrast to the former kind of evolution, automatic and mechanical, a *new evolution* reveals itself in humankind, composed of three factors: invention, education (transmission of acquired knowledge) and socialization (convergence on oneself). This new mode of evolution does not pertain only to external observation, but primarily to 'introspection'.[47]

Teilhard's criticism bears on the reduction of evolution to a mere 'Darwinian survival'.[48] As regards the human organism, the issue is not only about surviving by adapting to his environment, but of 'super-living' in transforming this environment. Teilhard concedes that the struggle for existence presupposes a 'tenacious sense of conservation, of survival'.[49] For humans, however, there exists, more essentially, a 'basic polarization' expressed precisely in a 'zest for life'. In Teilhard's view, Darwin gives too much importance to the competition between beings, while in fact it is biological convergence that wins out in significance over the struggle for life.

Because of this insight, we must readjust our conception of matter, to respect the fundamental solidarity between the human being and the rest of the world. Teilhard extrapolates the fundamental human experience of freedom back to matter. Hence, he writes: matter tends, 'in virtue of some initial (and, because initial, inexplicable) disposition of the *Weltstoff* to become organized, to become complex, to become interiorized.[50] This seems to go in the direction of a Lamarckian biology. Teilhard in fact speaks explicitly of a 'new form of speciation', which is demonstrated by the 'accumulation and the transmission of something learned'.[51] He elaborates this by adding that a 'common human foundation' arises, which may even have, in a retro-active manner, a chromosomal influence.[52] An important text in *Le Phénomène humain* makes his vision of these things clearer. He distinguishes between a Darwinian biology (chance and environmental selection) of 'little complexes' and a Lamarckian biology of 'large complexes'.[53] As regards the pre-human zones of life, the neo-Darwinians get things right, with their idea of an 'automatic' appearance of life. From the emergence of human beings onwards, however, 'it is the

neo-Lamarckians who have the better of the argument'.[54] Darwinian evolution puts the accent on the conservation of organisms, while human
evolution valorizes transformation. Hence, evolution, 'from being passive,
tends to become active in the pursuit of its purpose [*en se finalisant*]'.[55]
Biological finality, it must be recalled, is not noticeable everywhere. It
makes itself felt at certain levels of complexity. In Teilhard's terminology,
the forces of choice and of internal direction increasingly prevail over
mechanical processes. This aspect, this shift, could still be modest, even
un-noticeable, to the scientific view situated at a distance. It is this aspect,
however, that constitutes the power to renew the world. Understanding
evolution requires a global vision.

6. Christ, Source of Evolution

Up till now, the Christian dimension has not been explicitly dealt with.
One needs to recall however that it is difficult to fully understand Teilhard's
thought if one disregards this central element of his life. We have already
mentioned the role within his research of a mystical aspiration towards
the absolute. One may think of this aspiration as primarily a search for
meaning.

In the lecture already quoted, 'Science and Christ', he says that Christ
'fills this empty place which has been distinguished by the expectation of
all Nature'.[56] If we understand the progress of the world as a synthesis that
tends towards the unity of a common centre, we grasp also that the centre
is at the same time internal and external to this progress of the world.
Evidently, the difficulty consists in holding together this immanence and
this transcendence. Teilhard has been accused frequently by his adversaries
of immanentism or of pantheism. He defended himself against this accusation, particularly in a text of 1946, entitled 'Outline of the Dialectic of
Spirit'. He first recalls the rise of the Universe where evolution 'assumes
a strictly *convergent* form which, towards its peak, produces *a point of
maturation* (or of collective reflection)'.[57] But this aspect, seen first as simply immanent to evolution, 'presupposes behind it, and deeper than it, a
transcendent – a divine – nucleus'.[58] There is indeed a dialectic: the progress of the world does not by itself lead to the effective realization of this
desired communion. The combination of the elements of the world does
not produce anything more than an element of this world. Humanity, however, aspires to 'more'. It aspires not just to survive (*survivre*) but to super-
live (*super-vivre*). This added aspiration can only be given to humanity
from beyond the world, by God.

The God of Teilhard is a God who enters into the world to be one, to be
incorporated, with it. 'If the universe is rising progressively higher towards
unity, it is therefore not only under the influence of some external force,

but because in that unity the transcendent has made itself to some degree immanent'.[59] God comes to inhabit the world and to transform it from the inside. This divine design expresses itself in the form of a universal communion. For Teilhard, every existent aspires to unity. The metaphysical scheme underlying his thought is of a 'creative union'.[60] In the beginning, there was multiplicity, but this multiplicity tends towards the one. This aspiration towards unity is at the same time an interior tendency to being and also an attraction towards an ultimate communion, the 'Omega point'. His metaphysical scheme represents at the same time the necessary outcome of the development of being, which he calls natural, and also a force exterior to the world that operates despite the tendency to dispersion, opposing the tendency to unification. Without doubt, nothing guarantees in advance the victory of the forces of unification. Teilhard's optimism is founded on his meditation on the victory of Christ over death. It is because life overrides death that it is *reasonable to hope* in the future salvation of humanity. So Teilhard does indeed take into account the existence of the forces of disintegration, but he believes that they will not have the last word.

It is true that these views do not result directly from the phenomenological observation of the world. Teilhard's talk of the 'irresistible' character of progress must be understood in the sense of an act of faith. Such faith expresses a hope. His concern is to show that this hope is not arbitrary. He invites his readers to look at the unfolding of events in the world to verify the relevance of this hope. The encounter between theological hope and the observation of the world makes Teilhard accord a central importance to the figure of Christ, God incarnate, dead and risen. The God of Teilhard is not only a creator, seen as a first cause, an abstract principle of being. For Teilhard, God is personal. God moves the world only by participating from the interior in the unfolding of its history.

7. Conclusion

Teilhard's contribution to scientific knowledge of the world is not negligible. The question whether his 'science of the human being' is relevant remains open. He certainly contributes important elements of reflection regarding human beings and their place in nature.

Classic science is reductionist: it tries to relate complex phenomena, particularly pertaining to the living world, to simple elements, elementary particles and fundamental forces. For several centuries, this approach has shown its effectiveness. There is no serious reason to think that this style of doing science will not continue in the future. Nevertheless, as Alfred North Whitehead has stressed, this mode of explanation misses many elements of our experience. Is it possible to develop a more global science, a hyper-physics, as Teilhard would say – a hyper-physics that re-integrates these elements? This is debatable. It seems that such a new approach does not arise from science itself. At this level, the epistemological reflection of Teilhard remains insufficient. It is helpful to highlight, more clearly than he did, what distinguishes the human phenomenon from other phenomena in the world, that is what distinguishes what arises from a scientific *explanation* and what arises from the *interpretation* made possible by human *freedom*.

This distinction allows the critical evaluation of certain suggestions that claim to draw inspiration from Darwinism to justify a vision of the world that Christian Theology can only refute. It is an abuse of Darwinism, for example, to deduce from it an interpretation that denies all specificity to the human person. To make of the human being a mere constituent of the world is to run the risk of instrumentalizing it. It runs the risk of reducing it to the status of a thing, in the same way as totalitarian political systems tried to do. Admittedly, a close comparison between Darwinism and Totalitarianism is clearly inappropriate. One must, however, be aware of the deviations that are possible once the validity of the theory in its own domain is not sufficiently distinguished from the extrapolated interpretation that one draws from it.

In other suggestions that allegedly originate from Darwinism, one may notice aspects that are less extreme: a tendency to fatalism, even to pessimism. John Haught writes: 'even though a pessimistic interpretation of the cosmos is more the product of myth than of science, physicists and evolutionary biologists have generally displayed their ideas in such a way that tragedy seems to be their most natural setting.'[61] Consider, for instance, Daniel Dennett. In spite of the fact that his reflection is very rich, his vision remains explicitly 'mechanical'.[62] One wonders whether, in his system, a novelty is really possible. The great number of components, associated with the game of chance, means that many combinations are possible, many more than we can imagine. All combinations, however, remain enclosed within a determined frame.

Biblical tradition gives a prominent place to the freedom of the human agent. The human person is the only creature created in the image of God, a God who is himself a creator. Because of this fact, neither the sense of human existence nor the future of the world is determined beforehand, independently of the freedom of the human agent. The biblical notion of 'God's design' expresses the divine will of a universal salvation, without prejudice to the material forms that this salvation could take. Human freedom, however, is realized within a world. Teilhard has the merit of being the one who recalled the fundamental solidarity that unites humanity to the universe.

The main contribution of Teilhardian thought is not on the level of knowledge of the phenomena of the world. It is more in the sense of a hope breathed into a 'world inhabited by anguish'.[63] This is in line with the opinion of Theodosius Dobzhansky, one of the fathers of the Synthetic Theory. After critiquing Teilhardian orthogenesis on the scientific plane, Dobzhansky writes in the conclusion of his work on humanity in the light of evolution: 'To modern man, so solitary, spiritually imprisoned in the midst of this vast universe apparently denuded of sense, the notion of evolution of Teilhard de Chardin appears like a ray of hope.'[64] Teilhard shows clearly that there is no opposition in principle between the Christian tradition and an evolutionary vision of the world, on condition that the latter is not understood in a closed way. The knowledge of the mechanisms of evolution does not dispense us from the freedom to give meaning to our presence in the world.

Notes

1 Teilhard de Chardin, *The Human Phenomenon*, trans. Sarah Appleton-Weber (Brighton-Portland: Sussex Academic Press, 1999), 3.
2 O. Rabut, *Dialogue avec Teilhard* (Paris: Cerf, 1958), 142.
3 *The Human Phenomenon*, 3.
4 David Grumett, *Teilhard de Chardin. Theology, Humanity and Cosmos* (Leuven: Peeters, 2005), 5.
5 See Gustav Martelet, *Teilhard, prophète d'un Christ toujours plus grand* (Bruxelles: Lessius, 2005).
6 Peter Medawar, 'The Phenomenon of Man', *Mind*, January 1961; reprinted in: Peter Medawar, *The Strange Case of the Spotted Mice* (Oxford: Oxford University Press, 1996), 1–11.
7 Quoted in R. Speaight, *Teilhard de Chardin. A Biography* (London: Collins, 1967), 273.
8 George Murray, 'Teilhard and Orthogenetic Evolution', *Harvard Theological Review*, 60 (1967), 281.
9 Ludovico Galleni, 'Relationships between Scientific Analysis and the World View of Pierre Teilhard de Chardin', *Zygon*, 27/2 (1992), 153.
10 See J. Piveteau, *Le Père Teilhard de Chardin savant* (Paris: Fayard, 1964). A systematic study of Teilhard's purely scientific work is still to appear.
11 These works have been edited by Karl and Nicole Schmitz-Moormann and published by Walter Verlag (vol. 11).
12 Teilhard de Chardin, *The Human Phenomenon*, 1.
13 Christian de Duve, *Poussière de vie* (Paris: Fayard, 1996), 476; original version: *Vital Dust: life as a cosmic imperative* (New York: Basic Books, 1995).
14 *Ibid.*, 478.
15 Jacques Monod, *Chance and Necessity*, trans. A. Wainhouse (Penguin, 1971), 180; original version: *Le hasard et la nécessité* (Paris: Seuil, 1970). Christian de Duve is very critical of Monod: 'on the scientific level, I feel much closer to Monod than to Teilhard. But it is true that I have opted in favor of a meaningful Universe and not one emptied of sense' (de Duve, *Poussière de vie*, 494).
16 Murray, 'Teilhard and Orthogenetic Evolution', 289.
17 Galleni, 'Relationships between Scientific Analysis and the World View of Pierre Teilhard de Chardin', 155.

18 Georges Gusdorf, *Introduction aux sciences humaines* (Paris: Belles lettres, 1960), 399.
19 L. Galleni, 'How Does the Teilhardian Vision of Evolution Compare with Contemporary Theories?' *Zygon*, 30/1 (1995), 28.
20 *Ibid.*, 29.
21 Teilhard de Chardin, *The Heart of Matter*, tr. Rene Hague (London: Collins, 1978), 16.
22 Teilhard de Chardin, 'A Note on Progress', in: *The Future of Man*, trans. Norman Denny (New York, Image Books Doubleday, 2004), 3.
23 These two elements bring together the intuition of Teilhard and that of Alfred North Whitehead. This proximity has been noted several times. Joseph Needham thinks that Teilhard 'could have gained much from Whitehead's organic philosophy' (quoted in R. Speaight, *Teilhard de Chardin. A Biography*, 273). Ian Barbour studied this issue in: 'Five Ways of Reading Teilhard', *Soundings*, II/2 (1968): 115–45; and 'Teilhard's Process Metaphysics', *Journal of Religion*, 49 (1969): 136–59, reprinted in: E. Cousins (ed.), *Process Theology. Basic Writings* (New York, 1971), 323–50. See also the special issue of *Process Studies* (35/1, October 2006), partially devoted to Teilhard.
24 Teilhard de Chardin, *The Human Phenomenon*, 27.
25 See Edouard le Roy's lecture *L'Exigence idéaliste et le fait de l'évolution* (Paris, 1927).
26 In the original French: 'devenir, progrès, jaillissement perpétuel, incessante genèse, tendance créatrice épanouie en gerbe toujours montante', ibid., 34.
27 Ibid., p. 44.
28 'The Human Rebound of Evolution', in: Teilhard de Chardin, *The Future of Man*, 199.
29 'Some Reflections on the Spiritual Repercussions of the Atom Bomb', in: Teilhard de Chardin, *The Future of Man*, 135.
30 Ibid., p. 138.
31 David Grumett, 'Teilhard de Chardin's Evolutionary Natural Theology', *Zygon* 42/2 (2007), 529.
32 'Some Reflections on the Spiritual Repercussions of the Atom Bomb', in: Teilhard de Chardin, *The Future of Man*, 187.
33 Teilhard de Chardin, *Science and Christ*, tr. Rene Hague (London: Collins, 1968), 21–36.
34 Ibid., p 29.
35 Ibid., p. 30.
36 Ibid.,p. 31.
37 See Galleni, 'Relationships between Scientific Analysis and the World View of Pierre Teilhard de Chardin', 155.
38 Teilhard de Chardin, *The Vision of the Past: The basis and foundations of the idea of evolution*, trans. J. M. Cohen (London: Collins, 1966), 137.
39 Ibid., p. 136.
40 Teilhard de Chardin, 'The New Spirit', in: *The Future of Man*, 79.
41 Ibid.
42 Teilhard de Chardin, 'Evolution of the Idea of Evolution,' in: *The Vision of the Past*, 246.
43 Teilhard de Chardin, 'Man's Place in the Universe,' in: *The Vision of the Past*, 216.
44 Teilhard de Chardin, 'Hominization and Speciation,' in: *The Vision of the Past*, 260.

45 Teilhard de Chardin, 'The Energy of Evolution', in: *Activation of Energy*, trans. Rene Hague (San Diego: Harvest Book, 1978), 363.
46 Ibid., pp. 363–4.
47 Ibid., p. 385.
48 Teilhard de Chardin, 'The Activation of Human Energy', in: *Activation of Energy*, 391.
49 Teilhard de Chardin, 'The Zest for Living', in: *Activation of Energy*, 233–4.
50 Teilhard de Chardin, 'The Reflection of Energy', in: *Activation of Energy*, 324.
51 Lettre à Pierre Leroy, 6 mai 1953, *Lettres familières de Pierre Teilhard de Chardin mon ami. Les dernières années (1948–55)*. (Paris: Le Centurion, 1976), 191.
52 Ibid., p. 192.
53 Teilhard de Chardin, *The Human Phenomenon*, 97.
54 Teilhard de Chardin, 'The Human Rebound of Evolution', in: *The Future of Man*, 196.
55 Ibid., p. 201.
56 Teilhard de Chardin, *Science and Christ*, 34.
57 Teilhard de Chardin, 'Outline of a Dialectic of Spirit', in: *Activation of Energy*, 144.
58 Ibid., p. 145.
59 Ibid., p. 148.
60 See Teilhard de Chardin, *Writings in the Time of War*, trans. Rene Hague (London: Collins, 1968), 151–76.
61 J. Haught, *God after Darwin* (2nd rev. ed. Westview Press, 2007), 115.
62 Daniel Dennett, *Darwin's Dangerous Idea* (Simon & Schuster, 1996).
63 M. Barthélémy-Madaule, 'La problématique teilhardienne,' in: *Teilhard de Chardin, son apport, son actualité* (Paris: Le Centurion, 1982), 99.
64 T. Dobzhansky, *L'homme en évolution* (Paris: Flammarion, 1966), 393.

Chapter 6

BERNARD LONERGAN'S TRANSFORMATION OF THE DARWINIAN WORLDVIEW

PATRICK H. BYRNE AND FRANK BUDENHOLZER

1. Lonergan as a Catholic Thinker

When it comes to the relationship between Darwinism and their faith, Catholics often now rely upon a commonplace: 'Evolution and creation are not mutually exclusive. God uses evolution to create living things.' Though few are aware of it, their commonplace echoes the traditional notion of God's instrumental causality, which has a long history in Catholic thought. Instrumental causality means that God indirectly causes certain things by more directly causing their causes.

At this level of generality there can be little objection. Yet the tensions between evolutionary thought and Catholic thought quickly become specific, and seldom remain at the level of generality of the commonplace. As other essays in this volume have shown, Catholic tensions with evolutionary thought never reached the level of vehement and blanket opposition that characterizes much of fundamentalist Protestant thought. Nor has Catholicism had to suffer anything quite like the trauma of a second Galileo affair with regard to Darwinism.

Nevertheless, the general the idea of instrumental causality alone does not meet the several more specific challenges that arise. Among other things, there is a great diversity among Darwinian thinkers. Some hold a kind of minimalist scientific approach that leaves aside metaphysical and theological questions for other disciplines; others regard Darwinian theory as a totalizing, materialistic answer to all questions, which eliminates the need for 'the God hypothesis'. Clearly, 'God uses evolution to create living things' cannot be reconciled with this last variety of Darwinism. In addition, the problems of randomness *versus* divine purpose, and of the special status of human beings in the order of creation/evolution, remain in uncomfortable tension with certain varieties of Darwinism. Clearly something more nuanced than the commonplace about instrumental causality is called for.

In this chapter, we propose to show how Bernard Lonergan developed a nuanced, philosophical account of world process, including evolution, which he referred to as 'emergent probability'. His account is compatible with all of the genuine advances of Darwinian science, and yet avoids the non-scientific assumptions of several thinkers that would seem to make Darwinian science incompatible with Catholic faith.

As with most things, Bernard Lonergan approached issues concerning biological evolution and Darwinism self-consciously as a Catholic thinker. Yet the very phrase 'Catholic thinker' is likely to evoke disturbing images of someone who rejects any new idea superficially thought to be incompatible with Catholic doctrines. Such of course was not Lonergan's approach. For him, the first task was learning to better understand the subtleties of the Catholic tradition. Not only did he consider how the Catholic tradition might inform thinking about contemporary issues; his thinking about contemporary issues deepened his understanding and appreciation of the tradition itself. This meant that Lonergan came to his reflections on evolution by a circuitous route. He did not initially set out to understand how the new developments in biological science are related to Catholic thought. Rather, as a young man he was inspired by the encyclicals of the 1930s that stressed 'the *social* need of philosophy'.[1] In a lengthy, unpublished essay from his early student days, Lonergan set forth his first preliminary sketch of his Catholic philosophy of society and history. His approach diverges from the tendency in Darwinism to focus solely on the material forces of the struggle for existence, survival and extinction. In Lonergan's early essay, there is a more nuanced account of the complex dynamic tension in which human intelligence builds upon nature, sin destroys and grace transforms. These would later become key components in his evolutionary vision of 'emergent probability'.

A few years later, Lonergan pushed his understanding of grace and its role in the transformation of human history to greater depths as he took up his dissertation researches. These were his first efforts in 'reaching up to the mind of Aquinas', an effort that made him 'capable of grasping' what the tradition really is, 'but also opened challenging vistas' on how to think about new developments such as critical historical method and biological evolution.[2] In Aquinas's writings on grace, Lonergan encountered profound and nuanced insights about God's instrumental causality. Among the many things that Lonergan discovered through his researches, two were especially significant for his later reflections on evolution: the radical contingency of events in the natural and human worlds, and the precise distinction between the natural and supernatural orders. Regarding the former, Lonergan discovered that Aquinas situated human freedom and divine causality in a fundamentally non-systematic and contingent world, and that this was essential to Aquinas's 'thinking out of the Christian universe'.[3] The notion of a non-systematic and contingent world would later become a central feature of Lonergan's notion of emergent probability. On the other hand, from the 'theorem of the supernatural', Lonergan found in Aquinas a basis for both the proper autonomy of the methods of natural science from interference by theology, as well as a basis for bringing these disciplines into fruitful interaction.[4] Once Lonergan finally comprehended Aquinas's achievements and their ramifications, this allowed him to distinguish and yet maintain a fertile tension between science and religion. Importantly for purposes of this chapter, it also meant that Lonergan saw no need for the Catholic tradition to invoke divine intervention or design as a premise within the realm of natural scientific explanation.

In summary, Lonergan found the key ideas that would lead him to a deeper way of understanding natural evolution through his probing of the meaning of human history. In the interplay of intellectual creativity, freedom, sin and redemptive grace, Lonergan arrived at an understanding profoundly informed by his Catholic heritage. On the basis of his studies, Lonergan developed his unique theory of human cognition and its distinctive worldview: 'emergent probability.'

2. Worldviews, Emergent Probability and Lonergan's Cognitional Analysis

The physical and life sciences have been remarkably successful in explaining the world we live in, hence people of our age would argue for a 'scientific' worldview. Yet this scientific worldview is not simply the sum of all scientific knowledge. Rather, the scientific worldview arises from the success that science has already experienced as a methodology, and then presumes that (1) scientific method is the best method for gaining knowledge of the material world and, in its stronger forms, (2) that the only really true knowledge is knowledge gained through the scientific method. An even stronger version holds that a certain subset of scientific knowledge and methodology can be taken as uniquely competent to describe the world in which we live. Thus we will speak of an 'evolutionary worldview' or of a 'Darwinian worldview'.

Lonergan also formulates a worldview. However, Lonergan begins not with a particular instance of scientific method but rather with a much more general analysis of human knowing and human cognition. He then argues that there is a relationship between the structure of human knowing and the nature of the known. Lonergan's approach is what might be called a 'bottom-up' approach. It begins with an analysis of the nature of human knowing and then argues for the complete intelligibility of all that is. Lonergan set forth his cognitional theory and worldview in his masterwork, *Insight*. It begins with an extended reflection on a wide range of practices in modern scientific methods, culminating in his own philosophical account of evolution and world process.

Among the practices in scientific method, Lonergan gives enquiry the place of greatest prominence. While observations, hypotheses, theories and laws all have important roles in modern scientific methods, much more fundamental than any of these is enquiry, questioning, wonder. As Lonergan puts it, 'There is, then, common to all human beings the very spirit of enquiry that constitutes the scientific attitude'.[5] The most basic thing that scientists do is to inquire and to pursue insights and hypotheses that are possible answers to those questions. Yet, scientific insights and their hypotheses are not isolated monads. Just as they arise from questions about experiences, they also give rise to still further questions about their own correctness. These further questions stimulate a self-correcting, cyclical process that heads towards verified scientific knowledge in the fullest sense.

This means that scientific observation and experimentation are not ends in themselves; rather empirical research is pursued within a context that is first established by scientific questions. Therefore scientific verification is not merely a matter showing that theoretical predictions are borne out by experimental data. This naïve version of verification has been roundly criticized by the twentieth-century philosophers of science.[6] For Lonergan it is questioning, not sense data as such, that holds the key to verification. Enquiry dictates which observations are to be sought and how they are to be regarded. Verification is less a matter of 'matching' hypotheses to data than of answering all the further pertinent inquiries. The scientist can reasonably affirm that her or his understanding of nature is correct only when these further inquiries are fully answered.

Lonergan went on to draw attention to fundamental differences in methodology among different areas of science. However, from the fundamental role that enquiry plays in directing scientific investigation, he argued that all scientific method is 'heuristic'. By this he meant that inquiries anticipate different types of insights, and that scientists use these anticipations methodically to guide them as they seek answers. While acknowledging the many varieties and great differences among the methods employed in different branches of science and individual scientists, Lonergan proposed that there are two basic kinds of heuristic methods commonly used by all natural sciences, and a third kind employed specifically in the biological sciences. All natural sciences, he argued, employ what he called classical and statistical methods.[7] In the biological sciences, it is necessary to add a third kind of method, a genetic method that seeks correct understanding of development – embryological development, for example.[8]

The first kind of scientific heuristic method – which Lonergan dubbed 'classical heuristic method' – pursues insights into the intelligible correlations among events and things. In physics, these correlations are expressed in equations that relate variables to one another. These relationships play so fundamental a role in modern science that we emphasize their role by use of a juridical metaphor – 'law' of science. For example, in physics we speak of Newton's 'law' of gravitation and the 'laws' of conservation of energy and momentum.' In chemistry there are similar correlations, such as the 'law' of balancing oxidation and reduction states in chemical reactions and in biology Darwin is credited with the 'law' of natural selection.

But the metaphor of law can lead to what Lonergan called an 'oversight of insight'.[9] That is to say, it is easy to overlook a most important feature of the equations and other discoveries of classical methods, namely: these correlations are highly *conditioned*. Classical correlations are extremely generic, and manifest themselves quite differently, depending upon the environmental conditions. The classic example is Newton's 'laws'. The very same 'laws' manifest themselves in very different and indeed incompatible ways under different conditions. Depending upon the relative energies, momenta and positions of just two celestial bodies, their orbital paths could be hyperbolic, parabolic, elliptical or circular. Likewise, the 'laws' of relationships among chemical elements lead to very different kinds of chemical reactions, depending upon the different conditions of temperature, concentration, pH level and so on.

Lonergan uses the general features of classical correlations to show how scientists approach the explanation of organized complexity. He focuses upon the cycles or 'schemes of recurrence' that populate so much of the earth and outer space.[10] His analysis of cycles or recurrent schemes includes but goes beyond biological phenomena. Each and every movement within such cycles is in accord with and explained by a conditioned classical correlation (or 'law') discovered through use of classical methods by physicists, chemists, biologists and so on. Such cycles or schemes are formed and explained because of the different ways classical correlations can be combined to form sequences of events. This wide variation of combinations is possible precisely because classical correlations are highly conditioned, and can have many different manifestations under different conditions.

Lonergan noted further that throughout the universe, simpler cycles provide the conditions for the recurrence of ever more complex cycles. For instance, the earth's supply of light and heat energy is conditioned by the fusion cycles in the interior of our sun. Hence, the solar fusion cycles form conditions for the terrestrial hydrological cycles (evaporation, cloud formation, precipitation, water flow, evaporation etc.). The hydrological cycles distribute and replenish water supplies that form the conditions for the cycles for the growth, reproduction and evolution of plants. Plant cycles in turn constantly replenish supplies of carbohydrates consumed by herbivorous animals. The consumed carbohydrates are broken down and provide the conditions for Krebs cycles in the interiors of animal cells, and the Krebs cycles provide the conditions for the recurrence of ATP cycles.

There is then a long, complex network or series of conditioned schemes of recurrence reaching from the interior of the sun to the interior of animals' cellular functionings.

One of Lonergan's most ingenious observations was that these networks of functional interdependence imply sequences of emergence. The simpler cycles can begin to function without the presence of the more complex cycles. They set conditions for the emergence of more complex cycles, and this possibility can recur over and again. When it does, there is a 'conditioned *series* of schemes of recurrence'. This conditioned series of emergent cycles is the *key idea in Lonergan's way of speaking of the intelligibility of the wholeness of evolution*. Notice, this idea is not based upon any specific results of scientific investigations, but rather upon the very general features of classical correlations arrived at through the employment of classical heuristic methods.

The idea of a conditioned series of schemes of recurrence provokes an interesting question: Is the whole universe therefore just one big complex cycle, one big deterministic, totalizing system? Lonergan's answer is, No. He argues instead that the universe has a vast, non-systematic, random dimension to it, an idea that he obtained from his studies of Aquinas's attempt to think about 'a Christian universe'. Since cycles of complexity can only begin to function once their proper conditions have arisen, they must rely upon some other source to provide those conditions. In general, this means that these sets of conditions arise and fall away in random, non-systematic fashions.[11]

During the nineteenth century, therefore, scientists began to develop the second kind of scientific method, statistical method, to investigate the intrinsically non-systematic and random dimensions of nature. Statistical methods seek to understand populations of events and things. Statistical method goes beyond determining actual frequencies, and seeks to discover *ideal relative* frequencies (called *probabilities*). The actual frequencies of events will fluctuate randomly around the ideal frequencies (probabilities).

Lonergan's reflections on statistical methods cast light upon the meaning of randomness, a notion that is especially central to the neo-Darwinian synthesis. Randomness has proved notoriously difficult to define, and it is often badly misunderstood. Physicist Stephen Barr makes exactly this point:

> In common speech, 'random' is often used to mean 'uncaused,' 'meaningless,' 'inexplicable,' or 'pointless.' And there is no question that some biologists, when they explain evolution to the public or to hapless students, do argue from the 'randomness' of genetic mutations to the philosophical conclusion that the history of life is 'unguided' and 'unplanned.' Some do this because of an anti-religious animus, while others are simply careless . . . [But the] word 'random' as used in science does not mean uncaused, unplanned, or inexplicable. It means *uncorrelated*.[12]

Lonergan relied on a similarly qualified notion of randomness as he developed his account of emergent probability. For him 'a situation is random if it is any whatever provided specified conditions of intelligibility are not fulfilled'.[13] In other words, randomness is defined not absolutely, but in relation to some 'specified conditions of intelligibility'.

Hence, there is not just one kind of randomness; there are many. There are as many kinds of randomness as there are kinds of patterned expectations from which actual events can diverge. Randomness is always *relative* to some sort of pattern (say the curve on a graph). The kind of randomness that is relevant to neo-Darwinian theories of evolution has to do with the emergence of biologically advantageous characteristics in their immediate environment. A central tenet of Darwinism is that the biological opportunities of an environment do not directly cause inheritance of advantageous characteristics. In other words, the origination of heritable genetic variations is random relative to their adaptive advantage in the immediate environment.[14] If a relatively random series of mutations coincidentally happens to have adaptive advantage in the environment, then it will shift probabilities of survival and propagation of its possessors and their progeny. But this series of mutations is a kind of happy accident (the *per accidens* that Aquinas adapted from Aristotle). It is not directly caused by the adaptive opportunities available in the immediate environment. There is no direct correlation between the adaptive potentialities of the environment and the series of mutations that are favoured by those potentialities. Neo-Darwinians commonly express this tenet by saying that the series of genetic mutations is 'not directed'.

Technically speaking, then, this is the type of randomness that is required by neo-Darwinian explanations: randomness of the series of inheritable mutations *relative to* adaptive potentialities in the immediate environment. It is a quite specific and relatively limited assertion of randomness. But to claim that genetic variations are absolutely random relative to every possible intelligibility is neither needed by neo-Darwinian science nor could it be verified on purely empirical grounds.[15]

Lonergan brings his analyses of the two methods together to form his worldview. Classical methods explain how and why organized complexity functions. Statistical methods analyse the probabilities of conditions coming together for the emergence and survival of complex cycles. Schemes of recurrence arise when appropriate conditions are assembled at in the same vicinity at the same time. This assembly occurs in relatively random and non-systematic ways, and yet in ways that conform to the ideal frequencies of probabilities. In other words, there are probabilities for events coming together to make possible the emergence of new organized schemes of recurrence.

Even more importantly, once simple schemes occur, they themselves can constitute a non-systematic collection of conditions for the emergence of still more complex schemes. This means that the emergences of lower and simpler schemes *actually change the probabilities* for the emergence of those subsequent, more complex schemes. Lonergan shows how emerging complexity actually increases the probability of the emergence of still greater complexity.[16] Hence, not only are there sequences of increasingly complex schemes, but there are also sequences of increasing probabilities.

'Emergent probability' is Lonergan's term for the evolving universe that becomes ever more fully known through the combined efforts of classical and statistical scientific methods. As he puts it, 'Emergent probability is the successive realization in accord with successive schedules of probability of a conditioned series of schemes of recurrence'.[17] This worldview is called 'emergent' because schemes or cycles of increasing complexity emerge, begin to function, and survive as long as their requisite conditions are in place. It is associated with probability because the conditions for the schemes come together non-systematically and relatively randomly, but nevertheless do so in compliance with ideal frequencies. Finally, it is called 'emergent probability' because higher probabilities emerge along with the increasing complexity of schemes.

3. Connections with Neo-Darwinism and Further Implications

Lonergan's account of emergent probability shares many important features with the Darwinian worldview, and Lonergan bestows upon Darwin some of the highest praise in the entire book.[18] Nevertheless, he does differ from Darwin in certain important ways.

First and foremost Lonergan differs from Darwin in the basis for his account of world process. Darwin himself developed his theory of evolution on the basis of his extensive observations and readings about biological, geological and even human population phenomena. Subsequently the neo-Darwinian synthesis was crafted at the beginning of the twentieth century when Mendelian genetics was rediscovered. Data from extensive genetic experiments and theories, as well as the insights of contemporary molecular biology and chemical biology, were integrated with classical Darwinian explanations. While Lonergan was well-informed about the natural phenomena and developments in neo-Darwinian science, his own observations focused primarily on *how scientists do science*, rather than on the evolutionary data from the natural world itself. In other words, Lonergan focused more on scientific methods and practices, rather than on the data and results of scientific method. He developed his evolutionary account from his reflections about the implications of scientific methods. It is important to realize that Lonergan's approach is not somehow in competition with Darwinian science. As a scientific theory, neo-Darwinism begins with observation and adds scientific understandings. This is as it should be. Lonergan on the other hand developed what we might call a meta-theory of evolution. Lonergan's meta-theory and Darwinian science will only come into conflict if either goes beyond the bounds of its own competence.

Thus, one of the big advantages of Lonergan's approach is its independence from the present state of evolutionary science. His approach does not have to assume that the present state of neo-Darwinian science is the last word on the matter. It can allow that scientific methods will lead to great alterations in the understanding of evolutionary processes. By focusing instead on the methods of science, Lonergan's approach avoids the God-of-the-gaps problem. His approach does not need to assume that there will be explanatory gaps that can only be explained by God's creative interventions. He can grant that all organic structures will be found to have come about through relatively random mutations and natural processes of differential survival and inheritance.

Still, it might seem that Lonergan has accomplished very little by saying that the evolution of the cosmos has the structure of emergent probability. After all, he himself explicitly acknowledges that this is a general, heuristic notion, and that the vast wealth of details must be filled in by empirical scientific researches in different fields. At each stage the abstract classical laws as well as the probabilities of emergence and survival have to be discovered and verified using the more specific scientific techniques appropriate to each level. Emergent probability will not dispense us from the scientific work of correctly understanding the actual mechanisms of evolution.

Yet Lonergan's analysis does yield its own important philosophical conclusions. First and foremost, Lonergan argues that the evolving universe is intelligible. Because science is fundamentally a matter of enquiry seeking verified explanatory insights, science is therefore seeking to understand the intelligibility of the natural world. Spontaneously scientists act as though the universe is intelligible. They engage in their endeavors with the implicit faith that their efforts to understand the universe will pay off. As Albert Einstein once said, 'The most incomprehensible thing about the universe is that it is comprehensible'. No matter what the ultimate outcomes of methodical scientific enquiry, no matter how many imperfect hypotheses are abandoned in favour of better ones, the entire enterprise of natural science is a quest to know the intelligibility of the evolving universe.

Lonergan's conclusion stands in tension with one of the most pervasive philosophical assumptions usually associated with Darwinism, namely, that evolution is a purely material process calling for a purely materialistic explanation. Most authors speak of Darwinian evolution and its explanatory power under the heading of a 'materialistic' science or of its 'material' laws or principles or mechanisms. This is true not only of those who claim that Darwinism eliminates the validity of theistic belief. Even believers like cell biologist Kenneth Miller speak of Darwinian evolution as material-istic.[19] If one assumes that evolutionary science is purely materialistic, this poses considerable difficulties for thinking about how God, a purely spiritual being, can have any relationship with the world investigated by scientific methods.

Lonergan's approach of grounding scientific method in enquiry and explanatory insight shifts the focus rather dramatically. Modern science seeks not 'purely material laws' but rather the intelligibilities that explain why things happen as they do. Brute matter does not explain anything at all, and it especially does not yield scientific explanations. According to Lonergan, materialism is just another example of 'extra-scientific opin-ion'.[20] an extra, metaphysical assumption added over and above the intel-ligibilities that scientific methods discover and seek to verify. If the world of modern science is fundamentally intelligible rather than material, this changes the God-world relationship quite significantly. So it is not a ques-tion of selecting either neo-Darwinism or an emergent probability world-view, provided neo-Darwinism does not range beyond strictly scientific pronouncements.

Secondly, neo-Darwinian explanations (purged of their materialistic metaphysical assumptions) form a specialized subset within the broader field of emergent probability. Darwin's basic insight of inherited charac-teristics leading to differential levels of reproduction and hence, within a given ecological niche, the survival or extinction of certain classes of organisms is well established. The neo-Darwinian mechanisms of genetic mutation and expression, selection, differential reproduction and the details of contemporary molecular biology and molecular genetics are all specialized instances of this general evolutionary pattern of a con-ditioned series of schemes of recurrence. But emergent probability is not restricted to the phenomena of biological and biochemical recurrent schemes. Evolution of the complex schemes of living organisms comprises only a portion of all the schemes that emerge, recur and pass away. In his recent *The Emergence of Everything*, Harold Morowitz describes twenty-eight key steps in the development of the cosmos – from the big bang, through the emergence of the solar system, the beginnings of life, right up through the emergence of the human person and culture. Each of these is a stage in the general dynamism of emergent probability.[21] The general features of emergent probability characterize the whole evolving universe, and are present in the more specialized neo-Darwinian features of evolving terrestrial organic life.

Third, emergent probability is a worldview that anticipates the ever-increasing complexity of the universe and of biological evolution. This is in stark contrast to a flat materialistic version of Darwinism that does not really know how to deal with the fact that there is increasing complexity in the universe. If everything is just matter in motion, then increasing complexity seems an illusion at best. By way of contrast, our own experience as knowers and our understanding of the universe as it actually exists suggest that the increase in complexity is not an anomaly to be explained away, but rather a basic fact of the developing universe. Emergent probability draws attention to the evolving universe as a 'conditioned *series* of schemes of recurrence'. The earlier, simpler schemes set conditions for the subsequent emergence of more complex cycles, and this possibility can recur over and again. Just as experience leads to insight and clusters of insights lead to higher viewpoints, so there exist in the actual world higher levels of schemes, which integrate recurring events that would otherwise only be regarded as happy random coincidences. This of course constitutes a rejection of the simplistic reductionism that is often assumed by many contemporary neo-Darwinians.[22] There do exist various levels and each new level integrates properties that are found on the lower levels. However, each new level – whether the molecular, living systems or human persons – is equally real and will have its own properties. There is no purely scientific reason for giving ontological priority to any one level, and especially not to the level that is presumed to be that of the smallest pieces of matter.

On the other hand, like Darwinism, emergent probability does not imply a determinate plan; it does not envision a pre-determined future somehow pulling the universe into increased complexity. Rather, the steady increase in complexity comes about in accord with the empirical statistics that are the basis of emergent probability. As Lonergan puts it, the universe has 'an upwardly *but indeterminately* directed dynamism'.[23] It is 'an incomplete universe heading toward fuller being', but in a radically, indeterminate fashion.[24] A question that has perturbed thinkers since the beginnings of the modern period is that of direction. It has seemed that to acknowledge direction is to presume the future as a known, in ways that violate the integrity of scientific investigation. The finality of emergent probability both acknowledges a general direction of increasing complexity, while at the same time respecting the intrinsic relative randomness of the universe. Hence, emergent probability also respects the proper scientific agnosticism about the unknown details of the ultimate future of the universe. It waits upon the universe to determine that ultimate future, and it leaves to future scientific research the detailed explanations of how the mechanisms involved in the evolution of universe and of life within it.

4. Evolution and God as Creator

To say that the actual course of evolution is random relative to the perspective of the combined natural sciences does not necessarily rule out the possibility that it may have intelligibility, value and purpose that transcends the specialized intelligibilities sought by those sciences. Lonergan went on to explore how this can be so. He proposed a way of thinking about the compatibility of a divinely authored transcendent purpose and a radically contingent, randomly evolving universe that is compatible with neo-Darwinian, scientific understandings.

Lonergan's approach begins by asking different kinds of questions than those pursued by the standard forms of the intelligent design argument. While the standard arguments attempt to show that this or that pattern in the natural world can only be explained by postulating the intervention of a divine designer, his alternative approach shifts the focus by asking whether the entirety of the evolving world itself has an explanation. Any particular instance of organized complexity may very well be explainable in virtue of a series of relatively random transmutations and propagations. Still, each and every instance of organized complexity is but a component in the whole of the course of evolution. To ask about the entirety of the course of evolution is to ask questions very different in kind from questions about the origins of this or that design. These further questions are not about how this or that complex pattern evolved from a predecessor, or even how it is related to a series of predecessors. Rather, questions about the whole of evolution are questions such as: Why does the natural, living world evolve at all? Why is it not static, with every living being present and perfectly adapted from the start, as was assumed for so many centuries before Darwin? Why does it actually evolve in the ways that it does? Why does current science indicate that it evolves according to neo-Darwinian, rather than say through Lamarkian mechanisms? Why is the universe a 'world process in which the order or design is constituted by emergent probability'?[25] Why indeed are the 'laws' of physics, chemistry and biology the way they are, rather than having some other conceivable form? Such questions do not ask for an explanation of this or that pattern or organism within the evolutionary history of the world; they ask for an explanation of the actual, contingent evolutionary history of the world itself. These are questions that can only be answered by asking about what might transcend the evolving universe. They are questions about God.

So, if the design of the evolving universe is emergent probability, what must God be like? We think it is best to begin with the frank admission that human beings cannot have *any* very determinate idea of what God is like. God is utterly beyond human comprehension. No matter what way we have of conceiving of God, that is not what or who God is. Our ways of conceiving of God all pale in comparison to what God is. Much of the discussion about science and religion and intelligent design has suffered dearly from a failure to admit this fact at the very outset. And yet it is desperately important for Christians and Catholics to try to talk about God in the least inadequate way possible.

Perhaps not surprisingly, when Lonergan himself turned to the nigh impossible task of talking about God, he turned to the ecstasy of scientific discovery as his modest point of departure. He wrote, so movingly,

> Our subject has been the act of insight or understanding, and God is the unrestricted act of understanding, the eternal rapture glimpsed in every Archimedean cry of 'Eureka!'[26]

For Lonergan, the rapture of unlimited understanding is the beginning point for a least inadequate way of talking about God. God can be conceived analogically as an *unrestricted* act of understanding that totally understands and therefore can be said to be totally enraptured with every single person and organism and mutation and elementary particle decay in the entire story of the universe. For Lonergan, God's understanding of all that is, is one with God's act of creation. And God's act of creation is not the fabrication of a world that somehow runs on its own, but the maintenance in being of all that ever was and ever will be. Thus for Lonergan, God is not one who looks down upon the universe from afar. He rather conceives God's unrestricted understanding as an intensely intimate identification with the intelligibility of everything about every thing.

Lonergan explores the implications of this analogical conception in great detail.[27] Towards the end of that exploration, he proposes that virtually all of the things that can be said about this unrestricted understanding are the sorts of things that traditional theists would ascribe to God, although with subtle refinements. Among other things, God's unrestricted act of understanding would intimately understand the actual, evolving world in all its myriads of details, with its unique relatively random patterns of intricate twists, turns, transmutations and dead ends. 'So it is that every tendency and force, every movement and change, every desire and striving is designed to bring about the order of the universe in the manner in which in fact they contribute to it'.[28] God's understanding would also encompass *how* to actualize the actual order of the course of the evolving world (because if God did not understand this, something would be missing from God's understanding, and it would not be unrestricted).

Most importantly, however, passionate, unrestricted understanding would understand *why* this design is being realized. That is to say, God would understand the transcendent value and purpose that would make it worthwhile to realize the *actual*, emergent probability, that is the actual evolution of sequences of events from out of all the others that *could* have been selected. Because of this unrestricted understanding of that value, then, God's creative choice would not be arbitrary or absolutely random. What would be properly regarded as relatively random as far as the methods of the natural science are concerned, would be comprehended as special and important and transcendently valuable and worth realizing by the unrestricted act of understanding. As Lonergan puts it, God's unrestricted understanding 'is the ground of value, and it is the ultimate cause of causes for it overcomes contingence at its deepest level'.[29]

In other words, God conceived as unrestricted understanding would bring about each particular complex cycle and organism by bringing about the entirety of evolution, in which each instance of organized complexity is a component. Only an unrestricted act of understanding could do what no human mind can do – intimately understand each and every one of the myriads of intricate details and connections as components in the whole actual course of evolution – not one by one, but by understanding the wholeness, the order, the design universe itself. Because of its unrestricted-ness, God's act of understanding would also understand every other evolutionary course that might have been picked out of the 'grab bag' of 'all the possible sequences of events compatible with the laws of physics, chemistry and biology'. And it would understand the reason and purpose and value of selecting one over all other possibilities, a reason and purpose so profound and transcendent that every event, every cycle and every thing is made precious beyond human comprehension.

Hence Lonergan's approach does more than just assert the compatibility of theistic faith and evolutionary science. Beyond this, Lonergan shows *how* it is possible to reconcile the affirmation of divine purpose with an evolving world shot through with scientific randomness and contingency. The ultimate design, meaning and purpose of the evolving world have a transcendent meaning and value. It would require an unrestricted understanding in order to comprehend that value and purpose. All human understandings fall short of that unrestricted sweep. For human understandings, therefore, the design or purpose of the evolving universe will remain the 'mystery of mysteries'.[30]

There is, however, a problem. To many, belief in transcendental purpose in the universe along with an acceptance of radical contingency would seem to be a flat out contraction. Furthermore, this is not simply an esoteric philosophical problem but seems to go to the heart of the faith experience of many believers. It did not have to be that life evolved on this planet Earth. It did not have to be that the person that I am was conceived and allowed to grow up and mature to ask these sorts of questions. What happens to the traditional understanding of Providence in a world where things could have been very different?

The key to understanding the relationship of a contingent world order and God's transcendent purpose is to understand God's relationship to creation and especially to time. Everything that is ultimately depends on God. To use Lonergan's own words in *Insight*: 'God controls each event because he controls all and he controls all because he alone can be the cause of the order of the universe on which every event depends.'[31] Such an understanding would seem to indicate a world order in which there is no contingency, where everything is decided in some mysterious way by God. If our image of God's relation to creation is of a God within time, then we would seem to have to choose between, on the one hand, allowing creation some space outside of God's control and, on the other hand, having creation completely determined in every detail by an earlier decision of God. The first option would seem to deny that God is the source of all being and the second option seems to make a charade of human freedom and the contingency that seems part and parcel of our universe.

Lonergan suggests another option. God is eternal. God is one and simple and in God there is no change. All time is related to God as an eternal present. If this is the case, there is the possibility of God's creative will being the source of true contingency. God wills all events in this cosmos, but God can will them contingently. To believe God is the source of all being and to accept the reality of finitely random events is not a contradiction. In this scenario, life did not have to evolve on planet earth – there could have been other developments. Evolution on this planet did not have to lead to the human race. Something catastrophic could have intervened. We, the authors, and you, the reader, could have not been here to write and read this paper. Something unexpected could have intervened. But the fact is that each of these contingent events is willed by God, not deterministically but contingently.[32] This is what Lonergan means by God's plan and God's providence. 'From the viewpoint of unrestricted understanding, the non-systematic vanishes to yield place to a fully determinate and absolutely efficacious plan and intention'.[33] Thus we affirm both a divine plan and the real possibility of contingent future development, or of future decline and catastrophe.

5. Conclusion

In this paper, we have attempted to indicate how the thought of Bernard Lonergan, specifically his theory of world, process as emergent probability and his philosophy of God as creator and source of intelligibility, provides a framework that is both appreciative of the scientific developments of neo-Darwinian science and open to faith in a creator God. In conclusion, we make two comments.

First, the conviction of ultimate meaningfulness lies at the heart of the faith-lives of a great many people. It is a most important and valid source for further reflection on the questions of the purpose of the evolving world. Yet by itself, it is not yet an appropriate basis for a philosophical argument, and still less is it appropriate for introduction into methodical scientific investigations. This observation implies a double-limitation. On the one hand, the premise that being is completely intelligible is undecidable from the viewpoint of the scientific methods themselves. For that very reason, the scientist as scientist ought not to pronounce upon the existence or non-existence of a transcendent meaning or purpose or designer of evolution. On the other hand, this also means that it is inappropriate to introduce premises about transcendent value or purpose or their divine origin into the conduct of scientific investigations. Both are unwarranted intrusions of one kind of pursuit of human knowledge into the field of another. Believers may esteem the achievements of empirical scientists, but appropriately reject their denials of the transcendent as going beyond empirical justification. Scientists as human beings may deny or affirm transcendent purpose and divine authorship, but as scientists they should recognize that these matters are distinct from empirical scientific knowledge proper. It is for this reason that scientists have properly opposed attempts to introduce intelligent design arguments into scientific explanation.

Secondly, for Christians, as for all believers in the monotheistic traditions, there is the conviction that our knowledge of God is not limited to the results of our scientific and philosophical investigations. Christians believe that God not only is the creator of the universe but also that God has chosen to have a special, what we can call personal, relationship with the human species on this planet. Humans are special and, as far as we know, are unique among the animal species on planet earth. We can know, we can study science, we have the ability to make truly free decisions and we can love and be loved. Christians believe God has turned directly towards us, spoken to us in revelation and asks for our response. Christians believe that God has intervened in our messy, contingent history in the person of Jesus Christ. Ultimately each individual will have to answer for him or herself whether they believe God in fact has entered into this special relationship with human persons. We simply suggest that, for Christians, the ultimate answer to the questions: 'Is there a Divine purpose? Does God really care?' will be based first and foremost on the experience that God has reached out in a personal way to us as human persons.

Notes

1 Bernard Lonergan, '*Pantôn Anakephalaôsis* [The Restoration of All Things]', *Method: Journal of Lonergan Studies*, 2 (1991): 155.
2 *Insight*, 769.
3 Bernard Lonergan, *Grace and Freedom: Operative Grace in the Thought of St Thomas Aquinas*, Collected Works of Bernard Lonergan, vol. 1, edited by Frederick E. Crowe and Robert M. Doran, (Toronto: University of Toronto Press, 2000), 84. Aquinas uses the term *per accidens* derived from Aristotle. See ibid., 75–86, 116–18. For a brief summary, see also Patrick H. Byrne, 'The Fabric of Lonergan's Thought', *Lonergan Workshop*, 6 (1986), 22–32.
4 *Grace and Freedom*, op. cit., 17–20. See also J. Michael Stebbins, *The Divine Initiative: Grace, World Order, and Human Freedom in the Early Writings of Bernard Lonergan*, (Toronto: University of Toronto Press, 1995), 78–81.

5 *Insight*, 197.
6 See Frederick Suppe, 'The Search for Philosophical Understanding of Scientific Theories', 17–27, 66–94 in: *The Structure of Scientific Theories*, (Urbana, IL: University of Illinois Press, 1974).
7 *Insight*, 60–88.
8 *Insight*, 484–92. Even though genetic method is crucial to biological and evolutionary science, it is not possible to summarize Lonergan's long discussion in this article. However, its inclusion would not alter the general features of the argument that follows.
9 *Insight*, 70.
10 *Insight*, 141.
11 *Insight*, 131; see also 109ff and 149–50.
12 Stephen Barr, 'The Design of Evolution', *First Things* 156 (October 2005), 10, emphasis added.
13 *Insight*, 74. This definition can be shown to be a more general version of the definition of randomness widely accepted in the field of information theory. See by Gregory J. Chaitin 'Randomness in Arithmetic', *Scientific American* 259, No. 1 (July 1988), 80–5.
14 This of course does *not* mean that their differential *survival* is unrelated to environmental advantage.
15 For further details, see Patrick Byrne, 'Evolution, Randomness, and Divine Purpose: A Reply to Cardinal Schönborn', *Theological Studies*, 67 (2006), 653–65.
16 The argument for this claim is beyond the limits of this article. See *Insight*, 143–51.
17 *Insight*, 148–9. Lonergan remarks that this intelligible design becomes a '*generalized* emergent probability' once genetic heuristic method is added to the classical and statistical, ibid., 487, emphasis added.
18 *Insight*, 154–5.
19 Kenneth R. Miller, *Finding Darwin's God*, (NY: HarperCollins Publishers, 1999), 217. He writes: 'God can carry out the work He chooses to in a way that is consistent with the fully materialistic view of biology'. For Lonergan a *fully intelligible* view of biology is needed.
20 *Insight*, 424.
21 Harold Morowitz, *The Emergence of Everything*, (NY: Oxford University Press, 2002).
22 Frank Budenholzer, 'Some Comments on the Problem of Reductionism in Contemporary Physical Science', *Zygon*, 38 (2003), 61–9.
23 *Insight*, 659; also 497.
24 *Insight*, 471.
25 *Insight*, 125, emphasis added. See also 139.
26 *Insight*, 706.
27 See *Insight*, 680–7.
28 *Insight*, 688, emphasis added; see also 673.
29 *Insight*, 679–80.
30 See *The Origin of Species*, 25; see also *Voyage of the Beagle*, (Garden City, NY: Doubleday & Company, Inc., 1962), 379.
31 *Insight*, 664.
32 *Grace and Freedom* (2000), 108–10.
33 *Insight*, 665.

Part Two

PHILOSOPHICAL THEMES

Chapter 7

ON EVOLUTION AND INTELLIGENT DESIGN

Nicholas Rescher

1. Being Intelligently Designed

This chapter is intended to make two principal points: (1) that there is a decided difference between being designed *intelligently* and being designed *by intelligence*, and (2) that evolution, broadly understood, is in principle a developmental process through which the former feature – being designed intelligently – can be realized. The conjoining of these items means that, rather than there being a conflict or opposition between evolution and intelligent design, evolution itself can be conceived of as providing an instrumentality of intelligent design.

To be intelligently designed is to be constructed in the way an intelligent being *would* do it. To this end, it need not be claimed that an intelligent being *did* do it. Being intelligently designed no more requires an intelligent designer than being designed awkwardly requires an awkward one.

At bottom, intelligent design is a matter of efficiency and effectiveness in goal realization. But what then when the entire universe is at issue? How are we now conceiving of the matter of aims and goals? The crux here is not afforded by the question 'Does the universe have a goal?' but rather by the subtler, purely conditional and hypothetical question: 'If we are to think of the universe as having a goal, then what could this reasonably be taken to be?' The issue here is one of a figuratively *virtual* rather than necessarily *literal* goal.

So to begin with we must ask whether or not it is reasonable to expect an intelligent agent or agency to produce a certain particular result. Clearly and obviously, this issue will depend on the aims and purposes this agent or agency could reasonably be expected to have. And so we must begin with the question: What is it that one could reasonably expect regarding the aims and purposes of an intelligent agent or agency?

Now what would obviously have pride in place in the evaluative pantheon of such an intelligence is intelligence itself. Surely nothing has higher value for an intelligent being than intelligence itself and there is little that would be worse than 'losing its reason'. Intelligence and rationality is the paramount value for any rational creature: a rational being would rather lose its right arm than lose its reason. And of course a rational being will thereby only value something it regards as *having* value; it would not value something that it did not deem valuable. It will thus only value rationality in itself if it sees rationality as such as a thing of value. And so in valuing their rationality, truly rational creatures are bound to value rationality in general – whenever it may be found. The result of this will be a reciprocal recognizance among rational beings – as such they are bound to see themselves as the justly proud bearers of a special value.

And here the only response to the question of a conceivable goal for world-development that has a scintilla of plausibility would have to take the essentially Hegelian line of locating the crux of intelligent design in the very factor of intelligence itself. Implementing this idea calls for locating the 'virtual' goal of the universe in its providing for the development of intelligent beings able to achieve some understanding of its own ways and operations. One would accordingly inquire whether the world's nature and *modus operandi* are so constituted as to lead with efficiency and effectiveness to the emergence of intelligent beings. Put in technical jargon the question is: Is the universe noophelic in favouring the interests of intelligence in the course of its development.

A positive response here has deep roots in classical antiquity – originally in Plato and Aristotle and subsequently in Aristotelianizing neo-Platonism. It emerges when two ancient ideas are put into juxtaposition – first is that it is love that makes the world go round, and the second is that such love is a matter of understanding, so that its crux lies in an *amor intellecualis* of sorts. On this perspective, self-understanding, the appreciation through intelligence of intelligence, would be seen as the definitive aim and *telos* of nature's ongoing self-development. Such a position is, in effect, that of an updated neo-Platonism. And it represents a tendency of thought that still has potential relevancy.

2. *Intelligence within Nature*

From this perspective, intelligent design calls for deliberations that envision the prospering of intelligence in the world's scheme of things. But just what would this involve?

Of course, the emergence of living organisms is a crucial factor here. And an organically *viable* environment – to say nothing of a *knowable* one – must incorporate orderly experientiable structures. There must be regular patterns of occurrence in nature that even simple, single-celled creatures can embody in their make-up and reflect in their capacities. Even the humblest organisms, snails, say, and even algae, must so operate that certain types of stimuli (patterns of recurrently discernible impacts) call forth appropriately corresponding types of response – that such organisms can 'detect' a structured pattern in their natural environment and react to it in a way that proves to their advantage in evolutionary terms. Even its simplest creatures can maintain themselves in existence only by swimming in a sea of regularities of exactly the sort that would be readily detectable by intelligence. And so nature must cooperate with intelligence in a certain very particular way – it must be stable enough and regular enough and structured enough for there to be appropriate responses to natural events that can be 'learned' by creatures. If such 'appropriate responses' are to develop, nature must provide suitable stimuli in a duly structured way. Nature must thus present us with an environment that affords sufficiently stable patterns to make coherent 'experience' possible, enabling us to derive appropriate *information* from our structured interactions with the environment. Accordingly, a world in which any form of intelligence evolves will have to be a world that is congenial to the probes of intelligence. To reemphasize: a world in which intelligent creatures emerge in a natural and efficient way through the operation of evolutionary processes must be a substantially intelligible world.

But there is another side to it above and beyond order. For the world must also be varied and diversified – it cannot be so bland and monotone that the stimulation of the sort of challenge-and-response process required for evolution is not forthcoming. All in all, then, a universe with intelligent creatures must be intelligence-congenial: it must be just the sort of universe that an intelligent creatures would – if it could – endeavour to contrive, a universe that is intelligently designed with a view to the existence and flourishing of intelligent beings.

And so, to make the evolutionary emergence of intelligent beings possible, the universe must afford a manifold of lawful order that makes it a cosmos rather than a chaos.

A world in which intelligence emerges by anything like standard evolutionary processes must be a realm pervaded by regularities and periodicities regarding organism-nature interaction that produces and perpetuates organic species. On this line of deliberation, then, nature admits cognitive access not just because it has laws (is a *cosmos*), but because it has *relatively simple* laws, and those relatively simple laws must be there because if they were not, then nature just could not afford a viable environment for intelligent life. But how might an intelligence-friendly *noophelia* world come about? At this point, evolution comes upon the stage of deliberation.

There are many ways in which an organic species can endure through achieving survival across generations – the *multiplicity* of sea turtles, the *speed* of gazelles, the *hardness* of tortoise shells, and the *simplicity* of micro-organisms all afford examples. But, among these survival strategies, intelligence – the resource of intelligent beings – is an adaptive instrumentality of potent and indeed potentially optimal efficacy and effectiveness. So, in a universe that is sufficiently fertile and complex, the emergence of intelligent beings can be seen as something that is 'only natural' under the pressure of evolutionary processes.

After all, in order to emerge to prominence through evolution, intelligence must give an 'evolutionary edge' to its possessors. The world must encapsulate straightforwardly 'learnable' patterns and periodicities of occurrence in its operations – relatively simply laws. A world that is too anarchic or chaotic for reason to get a firm grasp on the *modus operandi* of things will be a world in which intelligent beings cannot emerge through the operations of evolutionary mechanisms. In a world that is not substantially lawful, they cannot emerge. In a world whose law structure is not in many ways rather simple, they cannot function effectively.

A world in which intelligence emerges by anything like standard evolutionary processes must thus be a realm pervaded by the regularities and mid-length periodicities regarding organism-nature interaction that produces and perpetuates organic species. On this line of deliberation, then, nature admits cognitive access not just because it has laws (is a *cosmos*), but because it has *relatively simple* laws, and those relatively simple laws must be there because if they were not, then nature just could not afford a viable environment for intelligent life.

On the other hand, however, in a world without significantly diversified phenomena intelligent creatures would lack opportunities for development. If their lifespan is too short, they cannot learn. If too long, there is too slow a pace of generational turnover for effective development – a sort of cognitive arteriosclerosis. Accordingly, nature's own contribution to the issue of the intelligibility of nature has to be the possession of a relatively simple, uniform and systematic law structure with regard to its processes – one that deploys so uncomplicated a set of regularities that even a community of inquirers possessed of only rather modest capabilities can be expected to achieve a fairly good grasp of significant parts of it.

In sum, for nature to be intelligible, there must be a coordinative alignment that requires cooperation on both sides. The analogy of crypt-analysis is suggestive. If A is to break B's code, there must be due reciprocal alignment. If A's methods are too crude, too hit and miss, he can get nowhere. But even if A is quite intelligent and resourceful, his efforts cannot succeed if B's procedures are simply beyond his powers. (The cryptanalysts of the 17th century, clever though they were, could get absolutely nowhere in applying their investigative instrumentalities to a high-level naval code of World War II vintage.) Analogously, if mind and nature were too far out of alignment – if mind were too 'unintelligent' for the complexities of nature or nature too complex for the capacities of mind – the two just could not get into step. It would be like trying to rewrite Shakespeare in a Pidgin English with a 500 word vocabulary, or like trying to monitor the workings of a system containing ten degrees of freedom by using a cognitive mechanism capable of keeping track of only four of them. If something like this were the case, mind could not accomplish its evolutionary mission. The interests of survival would then have been better served by an alignment process that does not take the cognitive route. And so, if the development of intelligent beings is the aim, then evolution is a pretty effective means for its realization. What we have is a hermeneutic circle in which evolution productively explains the operation of intelligence, while nevertheless intelligence functionally explains the operation of evolution. On this perspective, the key that unlocks all of these large explanatory issues regarding the nature of the world is the very presence of intelligent beings upon its stage. For, if intelligence is to emerge in a world by straightforward evolutionary means, it becomes a requisite that that world must be substantially intelligible. It must comport itself in a way that intelligent beings can grasp, and thereby function in a way that is substantially regular, orderly, economical and rational. In sum, it must be the sort of world that intelligent beings would contrive if they themselves were world contrivers, so that the world must be 'as if' it were the product of an intelligent agent or agency.

And what evolution by natural selection does is to take some of the magic out of intelligence – to help de-mystify that presence of intelligence in the cosmos. But it manages to do this precisely to the extent that it itself qualifies as an intelligently construed instrumentality for the realization of intelligence.

3. The Reverse Side: Nature's Nootropism

But beyond the issue of the evolution *of* intelligence there is also that of intelligence *in* evolution.

The question from which we set out was: Is the world so constituted that its natural development leads with effectiveness and efficacy to the emergence of intelligent beings capable of achieving some understanding of its *modus operandi*? And the answer to this question, as we now have it, lies in the consideration that a world in which intelligent creatures emerge through evolutionary means – as ours actually seems to be – is pretty much bound to be so constituted.

One would certainly expect, on general principles, that nature's processes should proceed in a maximally effective way – on the whole and with everything considered comporting itself intelligently, subject to considerations of what might be characterized as a rational economy of effort.

And so, with rationality understood as being a matter of the intelligent management of appropriate proceedings, we would view nature as a fundamentally rational system. However, our expectation of such processual rationality is not based on *personifying* nature, but rather, *au contraire*, on our *naturalizing* intelligence. For to say that nature comports itself intelligently is not so much to model nature upon us as to position ourselves within the manifold of process that is natural to nature itself. Here there is no projection of our intelligence into nature. There is rather the envisioning of a (minute) manifestation of nature's intelligence in ourselves. Nature's nootropism is thus seen as perfectly *naturalistic* an aspect of its inherent *modus operandi*. In maintaining the thesis that nature's workings proceed *as though* intelligent agency were at work, we not so much conceive of nature in our terms of reference as conceive of ourselves as natural products of the fundamentally rational comportment of nature. Our rationality, insofar as we possess it, is simply an inherent part of nature's ratiotropism.

In sum, what we have here is not an anthropomorphism of nature but rather a naturomorphism of man.

And this crucial fact has two immediate implications in our present context: first that an intelligent being would want to arrange for a cosmos in which intelligent beings could evolve and thrive; and second that this *modus operandi* of this cosmos be accessible to intelligences. The world should, accordingly, be one whose laws and processes are themselves comprehensible insofar as other requirements permit. A universe designed *by* an intelligent being would accordingly be a universe designed *for* intelligent beings, and thus be user-friendly for intelligent beings. Their very rationality requires rational beings to see themselves as members of a confraternity of a special and particularly worthy kind. But what about rationality in nature?

When desirable outcomes of extremely small probability are being produced with undue frequency, we can count on it that some sort of cheating is going on. And so the question arises: Does nature exhibit a favourable bias towards the interests of intelligence by 'checking' in its favour, through so functioning, so as to render an intelligence-favourable result more probable than would otherwise be the case? The rise and diffusion of intelligent beings in the cosmos is – if not a demonstration, then – at least a plausible indication that this is indeed so, and that nature views rationality with favour. Indeed, regard for rational beings and care for the real interests of such beings at large is, to all appearances at once, among rationality's most basic commitments and among the most striking features of nature's *modus operandi*.

4. A Naturalistic Teleology

It would be a profound error to oppose evolution to intelligent design – to see these two as somehow conflicting and incompatible. For natural selection – the survival of forms better able to realize self-replication in the face of challenges and better able to overcome the difficulties posed by the world's vicissitudes – affords an effective means to intelligent resolutions. (It is no accident that whales and sophisticated computer-designed submarines share much the same physical configuration, or that the age of iron succeeded that of bronze.) The process of natural selection at work in the unfolding of biological evolution is replicated in the rational selection we encounter throughout the history of human artifice. On either side, evolution reflects the capacity to overcome obstacles and resolve problems in the direction of greater efficiency and effectiveness. Selective evolutionary processes – alike in natural (biological) and rational (cultural) selection – are thus instrumentalities that move the developmental course of things in ways selective of increasing rationality.

Yet why should it be that the universe is so constituted as to permit the emergence of intelligence? Three possible answers to the problem of nature's user-friendliness towards intelligence suggest themselves:

- The universe is itself the product of the creative agency of an intelligent being who, as such, will of course factor the interests of intelligence.
- Our universe is simply one item within a vast megaverse of alternatives – and it just so happens (by pure chance, as it were) that the universe we ourselves inhabit exhibits intelligent design and intelligence-friendliness.
- Any manifold able to constitute a universe that is self-propagating and self-perpetuating over time is bound, in due course, to develop in the direction of an intelligence-favouring dimension. The same sort of selective developmental pressures that make for the emergence of intelligent beings *in* the universe make for the emergence of an intelligent design *of* the universe.

Note that the first and the last of these prospects are perfectly compatible with each other, though both are incompatible with the middle alternative, whose bizarre character marks its status as that of a decidedly desperate recourse.

To be sure, if the world is intelligently designed, there yet remains the pivotal question: how did it get that way?

Here there comes a forking of the way into two available routes, namely: *by natural* means or by *super-* or *supra-natural* means. There is nothing about intelligent design as such that constrains one route or the other. Intelligent design does not require or presuppose an intelligent designer – any more than an inefficiently designed reality would require an incompetent designer. A naturally emerging object need not be made into an artefact by possessing some feature that artifice can *also* produce. Being intelligently designed no more demands an intelligent designer than saying it is harmoniously arranged requires a harmonious arranger, or saying it is spatially extended requires a spatial extender.

Against this background, it would appear that there is thus nothing mystical about our revivified neo-Platonism. It is strictly geared to nature's *modus operandi*. Insofar as teleology is at work, it is a naturalistic teleology.

Here, many participants in the debates about intelligent design get things badly confused. Deeply immersed in *odium theologicum*, they think that divine creation is the only pathway to intelligent design, and thereby feel impelled to reject the idea of an intelligently designed universe in order to keep God out of it. They think that intelligent design can only come to realization through the intermediation of an intelligently designing creator. But this view is simply incorrect. A perfectly natural impetus to harmonious coordination could perfectly well issue in an intelligently designed result. And so could the natural selection inherent in some macroevolutionary process.

5. *Intelligence as an Evolutionary Pivot*

The strictly hypothetical and conditional character of the present line of reasoning must be acknowledged. It does no more than maintain the purely conditional thesis that, *if* intelligent creatures are going to emerge in the world by evolutionary processes, *then* the world must be ratiophile, so to speak – that is, user-friendly for rational intelligences. It is not, of course, being argued that the world must contain intelligent beings by virtue of some sort of transcendental necessity. What is being claimed is the merely conditional thesis that, if a world evolves intelligent beings, then it must itself possess a substantial measure of intelligible order. For the question we face is why we intelligent creatures present on the world's stage should be able to understand its operations in significant measure. And the conditional story at issue fully suffices to accomplish this particular job in line with linking evolution and intelligent design.

In sum, then, we have the composite consequences of two theses: (1) that a complex world with organisms that develop by natural selection is going to be such that intelligent beings are likely to emerge, and (2) that a world which permits the emergence of intelligent beings by natural diverseness success is going to be an intelligently designed world. The following are the consequences:

• The fact that the world's realities proceed and develop under the aegis of natural laws: that it is a manifold of lawful order whose doings exhibit a self-perpetuating stability of processual function.

- The fact that the course of cosmic development has seen an ever-growing scope for manifolds of lawful order providing, step by step, the materials for their development first at the level of the laws of physics, and then, sequentially, the laws chemistry, of biology, of sociology etc.
- The fact that intelligent beings have in fact emerged – that nature's *modus operandi* has possibilized and facilitated the emergence of intelligence.
- The fact of an ever-deepening comprehension/penetration of nature's ways on the part of intelligent beings – their ongoing expansion and deepening of their underlying of the world's events and processes.

And so, the key that unlocks all of these large explanatory issues regarding the nature of the world is the very presence of intelligent beings upon its stage. For, if intelligence is to emerge in a word by evolutionary means, it becomes a requisite that that world must be substantially intelligible. It must comport itself in a way that intelligent beings can grasp, and thereby function in a way that is substantially regular, orderly, economical and rational. In sum, it must be the sort of world that intelligent beings would contrive if they themselves were world-contrivers, so that the world must be 'as if' it were the product of an intelligent agent or agency. But there is no way to take that 'if' out of it.

In the event, then, evolutionary noophelia is a position for which there is plausible basis of evidential substantiation.

6. Derailing Wastage as an Objection to Evolved Design

To be sure, there can be objections. One runs as follows: 'Is evolution by variation and survivalistic selection not an enormously wasteful mode of operation? And is it not cumbersome and much too slow?' Does this sort of worry not rule intelligence out of it?

Not really. For, where the objector complains of *wastage* here, a more generous spirit might see a Leibnizian Principle of fertility at work that gives a wide variety of life forms their chance for a moment in the limelight. (Perhaps the objector would not think much of being a dinosaur; but then many is the small child who would not agree.) Anyway, perhaps it is better to be a microbe than to be a Was not that just Is not – to invoke Dr Seuss. Or again, one person's wastage is another's fertility – to invoke Leibniz.

But what of all that suffering that follows the lot of organic existence? Perhaps it is just collateral damage that is left behind in the cosmic struggle towards intelligent life. But this is neither the place nor the time for producing a *Theodicy* and to address the theological Problem of Evil. The salient point is simply that the Wastage Objection is not automatically telling, and that various lines of reply are available to deflect its impact.

Now, on to slowness: is the evolutionary process not cumbersome and much too slow? Surely the proper response here is to ask: What's the hurry? In relation to a virtually infinite vastness of time, any finite initial time-span is but an instant. Of course, there must be time enough for evolutionary processes to work out. There must be *sufficiency*. But nothing patent is achieved by *minimality*, unless there is some mysterious collective reason way this particular benefit – an economy of time – should be given priority other desiderata such as variety, fertility or the like.

7. Intelligent Design Does Not Require Absolute Perfection

Yet another line of objection arises along the following lines: 'Does not reality's all too evident imperfection constitute a decisive roadblock to intelligent design? For, if optimal alternatives were always realized, would not the world be altogether perfect in every regard?'

Not at all! After all, the best achievable result for a whole will require, in various realistic conditions, a less-than-perfect outcome for the parts. A game with multiple participants cannot be won by every one of them. A society of many members cannot put each of them at the top of the heap. In an engaging and suspenseful plot, things cannot go with unalloyed smoothness for everybody in every character.

Moreover, there are generally multiple parameters of positivity that function competitively so that some can only be enhanced at the cost of others – even as to make a car speedier we must sacrifice operating cost.

With an automobile, the parameters of merit clearly includes such factors as speed, reliability, repair infrequency, safety, operating economy, aesthetic appearance and road-handle ability. In actual practice, however, such features are interrelated. It is unavoidable that they trade off against one another: more of A means less of B. It would be ridiculous to have a super-safe car with a maximum speed of two miles per hour. It would be ridiculous to have a car that is inexpensive to operate but spends three-fourths of the time in a repair shop. Invariably, perfection – an all-at-once maximization of every value dimension – is inherently unrealizable because of the inherent interaction of evaluative parameters. In designing a car, you cannot maximize both safety and economy of operation; analogously, the world is not, and cannot possibly be, absolutely perfect – perfect in *every* respect – because this sort of absolute perfection is in principle impossible to realize.

In the context of multiple and potentially competing parameters of merit, the idea of an all-at-once maximization has to give way to an on-balance optimization.

The interactive complexity of value is crucial here. For it is the fundamental fact of axiology that every object has a *plurality* of evaluative features, some of which will in some respects stand in conflict. Absolute perfection becomes, in principle, infeasible. For what we have here is a relation of competition and tradeoff among modes of merit akin to the complementarity relation of quantum physics. The over-all optimality of a complex whole may well require some of its constituent comportments to be less perfect than they would be if viewed in isolation, without reference to their larger context. This suffices to sideline the objection: 'If intelligent design obtains, why is not the world absolutely perfect?'

8. Conclusion

Our discussion has argued that evolution is not at odds with intelligent design, because the efficiency-tropism inherent in the *modus operandi* of evolutionary development actually renders it likely to issue in an intelligently designed product. Accordingly, evolution should not be seen as the antithesis of intelligent design. Nor is it inimical to a theology of an intelligent designer. In arranging for a developmental pathway to an intelligently designed world, a benign creator could well opt for an evolutionary process. So, in the end, evolution is neither in conflict with intelligent design nor yet with a theology of divine creation.

In closing, it must be stressed that noophelia can be entirely naturalistic; it is nevertheless altogether congenial to theism. To be sure, there is no reason of necessity why a universe that is intelligently designed as user-friendly for intelligent beings must be the result of the agency of an intelligent being any more than a universe that is clumsily designed for accommodating clumsy beings would have to be the creative product of a clumsy being. But while this is so, nevertheless, such a universe is altogether harmonious to theistic cosmogony. After all, an intelligently construed universe is altogether consonant with a cosmogony of divine creation. And so: *noophelia is not only compatible with but actually congenial to theism.* One cannot but think that the well-being of its intelligent creatures will rank high in the value-scheme of a benign creator. As should really be the case in general, approaches based on the study of nature and the reflections of theology can here be brought into alignment.

As regards the Catholic ramifications of the issue, it is certainly true that the Church emphasizes the distinction between body and soul, and views the latter, soul, not as a product of the physical causality of nature, but of a special act of creation on the part of God. But this, of course, need not (and indeed should not) be construed as creating an unmendable breach between doctrine and evolution, since there simply is no need to say that evolution creates souls but rather that it affords fitting opportunities for the creation of souls.

Appendix

The most eloquent exponent of nootropism is Teilhard de Chardin. Whether the evolutionary emergence of what he calls the noosphere will go as far as to reach the ultimate 'omega state' that he envisions could be seen as speculative and eschatological. Yet, the fundamental process of ratiotropic evolution that he envisions is there for all to see presently, irrespective of how far they may be prepared to venture into its speculative projection into a yet uncertain future. In their detail, the present deliberations are decidedly distant from those of Teilhard. But their tendency and motivating spirit is undoubtedly akin to his.

Notes

1 The neo-Platonists Plotinus and Proclus differentiated natural *phusikós* love, (*amor naturalis*), and psychic (*psychikós*) love (*amor sensitivus*) from intellectual love: erôs noerós (*amor intellectualis* or *rationalis*). In the end, their rendition of the Aristotelian idea that 'love makes the world go round' comes down to having a world developed conformably and sympathetically to the demands of the intellect in relation to intelligibility.

2 See William S. Dembski, *The Design Inference: Eliminating Chance Through Small Probabilities* (Cambridge: Cambridge University Press, 1998). The quarrel between orthodox Darwinians and Intelligent Design Theorists of the more conservative stamp is not over the question of evolution by chance selection but simply over the question of whether such selection is strictly random or bias-manifestingly skewed. What is at issue here is not a choice between science vs religion but a choice between two rival scientific theories.

Chapter 8

WEAK DARWINISM

Peter van Inwagen

I

I will begin with some remarks on the word 'evolution', in its biological sense. The word is ambiguous. In one of its senses, it purports to refer to a certain *phenomenon*, something that is 'out there in the world', and was out there long before there were human beings – like life, or gravity, or hydrogen fusion. (Whatever this phenomenon is, it is a purely biological phenomenon. I think it is necessary to say this, because I have heard it said, or heard things said that seem to imply, that the Big Bang and the formation of galaxies and stars and planets were early, pre-biotic manifestations of the phenomenon called 'evolution'.) In another of its senses, the word 'evolution' refers to a certain *theory* – something that, like all theories, is a human creation – a theory that purports to explain certain things out there in the world, namely the Darwinian theory of evolution.

I think that this ambiguity can be a source of confusion. Accordingly, I will use the word only in one of these two senses: the second. In fact, I will not use the word 'evolution' at all, not in isolation. I will use it only as a component of longer phrases like 'the Darwinian theory of evolution' or 'the theory of evolution', for when I say 'the theory of evolution' I shall mean the Darwinian theory. And when I use the word 'Darwinism', as I occasionally shall, that will be just another way of referring to the Darwinian theory of evolution. 'But isn't something called "the theory of evolution" a theory about a phenomenon called "evolution"?' The reader will see that when I give a statement of 'the theory of evolution', as I shall in a moment, the word 'evolution' will not occur in this statement. As I represent this theory, it is not about a phenomenon called 'evolution'. At any rate, I do not want to describe it that way, if only because I am not sure what phenomenon 'evolution' is supposed to be. The theory, as we shall see, explains, or purports to explain, lots of things, but which one of those things it explains, or which combination of them, is 'evolution' is not a question I know how to answer. (That is why I have come down on the 'theory' rather than on the 'phenomenon' side of the ambiguity.) So, in my usage at least, the word 'evolution' is not a serious part of the name 'the theory of evolution'. I use that name simply because it is the traditional name for the theory I want to discuss. But the word 'theory' is a serious part of that name, and I want to say something about *that* word.

I hope all of us know that, although one perfectly good meaning of the word 'theory' (both in science and in everyday life) is 'unproved hypothesis', the word has (only in science) a second and equally good sense: a theory in the second sense is an *explanation* (right or wrong) of something, and an explanation that has some real, usable internal structure. When, for example, we speak of the special and general theories of relativity, we do not mean to suggest that the things that those two formidable theoretical structures imply about items like distance and motion and acceleration and space and time and light and gravity are unproved hypotheses. Maybe those things have been proved and maybe they have not; our use of the phrase 'the *theory* of relativity' is entirely neutral with respect to that question. (This paragraph is, of course, a repudiation of expressions like 'Evolution is only a theory'.)

It is this second sense that the word 'theory' has in the phrase 'the theory of evolution'. The theory of evolution is an explanation of something – in fact, of many things. (The word 'explanation' has a stronger and a weaker sense. In the stronger sense, something cannot be an explanation of some phenomenon unless it is right. In the weaker sense, something can be a *wrong* explanation of a phenomenon: its being wrong does not stop it from being an explanation. I use the word in the weaker sense. When I say that the theory of evolution is an explanation of certain things, what I say is not meant to imply that it is the right explanation – or, of course, that it is not.) It is an explanation of things like the enormous complexity, the apparent exquisite design, and the vast taxonomic diversity that we find in terrestrial life. And it is not simply an explanation of such very general features of the biological world as those. It, or parts of it – some of that 'real, usable internal structure' that I said a theory must have – can be used to explain a vast range of particular facts about living things, facts like the fact that the males of various species of dabbling ducks have colourful plumage, strikingly different in the different species, or the fact that in most species that exhibit sexual dimorphism, the number of males and the number of females are about equal.

And what is this theory? In one respect, at least, it is almost unique among scientific theories in that it is very hard to find a statement of it. I will have to provide my statement of the theory. If anyone wants to provide an alternative statement, I will be happy to consider it. I contend that the theory of evolution comprises the following five theses.

1. There have been living things on the earth for a very long time – for about 600,000 times as long as a literal reading of the book of Genesis would suggest. The natural classes or taxa that these living things fall into, moreover, are, contrary to what Aristotle supposed, 'mortal': most species are extinct; even some phyla are extinct. With the passage of time, new taxa come into existence even as others go out of existence. When a new species comes into existence, the members of that species are in every case descended from the members of other species.
2. Any two living things, whatever taxa they may belong to, have common ancestors: you and a spider on that wall, for example. In fact, the two of you are rather closely related compared with a pair like you and one of the *E. coli* bacteria in your gut – which is, nevertheless, one of your relations.
3. Here are some data to be explained. First: for a very long time now, life on earth has exhibited enormous taxonomic diversity. Secondly: for a very long time now, the most complex organisms have been enormously more complex than the simplest ones. Thirdly: even in the simplest organisms, there is a lot of apparent teleology or apparent design. If physiologists want to know what some mysterious organ or organelle or system in a living thing is 'doing', it is almost always useful for them to ask what it is 'for' – to ask something along the lines of: 'If this organism had been designed by a team of biological engineers, why would they have included an item with these features in their design?' Fourthly: for a very long time now, the biosphere, the totality of living things, has embodied an enormously complex system of internal causal relations. (One might almost think of it – metaphorically, but the metaphor has a point – as itself an organism, an organism enormously more complex than the most complex non-metaphorical organism.) These four points constitute data to be explained. *How* are they to be explained? The answer to this question is a simple one. The *only* explanation of all this diversity and complexity and apparent teleology is that provided by the operation of random mutation and natural selection. Or, at any rate, that is the only purely biological part of the explanation. Of course the explanation will have to involve the physical 'boundary conditions' under which these biological mechanisms operate – such things as the chemical makeup and physical attributes of the earth, the effects of phenomena like continental drift and outgassing from volcanoes, the intensity of solar radiation at various times, and collisions of asteroids or comets with the earth. And the same is true, in miniature as it were, of even the minutest features of the biological world. Now, no doubt, many biological facts are simply due to chance, and there is no explanation of how they came to be that is more interesting than 'That's just how things happened to turn out'. But insofar as *any* particular matter of biological fact has an interesting

historical explanation, this explanation must be in terms of natural selection.

4. Mutations are mainly due to copying errors that occur during reproduction. They have only biochemical causes. If the laws of chemistry will permit a certain mutation to occur when a certain cell divides – if that mutation is a chemical possibility – *whether* the mutation will occur and *how probable* its occurrence is have nothing to do with whether its occurrence would be a 'good thing' for the descendants of that cell (or the descendants of the organism of which that cell is a part). Suppose, for example, that a certain species of toad faces extinction owing to climate change. Suppose that in the reproductive organs of a member of that species a new gamete is being produced, and (owing to ways in which genetic copying errors could occur in the species) three mutations, A, B and C might, as a matter of biochemical possibility, occur in that gamete. A would be lethal to any toad that incorporated it; B, if it should spread widely among the toads of that species over the next 100 generations, would, to a high probability, enable the species to avoid extinction; C, if it became widespread, would almost certainly hasten extinction. The probability of each of these mutations occurring is a matter of biochemistry, of molecular mechanics, and has nothing whatever to do with the effects it would have if it occurred.

5. All apparent design in nature, all complexity, all diversity, is produced by the gradual accumulation (directed by environmental pressure – that is, by natural selection) of small hereditary differences, differences due to random mutations or to the random recombination of genetic material. Notice that this is no more than a gloss on something said above in (3): The *only* explanation of all this diversity and complexity is that provided by the operation of random mutation and natural selection.

These five theses must suffice for a statement of 'the theory of evolution'. There is a lot more to be said, of course. For one thing, and it is the most important thing, I have said nothing about what natural selection is, or, if you like, about what the words 'natural selection' mean. A better term – I have heard Alex Rosenberg use this phrase – might have been 'environmental filtration'. Saying what 'natural selection' means would be too large an undertaking. I will simply have to suppose that my readers have some familiarity with the concept of natural selection. And many will protest that I should have said something about 'fitness', or about 'adaptation', or about genes and gene-frequencies, or about genetic drift, or about reproductively isolated populations, or about 'the unit of selection', or about 'spandrels', or about a dozen or so other matters. My only excuse for giving such a sketchy statement of the theory is that I have no space to say anything more.

II

I am somewhat sceptical about certain aspects of this theory – although by no means all of them. I will list some points on which the most committed Darwinian and I are in no disagreement. There are stylistic advantages in having a name for a convinced and orthodox Darwinian. I will call him Alex – in honour of Alex Rosenberg.[1]

First, Alex and I do not disagree about astronomy or geology or paleontology or, in general, the ages and histories of things. I have no stake in defending the literal truth of the chronology of creation in the book of Genesis.[2] Secondly, we are not in any disagreement about the 'common ancestry' thesis. Alex's picture of our family tree and mine are the same. Thirdly, we are not in disagreement about the importance of the concept of natural selection in biology, or about the pervasiveness of the operation of natural selection in the biological world. Darwinians are fond of quoting T. Dobzhansky's famous dictum: 'Nothing in biology makes sense except in the light of evolution.'[3] Or, as I would prefer to modify the dictum, given the scruples I expressed earlier about the ambiguity of the word 'evolution': 'Nothing in biology makes sense except in the light of Darwin's theory of evolution.' I am willing to accept this dictum in a certain restricted sense – something like this: 'We shall never understand anything about the biological world unless our biological theories give a central and essential role to natural selection. There are pervasive features of that world that would *make no sense* if natural selection had not played a central and essential role in its development.' Fourthly, Alex and I are not in disagreement about the thesis that only natural causes have been at work in the history of life. It is not my purpose to put forward some sort of 'intelligent design' thesis. I should say that, as a theist, I do, of course, believe that the universe has a designer. But I do not think that the truth of this thesis can be inferred from an examination of the biological world. (And of course, I do not think that it can be inferred from an examination of the biological world that the universe does *not* have a designer, a point to which I will return.) I do not think that the science of biology needs to appeal to anything supernatural. On this point, I agree with Cardinal Newman: 'I believe in design because I believe in God, not in a God because I see design.'[4] If I were going to look at the world and see design, independently of my theological convictions, it would be the laws of physics I would look at and not the contingent biological structures on the earth. But I do not find even the arguments for design, those that appeal only to the laws of physics – so-called fine-tuning arguments – all that compelling. Suggestive, perhaps, but hardly compelling. In any case, fine-tuning is not my topic.

But then what *do* Alex and I disagree about? Our disagreement is essentially about the following proposition, which I quote from my own earlier statement of the theory: The *only* explanation of all this diversity and complexity is that provided by the operation of random mutation and natural selection.

I do not mean to imply that I reject this thesis. I mean that I do not see any reason to accept it. Let us call it Allism – since it is essentially the thesis that natural selection does it all. I see no reason to be confident that natural selection has the prodigious power to organize nature, to produce biological complexity, to produce apparent design, that most biologists attribute to it. And I see no reason to be confident that natural selection *does not* have this power. I am just a sceptic about what natural selection can do at that grand level. Some scientists, who know far more about the issues involved than I, are more than sceptical about Allism. Here is a quotation from the English biologist, Brian Goodwin:

> [D]espite the power of molecular genetics to reveal the hereditary essences of organisms, the large-scale aspects of evolution remain un-explained, including the origin of species. There is 'no clear evidence . . . for the gradual emergence of any evolutionary novelty,' says Ernst Mayr, one of the most eminent of contemporary evolutionary bio-logists. New types of organisms simply appear on the evolutionary scene, persist for various periods of time, and then become extinct. So Darwin's assumption that the tree of life is a consequence of the grad-ual accumulation of small hereditary differences seems to be without significant support. Some other process is responsible for the emergent properties of life, those distinctive features that separate one group of organisms from another – fishes and amphibians, worms and insects, horsetails and grasses. Clearly something is missing from biology.[5]

I am not so sure as Goodwin is that 'something is missing from biology'. But I am also not convinced that *nothing* (or nothing that will not be supplied by future research carried out within the Darwinian paradigm) is missing from biology. I do not see why I should accept, rather than suspend judgment about, Allism. When I read books like the book by Goodwin from which this quotation was taken, or Michael Denton's *Evolution: A Theory in Crisis*, or Michael Behe's *Darwin's Black Box*, I find a great deal of what seems to me to be misplaced certainty that Allism is, and has been shown by their authors, to be false.[6] But I also find a great many data that, it seems to me, represent the world as looking different from the way we would expect it to look if Allism were true.[7] But it does not follow from this that Allism is in fact false – or even that its falsity is more probable than its truth. Let me tell you a cautionary tale from the history of science. This is the first of three cautionary tales I will tell you.

Newton thought that the orbits of the planets must be unstable unless very precisely adjusted at the Creation, and perhaps periodically *re*-adjusted, by God. This instability was supposed to be due to the per-turbation of each planet's orbit by the gravitational influence of the others. In the late eighteenth century, however, the great applied mathematician Pierre-Simon Laplace showed that nothing besides Newton's own laws – the laws of motion and the inverse-square law of gravitation – was needed to account for the observed stability of the planetary orbits. Roughly speaking, he showed that the orbital perturbations that worried Newton tend to cancel each other out. This was not something Newton had missed because he was an idiot. It was not an *easy* thing to discover: Laplace had to invent a whole new branch of applied mathematics, called perturbation theory, to demonstrate it.[8]

The lesson of this cautionary tale is: You cannot just look at a phenomenon and a theory and blithely say, 'That theory can't account for that phenomenon.' Not always – not in the case of every phenomenon that a theory provides no obvious account of. It is not always *evident* what a theory can account for: an account of a recalcitrant phenomenon may well be latent in a theory that suggests no obvious account of it.

And let us note that this cautionary tale would have the same point if Newton had postulated not a supernatural explanation of the stability of the planetary orbits but had rather proposed that some new physical principle, something besides his own laws of motion and law of universal gravitation, was needed to account for orbital stability.[9] It is for this reason that the arguments of anti-Darwinians like Goodwin and Behe and Denton do not convince me that Allism is false: it may well be that nothing besides natural selection is needed to account for all those recalcitrant data that these and other writers appeal to in their attempts to refute Darwinism.

My position is that we do not know this to be true. At present we should neither accept nor reject Allism. We should be agnostics about the power of natural selection to explain all the complexity, diversity and apparent teleology that we observe in the biological world. Let me ask you to do something. Let me ask you to consider a theory I will call *Weak Darwinism*. Weak Darwinism is simply Darwinism with Allism subtracted from it. To get a statement of Weak Darwinism, take my five-part statement of the Darwinian theory presented above, and replace the following statement in Part (3):

> The *only* explanation of all this diversity and complexity and apparent teleology is that provided by the operation of random mutation and natural selection.

with the statement

> The operation of random mutation and natural selection is at least a very important part of the explanation of all this diversity, complexity and apparent teleology – perhaps it is the whole explanation and perhaps not.

(And, of course, delete Part (5) – or preface it with the words: 'it may be that' or 'for all anyone knows'.)

Now suppose all biologists were to accept only Weak Darwinism. Would the science of biology be adversely affected? I do not see how it would be. But I am neither a biologist nor a philosopher of biology, and I would like to hear how the specialists would answer this question. One thing is certain, however: it would not prevent biologists from explaining particular biological phenomena in terms of natural selection. Consider, for example, a fact I alluded to in Part I, the fact that male dabbling ducks generally have showy plumage. Here is an explanation of this fact, an explanation in terms of natural selection:

> Many regions of North America are inhabited by more than one species of dabbling ducks. Hybridization sometimes takes place because the females, who are the mate-choosers, sometimes mistake males of another species for males of their own. The hybrid offspring are as a rule less viable than the intra-specific offspring and sometimes sterile, and this fact has led to selection pressure in favour of showy male plumage, distinct in each species, because such plumage enables females better to identify the males of their own species. Obviously, no such pressure operates on the females; in fact, the pressure is in the other direction, since a duck with showy plumage is more easily spotted by predators. Of course this second kind of pressure, this negative pressure, operates on the males too, but it's outweighed by the positive pressure that comes from its tendency to reduce mating errors. (Under most conditions, a male with showy plumage is more likely to be eaten before he reproduces; but, if he does reproduce, his offspring of both sexes will be less likely to be weak or sterile, and thus more likely themselves to reproduce. The latter effect predominates.) There are, however, certain isolated areas in which there is only one species of dabbling duck, and in those areas, of course, no mating errors can occur. There the negative or 'camouflage' pressure works unopposed among the males as well as the females, and in consequence the males of several species in several such areas have lost their showy plumage.

I am not in a position to tell you that this explanation is right.[10] I can say, however, that it is certainly a good explanation, if it *is* right – just the sort of explanation we expect from science. My point is that explanations of this sort would be as available to biologists who accepted only Weak Darwinism as they are to biologists who accept Darwinism. It looks to me as if, in the present state of our knowledge, Weak Darwinism has all the same observable consequences as Darwinism, and it is of course a weaker theory: Darwinism entails Weak Darwinism, but not vice versa. I do not know what the best philosophers of science say about this today, but when I was in graduate school they said that, if two theories had all the same observable consequences and one was stronger than the other, you should not adopt the stronger one. (This is not to say that you should adopt the weaker one; that is as may be.)

Why, then, do most biologists adhere to Darwinism? In my view, there are two reasons. First, people like to think they understand things – and, of course, they *do not* like to think they *do not* understand things. Hear my second cautionary tale.

Lord Kelvin, the great nineteenth-century physicist (nineteenth-century to a first approximation; he died in 1907), he in whose honour the Kelvin temperature scale is named, thought that the output of radiant energy from the sun must be due to the one mechanism he could identify as a possible source of such energy, gravitational compression. The sun is a ball of gas. The mutual gravitation of the particles of matter of which it is composed will tend to cause those particles to form themselves into a smaller, denser ball. That is, particles of matter will tend to fall inward towards their centre of mass. As a given particle falls, it loses potential energy and gains energy of motion or kinetic energy. Assuming that it hits other particles, this particle will probably strike off in other directions than downward: that is, the motion of the falling particles will be randomized and therefore express itself in the form we call heat. The gas that composes the sun will therefore become hotter as it is compressed, and when things get hot enough they begin to radiate. The rate at which a hot body radiates away energy depends on its surface temperature and surface area. The surface area of the sun is vast (about 6×10^{18} square meters) and it is very hot (its surface temperature is about 6000 degrees K or C, or well over 10000 degrees F). So the sun puts out a lot of radiant energy per unit of time. How long could it keep doing that for at more or less its present rate?

Lord Kelvin, being a physicist, was able to set up and solve differential equations, and he obtained what I am told is the right answer, given his assumption about the source of the energy: for something between twenty and forty million years. But that figure raised a problem. The paleontologists told him that there had been life on the earth for at least 200 million years. (We know now that the right figure is almost twenty times that.) And obviously life requires sunshine. So, Kelvin said, the paleontologists had to be wrong. What he did not know, however, was that, although the conversion of gravitational potential energy to radiant energy is indeed an important part of the story of where sunshine comes from, it is only one part of the story. There is another part, and it is considerably *more* important: most of the energy comes from the release of nuclear binding energy when atomic nuclei down in the sun's core bump into each other and fuse.[11] This source of energy is so potent that it easily permits the sun to have been shining for as long as the paleontologists said it must have been shining for. And this additional mechanism was not only unknown to Kelvin when he made his calculation, it was one he *could not* have known about. Knowing about it had to wait for fundamental discoveries in physics that would come along in their own good time.

The lesson is: Do not always assume that the mechanisms you have identified and can describe and know are at work in the production of a certain phenomenon are *all* the mechanisms that are at work in the production of that phenomenon. And Lord Kelvin should not have made the assumption he did. The work of the paleontologists was good science. Lord Kelvin ought to have reasoned this way: 'It seems that the sun has been shining for a lot longer than I can account for, given the mechanisms for producing heat that I know about. So there must be at least one mechanism for producing heat that I *do not* know about.' And this is exactly the sort of thing that people like Goodwin and Behe and Denton say about Darwin's theory in the light of the recalcitrant data with which they confront it. For my part, I have to say that I do not regard the cases as entirely parallel. Lord Kelvin's version of Allism (gravitational compression accounts for *all* the phenomena of solar radiation) was a quantitative theory, and it yielded precise numerical predictions – which, because they were precise, could be seen to be indisputably at variance with the fossil record. The Darwinian theory does not make precise predictions – not about such things as the generation of new taxa, at least. It is none the worse for that, but the fact needs to be recognized. And it is therefore much more difficult to say whether 'natural selection does it all' is really at variance with a given set of data than it is to say whether 'gravitational compression does it all' is really at variance with a given set of data. It is for precisely this reason that I am sceptical about Allism and not a denier of Allism.

I have just examined one reason I think a lot of people are Allists: the natural tendency to suppose that an understood and well-described mechanism that is clearly at work in the production of a phenomenon is the only mechanism at work in the production of that phenomenon. The second reason, I promised you, has to do with religion, or more exactly, with anti-religion. A good many proponents of Darwinism think that Darwinism (if true) shows that there is no God, that Darwinism is inconsistent with theism. And this is a conclusion that many of them are very happy with. But if it is evident that Darwinism is inconsistent with theism (they suppose this to be evident), it is at least much less evident that Weak Darwinism is inconsistent with theism. Who knows what the unknown mechanism or mechanisms at work in the development of life might be if there were such? To attribute apparent design in nature to a process of random mutation and the culling of populations by natural selection – a process that has operated over geologically vast stretches of time – seems, to many, to imply that there is no thought, no design behind nature. If there are evolutionary mechanisms other than natural selection, who can say what those mechanisms would seem to us to imply if we knew what they were? In any case, we *do not* know what they are, and an unknown can't seem to imply anything.

There is, moreover, the following sort of reasoning to be considered, reasoning I am sure has been present in the mind of more than one biologist: 'For whatever reason, we biologists have mostly embraced Allism. Allism is a part of Darwinism as it actually exists. Opposition to Darwinism has been mainly from religious quarters. If biology were to qualify the entrenched formulation of Darwinism in any way, that qualification would be perceived, certainly by religious people and perhaps by the general public, as a retreat by science and a victory for religion.'

I will not say much more about this, but I will offer you a sociological speculation. Suppose that religious belief had more or less died out many years ago – as many high-minded and progressive people keep predicting it will any moment now. My speculation is this: Allism would have died out too; the working theory of evolution in biology would be something like what I have called Weak Darwinism. There would be vigorous research programmes in biology searching for evolutionary mechanisms that operate alongside and in interaction with natural selection. I do not claim to know that this is true, of course. No one could know anything like that. But I do find it an interesting speculation, and it is one that I occasionally entertain with a considerable degree of hospitality.

'But can you really take seriously the thesis that most biologists accept a false biological theory? And who are *you*, who are not only not a biologist but not a scientist of any sort, to defend such a thesis?' I certainly can accept – and do accept and am willing to defend – the thesis that most biologists accept a theory that *may* be false. I might remind my readers that there are biologists (Goodwin, for example), and scientists in closely allied fields, who think not only that Darwinism *may* be false but that it *is* false.[12] But I will not explore the question: What should the lay person make of the fact that, although almost all biologists accept Darwinism, a few biologists (biochemists, geneticists . . .) reject that theory? I will instead tell a third cautionary tale, a tale showing that allegiance to a false theory can be pervasive in a particular science; here I am taking a false theory to be one against which there was evidence that should have rendered the theory at least doubtful.

Here is a quotation from what was once an important textbook (entitled *The Geological Evolution of North America*):

> The geosynclinal theory is one of the great unifying principles in geology. In many ways, its role in geology is similar to that of the theory of evolution, which serves to integrate the many branches of the biological sciences . . . Just as the doctrine of evolution is universally accepted among biologists, so also the geosynclinal origin of the major mountain systems is an established principle in geology.[13]

I want to emphasize that I am talking about the fairly recent past, and not about Lord Kelvin's day. *The Geological Evolution of North America* was published in 1960, when I was a freshman. The geosynclinal theory to which the text refers was an account of the origin of mountain ranges: huge troughs in the earth's surface (geosynclines) gradually fill with sediment till their content begins to sink under its own weight; eventually it breaks through into magma, and the interior heat of the earth pushes it back up and creates a mountain range. The forces that cause mountains to rise are thus essentially vertical. In the horizontal plane, the geosynclinal theory presents an essentially static model of the earth's crust – in contrast to the theory of plate tectonics, which is now considered to be the correct theory of the origins of mountain ranges. The geosynclinal theory was confidently affirmed for many decades by geologists, despite well-known evidence that ought to have made them at least take very seriously the idea that the earth's crust was, over geological time, very fluid in the horizontal plane.[14] This evidence was, however, ignored or ridiculed by most geologists. Many non-geologists, however, could see that there was something fishy about the geologists' professed certainty on this point. In fact, my fourth-grade teacher, Mrs Campbell, could. Having displayed to us nine-year-olds, with a paper cut-out, how neatly the coastlines of South America and Africa fit together, she reluctantly added, 'But the scientists tell us that it's just a coincidence, and we have to believe them.' Within ten years of the publication of *The Geological Evolution of North America*, the geosynclinal theory had vanished from geology almost as if it had never been.[15]

This third cautionary tale is not intended to imply that Allism is in the same sort of state as the state that the geosynclinal theory was in 1960. The geosynclinal theory was just wrong, wrong all the way through. The process that it contended led to the creation of mountain ranges was not even a part of the right story, and demonstrably so – whereas, as I have emphasized, natural selection is certainly at least a very important part of the story of how life on earth got into its present form. And, as I have repeatedly said, I at least do not want to say that it is not the whole story. The lesson of the third cautionary tale is simply this: it is possible for the consensus of opinion in a science to be wrong, and possible for outsiders to see that that consensus is wrong or that it should not at any rate be treated as decisive.

III

One point remains to be considered. It could be put in the form of an *ad hominem* argument, directed against myself: 'All right. You say that you don't know whether Darwinism (understood to include Allism) is true or false. So, for all you know, it's true. But Darwinism is inconsistent with theism. How, therefore, can you be a theist? Shouldn't you be, if not an atheist, then an agnostic?'

I reply that Darwinism is not inconsistent with theism.[16] The argument is simple. I will present it as a second *ad hominem* argument, the *homines* in question being Darwinists. 'You Darwinists believe that the actual world is a Darwinian world – that is, a world in which Darwin's theory is *true*. But actuality implies possibility: anything that is actual is possible. And God, if he exists, is by definition omnipotent. And an omnipotent being can create any possible object, even if that object is a whole universe or cosmos. Well, this Darwinian earth of ours (as you believe it to be) is a possible object – since it exists. Therefore, an omnipotent being could create it – and could create the whole physical universe of which it is a part. And if an omnipotent being *could* create a Darwinian world, then why should someone who thinks that the actual world is a Darwinian world regard that feature of the actual world as demonstrating that – as having even any tendency to show that – there is no God?' In fact, I maintain, *no* discovery of science (so far, at any rate) has the least tendency to show that there is no God. Nor has anything that, according to the best current science, *may well* be true any tendency to imply that there is no God. If anything we find in the world has any tendency to show this, it is the immense amount of suffering the world contains. This, of course, is the so-called problem of evil. But the fact that the world contains an immense amount of suffering is not a discovery of science.

Notes

1 Alexander Rosenberg is the R. Taylor Cole professor of philosophy and co-director of the Center for Philosophy of Biology at Duke University. On March 22, 2007, The Life Sciences and Religion Community Forum of Central Virginia, at Virginia Commonwealth University, organized a debate entitled 'Evolution and God', featuring Alex Rosenberg and myself. The main arguments of this paper derive from that occasion.

2 See Peter van Inwagen, 'Genesis and Evolution', in: *God, Knowledge & Mystery: Essays in Philosophical Theology* (Ithaca, NY: Cornell University Press, 1995), 128–62.

3 Dobzhansky used the phrase for the first time in his paper 'Biology, Molecular and Organismic', *American Zoologist* 4 (1964), 443–52.

4 John Henry Newman, *The Letters and Diaries of John Henry Newman, XXV*, edited by C. S. Dessain & T. Gornall (Oxford: Clarendon Press, 1973), 97. Note the indefinite article.

5 Brian Goodwin, *How the Leopard Changed its Spots: The Evolution of Complexity* (Princeton, NJ: Princeton University Press, 2001), xii–xiii.

6 Michael Denton, *Evolution: A Theory in Crisis* (Woodbine House Inc., 1996); Michael J. Behe, *Darwin's Black Box: The Biochemical Challenge to Evolution* (Simon & Schuster; 1998).

7 Goodwin alludes to some of these data when he says, 'New types of organisms simply appear on the evolutionary scene, persist for various periods of time, and then become extinct'.

8 See Charles Coulston, *Pierre-Simon Laplace, 1749–1827: A Life in Exact Science* (Princeton University Press 1997), Chapter 16.

9 Something of that sort did occur later in the history of astronomy: there are features of the planetary orbits that, it transpired, did require new physics for their explanation – but not the feature Newton was thinking of.

10 Biology is not my field, after all; I more or less copied it from an old biology textbook: William T. Keeton, *Elements of Biological Science* (New York: W. W. Norton & Co., 1969), 374.

11 More energy is needed to hold two or more nuclei together before they fuse than is needed to hold the one nucleus that is the product of the fusion together.

12 Examples of scientists in closely allied fields are Behe, a biochemist and Denton, a geneticist.

13 T. H. Clark and C. W. Steam, *The Geological Evolution of North America* (New York: Ronald Press, 1960), 43.

14 The nice 'jigsaw-puzzle fit' between the coastlines of South America and Africa was the most famous piece of evidence of this sort. But there was much, much more – including 'matching' mineral deposits along those same coasts, and species that had a clear evolutionary relation on opposite sides of the divide.

15 The great geologist Sir Harold Jeffreys continued to affirm the geosynclinal theory, and to insist that the evidence simply did not support the theory of plate tectonics, till his death in 1989.

16 Darwinism is of course inconsistent with literalism about the chronology of creation in Genesis. But then that sort of literalism was rejected long before the advent of modern geology and biology, by St Augustine and St Jerome – the translator who was responsible for the Vulgate Bible – and St Thomas Aquinas and many other important authorities. And those authorities have rather a good claim to be called theists. In my essay 'Genesis and Evolution', I said that Thomas Aquinas accepted the six-day creation story of Genesis as literally true. This statement was based on a statement about and a passage attributed to Aquinas in an essay by the great Church historian Jaroslav Pelikan ('Darwin's Legacy: Emanation, Evolution, and Development', in Charles L. Hamrum (ed.), *Darwin's Legacy: Nobel Conference XVIII* (San Francisco: Harper and Row, 1983).) In the footnote in which I cited Pelikan's essay, I said 'No citation of the words attributed to Aquinas is given'. The late Professor Norman Kretzmann, one of the greatest authorities on Aquinas of the last quarter of the twentieth century, later assured me that Pelikan was simply wrong: Aquinas was *not* a six-day literalist.

Chapter 9

DARWIN, ETHICS AND EVOLUTION

Harry J. Gensler

I begin by summarizing what Charles Darwin says about ethics. Then I consider some issues that evolution raises for moral philosophy; here I compare Darwin's views with alternative views and with the Catholic tradition. Like most Catholic thinkers, I am positive about evolution.[1] I am positive about Darwin's approach to ethics too, although I think it occasionally needs expansion or correction.

1. Darwin's Ethics

Darwin's *Origin of Species* (1859)[2] proposed that Earth's many biological species evolved from common ancestors by a process of mutation plus selection. Organisms randomly developed inheritable variations;[3] organisms with favourable variations were more likely to survive and produce offspring with similar features. Repeating this process many millions of times produced radically new life forms. Darwin argues that evolution explains a massive number of facts about organisms: comparative structure, embryology, geographical distribution and fossil records. But *Origin of Species* mostly avoids issues raised by the evolution of humans.

Darwin's *Descent of Man* (1871) focused on human evolution, with Chapters Four and Five discussing morality in an evolutionary framework. Darwin begins these chapters by saying that the moral sense (conscience), which has a rightful supremacy over other principles of human action, is the most important difference between humans and the lower animals. But analogues of morality exist in other social animals, such as ants and buffaloes. Many social animals show great concern for the welfare of their offspring or comrades, even risking their own safety. Wolves work together in packs and help each other. Dogs sympathize with another's distress or danger, and have something like a conscience; they can be models of fidelity and obedience. Baboons follow a leader and enjoy being with each other; this promotes their survival. With social animals, evolution encourages instincts and behaviours that benefit the group's survival chances.

Humans are social animals, living in families or groups. Like other social animals, we evolved social instincts. Humans are naturally sympathetic; we delight in helping others and are distressed by another's misery. We often show concern for others, especially our offspring and members of our own group. We tend to value the approval of others, internalize group values, and follow the leader. These social instincts are sometimes opposed by other impulses, such as lust, greed, hunger and vengeance, which at times can be anti-social. Primitive morality was instinctive and impulsive more than reflective and rational; people often lacked self-discipline and were swayed by arbitrary taboos. But primitive morality's biggest defect was to extend sympathy mainly to our clan or tribe, and to our own kind, but not to all members of our species; so we thought little of mistreating women or those of other races or tribes.

Over time, humans further developed their intellectual powers through language, observation, inductive reasoning, ends–means reasoning and abstract thinking. As a result, our primitive morality became more rational and less instinctive. We gained more self-discipline and learned more about the consequences of our actions. As human groups became larger, our circle of concern grew. Religion purified our social feelings and moral instincts. Increasingly we struggled towards a higher morality, supported by reason and directed to the welfare of others, where these 'others' gradually expanded to include all humanity, including its weakest members, and even animals. Our noblest attribute became our disinterested love for all living creatures. This higher morality is summed up in the golden rule, 'Treat others as you want to be treated.'

Darwin mentions Immanuel Kant, approving of his ideas about duty (its pure rational attraction, nobility and authority) and about respect for human dignity. Darwin also speaks well of David Hume and John Stuart Mill. Darwin accepts a modified form of Mill's 'greatest happiness' principle, in which we ought to promote the 'general good' of the species, seen not in terms of the balance of pleasure over pain, but rather in the rearing of the greatest number of individuals in full vigour and health.

So what is the natural history explanation of why we think morally? Evolution gave us two great gifts to promote our survival: social instincts and reason. Humanity used these two gifts over many centuries to move from a narrow concern for fellow tribal members towards a higher morality of inherent concern for everyone. We exhibit this higher morality in conscience and the term 'ought'; these have a rightful authority over other motivations and distinguish us from lower animals.

2. Is Altruism Innate?

Philosophers develop their views about morality in light of background assumptions about human nature. David Hume thought that a degree of altruism was built into us. In contrast, Thomas Hobbes thought that humans by nature were totally self-interested and incapable of intrinsic concern for others. Somewhere in the middle, John Stuart Mill held that genuine altruism, while not innate, was learnable. Darwin agrees with Hume and criticizes Mill, contending that if we admit (as we must) that altruism is innate in other social species, then there is no reason to deny that it is innate in humans too.

Does evolution favour the view that altruism is innate in humans? Many followers of Darwin answered no. Some so-called Social Darwinists saw evolution as a 'dog eat dog' struggle in which the strong survive and over-come the weak; so domination, not altruism, is built into us. Friedrich Nietzsche similarly argued that altruism goes against our nature and leads to frustration. Many argued that altruistic individuals had a lower chance to survive and thus would be eliminated in the evolutionary process.

What is the unit of evolutionary selection: the individual or the group? Some Social Darwinists thought in terms of the individual: altruistic individuals would be weeded out because of their reduced tendency to survive and reproduce. Darwin thought in terms of the group: altruistic groups have a stronger tendency to survive. Which side is correct? Con-temporary sociobiologists, like William Hamilton, Robert Trivers and Edward Wilson, think both sides are wrong; the unit of evolutionary selec-tion, they contend, is the gene.[4] Genes that are well adapted tend to be transmitted to future organisms; evolution promotes the survival of the fittest genes.

Consider a society of bees. The only female with offspring is the queen bee. But the female worker bees share the same genes (more or less) as the queen; by promoting the bee society, these female workers insure that copies of their genes are transmitted to future organisms. Something simi-lar holds for human society. We are biologically oriented to insure that copies of our genes are passed into the future. We can do this by having offspring ourselves or by helping those who have genes like ours to have offspring. We tend to provide greater help to close relatives since we share more genes with them.

Besides such *kin altruism* there is also *reciprocal altruism*, sometimes between different species. For example, some small fish act as 'cleaners' for larger fish, eating food from the gills of the larger fish; both sides benefit from this and developed an instinctive concern for the other side, since this promotes the survival of their genes. Other animals whose interests are connected, like humans, seem similarly to have evolved an innate tendency to cooperate with and show concern for each other.

So evolution would build a tendency to altruism into us, especially towards closer relatives or cooperation partners. The explanation is genetic: such altruism promotes the survival of our genes. Some talk about 'selfish genes'; evolution works as if genes promoted their survival by using the bodies of other beings. So does egoism rule? Some think this, but others hold that human benevolence is genuine and that 'selfish genes' is just a metaphor to explain how there evolved a tendency towards benevolence.

Sociobiology becomes complicated as it tries to explain (often using computer simulations) how humans developed a mix of altruism and egoism, and how this applies to how we treat close and further relatives and strangers. There is much controversy concerning the details and the larger question of how much human behaviour is innate and how much is due to socialization.

How does the dispute about the innateness of altruism relate to the Catholic tradition? Catholics see 'love your neighbour' as the core of how we ought to live; given that 'ought' implies 'can', this requires that we are capable (at least with grace) of loving our neighbour. Catholics further believe that such altruistic behaviour is not easy, since we have to struggle with egoistic tendencies, but that it brings a deep fulfilment in this life and in the hereafter. This tradition would be hard to reconcile with the views of Hobbes (who holds that humans are incapable of genuine altruism), some Social Darwinists (who hold that our nature is to dominate), and Nietzsche (who holds that altruism leads only to frustration). The views of Darwin and the sociobiologists, who think humans have an innate mix of altruism and egoism, are more compatible with Catholic thinking.

The Catholic tradition, while it seems to require that humans by nature have a mix of altruism and egoism, does not require that this mix be innate. Seemingly also compatible with Catholic thinking would be a view that sees altruism not as innate or instinctive but rather as part of a natural developmental process. Some explain our attraction to altruism by classical conditioning. Pavlov's dogs associated a bell with food, and later salivated when the bell rang without food. So too we associate pain behaviour (such as crying) with our inner distress, and later experience the same distress from observing another's pain behaviour; so we develop empathetic motivation to prevent in another what would cause pain if done to us. Or it could be that both explanations work together; perhaps altruism is natural to humans both because of how we evolved and because of classical conditioning.

More ultimately, in the Catholic tradition, we are oriented to love one another because we are made in the image and likeness of a loving God. But God can work through secondary causes.

3. Is and Ought

Moral philosophers sometimes use the term 'ethical evolutionism' to refer to the view that moral terms like 'good' and 'ought' are to be analyzed using evolutionary concepts: 'X is good' and 'X ought to be done' are taken to mean 'X accords with the main current of evolution'. On this view, moral principles can be deduced from scientific claims about evolution, thus giving them an objective, rational basis. This ethical evolutionism, while somewhat popular in the decades after Darwin, is among moral philosophers today unpopular – and this for three reasons.

First, if we want to analyze moral terms using purely descriptive notions, why use 'in accord with evolution' instead of 'socially approved' (cultural relativism), 'what I like' (subjectivism), 'what we would desire if we were ideally rational' (ideal observer theory), or 'what maximizes pleasure and minimizes pain' (utilitarian naturalism)? These definitions seem at least as plausible as ethical evolutionism.

Secondly, critics accuse ethical evolutionism of committing the *naturalistic fallacy*. It is wrong, they say, to identify the evaluative term 'good' with the descriptive term 'more evolved'. If something is *more evolved*, it is a further question whether it is *good*. Suppose that evolution moves us towards more misery (as some believe); would it follow that promoting misery was good? Depending on what the path of evolution is, it could be either good or bad to support it. Similarly, if evolution installed certain inclinations into us, we still need to ask which ones of these we ought to follow and which ones we ought to resist. A related objection is that ethical evolutionism violates Hume's law, which says that we cannot deduce an 'ought' from an 'is': we cannot prove moral conclusions solely from non-moral premises, since it is always consistent to accept the non-moral premises and yet reject the moral conclusion.

Thirdly, there are major disputes on which the 'main current' of evolution is, especially since evolution has many currents. Many evolutionists defend the dark side. Some Social Darwinists saw evolution as a 'dog eat dog' struggle in which the strong survive and overcome the weak. Human life, they thought, follows and ought to follow this same pattern; so it accords with nature and is right that strong individuals, businesses, social classes, races and nations struggle for supremacy and overcome the weak. The poor and the weak are unfit to survive; helping them violates the evolutionary process and thus is wrong. Such ideas fuelled Western capitalism, imperialism and racism. Friedrich Nietzsche had somewhat similar views; he thought humans, like other animals, evolved with the will to power and domination as their basic motivation. Nazis saw evolution as a struggle between races; they believed in the domination of Aryans over inferior races, which should be subjugated or eliminated. They also believed in a eugenic elimination of the weak or disabled (adults, children, infants or foetuses) in order to improve the race.

Darwin and the Catholic tradition would condemn such ideas. Darwin saw humans as evolving towards a 'higher morality' of love for all humanity, including its weakest members, and even animals; he summed up this morality in the golden rule, 'Treat others as you want to be treated.' To this, the Catholic tradition would say amen. Many in the Catholic tradition, from a faith perspective, see evolution as part of a larger Teilhardian progression. The cosmic process begins with God's initial moment of big-bang creation (the Alpha);[5] it continues through the biological emergence of ever higher species and then humanity, the emergence in salvation history of the God-man Christ, and humanity's growth in knowledge and love towards the culmination of the cosmic process in the second coming of Christ and the final Kingdom of God (the Omega Point). Love of God and neighbour accords with the cosmic process in the deepest way. Teilhard's ideas had a great influence on the Second Vatican Council (1962–65), especially on the *Church in the Modern World* document, which emphasizes change and speaks of Christians being 'on pilgrimage toward the heavenly city'.[6]

While Darwin contrasts (and insightfully so) the 'higher morality' of universal love with the 'lower morality' of concern for just one's group, he does not say that the higher morality is more correct because it is more evolved. He gives no hint that he defines moral terms using evolutionary concepts, or that he wants to deduce moral principles from scientific claims about evolution. So what we have called 'ethical evolutionism' does not get Darwin's endorsement (or the endorsement of many in the Catholic tradition).

Another view that appeals to some evolutionary thinkers, but gets little support from either Darwin or the Catholic tradition, is scepticism about ethics, based on the idea that ethics cannot be a rational enterprise because it cannot be based on science. This was the view of the logical positivists of old; they argued that any genuine truth claim has to be either analytic (true by language conventions, like 'All bachelors are single') or testable by sense experience (like 'There is snow outside'). Whatever fails this test is nonsensical; it says nothing that could be true or false. For example, 'Racism is wrong', being neither analytic nor empirically testable, must be nonsensical; it says nothing that could be true or false but only expresses emotion, like 'Boo on racism!' Logical positivism, however, led to so many problems that even its main supporters rejected it. For one thing, the view is self-refuting. The claim that every genuine truth claim is analytic or empirically testable is itself neither analytic nor empirically testable; by its own standard, it has to be nonsensical. Another problem is that science itself (including evolutionary science) needs value judgments like 'We *ought* normally to believe our sense experience' and 'Views are *better* if they are simpler and explain more'. Are these simply expressions of feeling and objectively no more true than 'A view is *better* if it accords with my horoscope'? A sceptic about values should in consistency be a sceptic about science.[7]

Darwin was not a sceptic about ethics, nor did he base the correctness of moral principles on scientific facts about evolution. He did not try to give an overall philosophical account of ethics; for this he depended on philosophers like Immanuel Kant and John Stuart Mill.[8] His task rather was to give a natural history account of how ethical thinking developed among humans.

4. How to Form Moral Beliefs

We can investigate moral beliefs from a descriptive or a normative perspective. Natural history is *descriptive*, relating how (and sometimes causally why) moral beliefs arose; natural history is an empirical science. Moral philosophy, in contrast, takes a *normative* perspective, proposing a method that we *ought* to follow for arriving at true or reasonable moral beliefs. The two studies, while different, interrelate. While Darwin focuses on natural history, he occasionally makes philosophical claims (and in my opinion sensible ones), for example, that one moral approach is *higher* than another; if asked to defend this claim, he would appeal not just to observation ('Look and see what this tribe believes') but to philosophical principles. In this section, I focus on the philosophical question: How *ought* we to form our moral beliefs?

Some have suggested a natural history test for proposed methods of forming moral beliefs: *the proposed method must make sense from a natural history standpoint*. Several philosophical views seem to fail this test. Take intuitionism, for example, which proposes that the basic moral truths are self-evident to a mature mind. Besides the problem that there is much disagreement about these truths, the view seems to fail the natural history test. How could the capacity to grasp self-evident moral truths have evolved? It seems difficult to answer this question. Or consider ethical evolutionism, which, as noted above, holds that 'X is good' means 'X accords with the main current of evolution'. If this view is correct, then how could primitive humans (or anyone who lived before the idea of evolution appeared) make moral judgments? Ethical evolutionism paradoxically makes no sense from a natural history perspective.

So how ought we to form our moral beliefs? Many philosophers today endorse some variation on the 'rationalized attitudes' approach: take your present attitudes, subject them to a rational criticism (where you try to be as consistent, informed, impartial and so forth as possible), and then see what attitudes you end up with.[9] Darwin seems to favour a method like this, where we take the instincts that we have as social animals and rationalize them. Such approaches require that we get clearer on how 'rationalizing' works – or, equivalently, on what 'rationality norms' we ought to follow in thinking through our moral beliefs. Here I will sketch the approach that I favour, one that emphasizes the golden rule and includes ideas from various philosophers.

In forming our moral beliefs, we first need to be *consistent*. This includes things like logical consistency among our beliefs, consistency between our ends and means, consistency between our evaluations of similar actions, and consistency between our moral beliefs and how we live and want others to live. Consistency also includes the golden rule, which requires that we treat others only as we are willing for ourselves to be treated in the same situation; if I do something to another and yet am unwilling that this be done to me in the same situation, then I violate golden-rule consistency. In addition, we need to be *informed* (understand the situation, alternative moral viewpoints and ourselves) and *imaginative* (have a vivid and accurate awareness of the situation of another). Science itself is subject to somewhat analogous rationality conditions (such as consistency and the previously mentioned 'Views are *better* if they are simpler and explain more'), thus demonstrating an important point of contact between morality and science.[10]

It is plausible that these three species of rationality – being consistent, informed and imaginative – would promote the survival of our genes and thus would somehow be programmed into us by the evolutionary process. For humans, inconsistency brings distress; psychologists speak here of 'cognitive dissonance'. Perhaps evolution programmed our minds to avoid inconsistencies, as it programmed our bodies to spit out many poisons; to see the need for consistency, imagine how it would paralyze us mentally if whenever we believed A we would also believe not-A. Being informed and being able to imagine another's perspective[11] would obviously promote survival too.

While the most important of these rationality conditions is the golden rule, the various conditions work together. Let us suppose that I am thinking about doing something to another and want to see if I can do this consistent with the golden rule. I would first try to understand the facts, especially about how my action would affect the other person. Then I would try to imagine myself, vividly and accurately, in the other person's place, on the receiving end of the action. Then I would ask myself, 'Am I willing that if I were in the other person's place in the reversed situation then this be done to me?' If I act in a given way towards another and yet am unwilling that I be treated this same way in the reversed situation, then I am inconsistent and violate the golden rule.

While Darwin's *Descent of Man* (1871) speaks of morality as being summed up in the golden rule, he also implicitly uses the rule in his *Voyage of the Beagle* (1837), which is about his five-year voyage around the world to collect biological data. The evil of slavery comes up repeatedly in this earlier work. Darwin recounts one episode where he stopped at a plantation in Brazil (from the entry for 27 April 1832):

> While staying at this estate, I was very nearly being an eyewitness to one of those atrocious acts, which can only take place in a slave country. Owing to a quarrel and a lawsuit, the owner was on the point of taking all the women and children from the men, and selling them separately at the public auction at Rio. Interest, and not any feeling of compassion, prevented this act. Indeed, I do not believe the inhumanity of separating thirty families, who had lived together for many years, even occurred to the person.

Darwin traces much of this blindness, in people who professed to love their neighbour as themselves and to try to do God's will, to a lack of empathetic imagination (from near the end of the 1845 edition):

> Those who look tenderly at the slave-owner, and with a cold heart at the slave, never seem to put themselves into the position of the latter; . . . picture to yourself the chance, ever hanging over you, of your wife and your little children – those objects which nature urges even the slave to call his own – being torn from you and sold like beasts to the first bidder!

Darwin's emphasis on the golden rule accords with Matthew 7:12 ('Treat others as you want to be treated; for this is the summary of the law and the prophets') and fits well with the Catholic tradition.

My opening paragraph noted that I was positive about Darwin's approach to ethics but thought it needed some expansion or correction in details. So we started with Darwin's natural history account of how moral thinking evolved in humans. We added scientific ideas about genetics and sociobiology, philosophical ideas about moral rationality and the golden rule, and theological ideas about how the evolutionary process could be viewed as part of a larger divine plan that goes from the first moment of God's big-bang creation (the Alpha) to the fulfilment of the cosmic process in the final Kingdom of God (the Omega). We might call the resulting view 'genetic sociobiological rationality golden-rule Christianized Darwinism'. Since this name is unwieldy, I will call the resulting view 'D+'. D+ fits well into the Catholic tradition.

5. Aquinas and Darwin

Talking about the Catholic tradition brings to mind St Thomas Aquinas (1224–74), who greatly influenced Catholic thought. Aquinas distinguished philosophy (which is based on human reason) from theology (which requires divine revelation). Correspondingly, his thinking about morality has two parts, which we might call his 'moral philosophy' and his 'moral theology'. His *moral philosophy* mostly follows Aristotle; its norms, called 'natural (moral) laws', are knowable from natural reason and do not require Christian revelation (which Aristotle lacked). Aquinas's *moral theology* requires Christian revelation (from the Bible and Church Tradition); it adds further religious norms and gives a religious context for viewing reason's natural laws. While these two areas should not conflict if approached correctly, they somewhat overlap, since both teach many of the same norms (e.g., that stealing is wrong – which can be based on either reason or revelation).

Here I will focus on Aquinas's moral philosophy. While it derives mostly from Aristotle, there is no necessity that Catholic philosophers build on Aristotle. Augustine built his moral philosophy on Plato, not on Aristotle; and Pope John Paul II stated 'The Church has no philosophy of her own nor does she canonize any one philosophy in preference to others.'[12] I would claim that the enhanced Darwinian approach to ethics (which I labelled 'D+') fits the Catholic tradition at least as well as does Aquinas's natural law approach (which I label 'NL'). I will here point out some features that they share.

First, the two approaches, while they tell different stories, both emphasize biology and our connection with lower animals. NL derives mostly from Aristotle, who was an outstanding biologist. Following Aristotle, NL holds that a human has both an animal soul and a rational soul; so a major part of humans is common to lower animals. NL adds that the good for humans also includes a strong animal aspect; NL divides human goods into three groups: goods common to all beings (like self-preservation), goods common to all animals (like sexual intercourse and raising offspring), and goods peculiar to rational beings (like knowing about God and living in society). Following Darwin, D+ explains that humans have much in common with lower animals because of our common descent; but humans greatly surpass lower animals in rationality. D+ explains the origin of human morality in terms of the social instincts that evolution instilled into us (and which we share with lower social animals) and the elevation of these instincts using human reason.

Secondly, both approaches assert that morality is natural to humans. The basic moral norms (including ones like the golden rule and love-your-neighbour) are objective, in some way built into us (especially into our inclinations, although we also have immoral and egoistic inclinations), and knowable by natural human reason (as opposed to being based purely on social convention or on divine revelation). Aquinas's NL explains how morality is built into our natural inclinations and into our reason, both of which are gifts to us from God. D+ accepts this too, but explains in greater detail what reason involves and how God used evolution to install inclinations and reason into us.[13]

Thirdly, both approaches, when combined with a faith perspective, see morality as part of a divine cosmic order. Aquinas fits NL into a framework whereby a loving God made us after his own image and likeness, to freely choose to live loving and moral lives, and to find our ultimate fulfilment in eternal happiness with God. A Christianized D+ would accept this but fit it into a larger cosmic process, which goes from the first moment of God's big-bang creation (the Alpha) to the fulfilment of the cosmic process in the final Kingdom of God (the Omega).

The central idea in both Aquinas and the Catholic intellectual tradition is the harmony between faith and reason. Pope John Paul II described faith and reason as 'like two wings on which the human spirit rises to the contemplation of truth'.[14] The pair, if understood properly, fit together harmoniously. While faith goes beyond what reason can tell us, reason prepares for faith and helps us to better understand faith. The Catholic intellectual tradition, when it is authentic, is open to new ideas that have a rational basis, whether these come from Aristotle or from Darwin.

Notes

1 We Catholics need to emphasize elements in our tradition that resist taking the biblical creation account literally. See Origen (75–6), Augustine (101), Galileo (241–4) and Teilhard de Chardin (326–9); these page references are to *The Sheed & Ward Anthology of Catholic Philosophy*, ed. James C. Swindal and Harry J. Gensler (Lanham, MD: Rowman & Littlefield, 2005).

2 The four books of Darwin that I refer to are available in various printed editions and online at http://www.gutenberg.org/browse/authors/d#a485 and http://darwin-online.org.uk on the Web.

3 Darwin and others of his time were weak about biological inheritance. Gregor Mendel (1822–84), an Augustinian monk, developed modern genetics, which enhanced our understanding of how evolution works. The recent Genome Project, which completely maps human genes, was another step forward.

4 See William D. Hamilton, 'The Genetic Evolution of Social Behavior I and II', *Journal of Theoretical Biology* 7 (1964): 1–52; Robert L. Trivers, 'The Evolution of Reciprocal Altruism', *Quarterly Review of Biology* 46 (1971): 35–57; *Social Evolution* (Menlo Park, Calif.: Benjamin/Cummings, 1985); and *Natural Selection and Social Theory: Selected Papers of Robert Trivers* (Oxford: Oxford University Press, 2002); and Edward O. Wilson, *Sociobiology: The New Synthesis*, 25th anniversary ed. (Cambridge, Mass.: Harvard University Press, 2000). A recent book explores altruism and the golden rule from a combined neurological, evolutionary and religious perspective: Donald W. Pfaff, *The Neuroscience of Fair Play: Why We (Usually) Follow the Golden Rule* (Chicago: Dana Press, 2007).

5 Darwin, by giving the first plausible non-theistic explanation of how humans could emerge, damaged the traditional argument from design for the existence of God. But recently the 'fine-tuning' or 'anthropic' version of the argument has appeared, based on the fact that the basic physical constants that govern the universe (like the gravitational constant 'g' or the strong nuclear force) have

to be within a very narrow range to make it possible for life to evolve. Steven Hawking gives this example: 'If the rate of expansion one second after the big bang had been smaller by even one part in a hundred thousand million million, the universe would have recollapsed before it ever reached its present size' (*A Brief History of Time*, tenth anniversary edition [New York: Bantam Books, 1998], 126) – which of course would have prevented the evolution of life. Is it not more reasonable to hold that the universe was caused by a great mind than that this precise combination of physical constants came about by chance? This reasoning has recently helped move two prominent atheists into becoming believers; see Anthony Flew (who was one of the most renowned anti-theism philosophers of the twentieth century), *There Is a God* (New York: HarperCollins, 2007), 113–21, and Francis S. Collins (a leading geneticist who directed the Genome Project), *The Language of God* (New York: Free Press, 2006), 63–84. See also Patrick Glynn, *God: The Evidence* (Rocklin, CA: Prima, 1997), 21–55, and Harry Gensler, 'God, Science, and the Golden Rule', in the *Catholic Philosophy Anthology*, 523–31. For a computer-game version of the argument, see http://www.jcu.edu/philosophy/gensler/genesis.exe (Windows only).

6 For an introduction to the ideas of Pierre Teilhard de Chardin, see 'Evolution and Christianity' in the *Catholic Philosophy Anthology*, 326–9.

7 Many today struggle with how (and whether it is possible) to base an objective ethics on evolution without committing the naturalistic fallacy; see *Issues in Evolutionary Ethics*, ed. Paul Thompson (Albany, N.Y.: SUNY Press, 1995), and *Biology and the Foundation of Ethics*, eds Jane Maienschein and Michael Ruse (Cambridge: Cambridge University Press, 1999).

8 While Darwin's *Descent of Man* seems to follow Kant about the objectivity and prescriptive authority of 'ought', his later *Autobiography* (1887) advocated following duty because this in the long run makes one happier. This book also talks about his transition from an Anglican theology student to an agnostic.

9 Ethicists who take this approach hold various views about the objectivity of ethical norms. I take a strong stand in favour of objectivity, since common sense supports it and since the arguments against objectivity, when clearly spelled out, are easy to attack (see the logical positivist argument mentioned above).

10 For more about rationality conditions, see my textbook *Ethics: A Contemporary Introduction* (London: Routledge, 1998), Chaps 7–9; my more technical *Formal Ethics* (London: Routledge, 1996); my logical formalization in *Introduction to Logic* (London: Routledge, 2002), Chap. 11; and my popular web page (http://www.jcu.edu/philosophy/gensler/goldrule.htm) on the golden rule. Much of my approach grew out of R. M. Hare's *Freedom and Reason* (Oxford: Clarendon Press, 1963).

11 Imagining another's perspective is a common and important human experience. A child pretends to be a mother or a cowboy. A chess player asks, 'If I were in my opponent's place, how would I respond to this move?' A writer dialogues with an imagined reader who misunderstands and raises objections. A teacher asks, 'How would I respond to this assignment if I were a student?' The ability to take another's perspective is especially important for applying the golden rule.

12 From *Fides et Ratio* in the *Catholic Philosophy Anthology*, 418.

13 An even wider D+ would include psychologists like Piaget and Kohlberg, who claim that people of all cultures go through a similar process of moral

development that involves the golden rule. See Jean Piaget, *The Moral Judgment of the Child*, trans. Marjorie Gabain (Glencoe, IL: Free Press, 1948), and Lawrence Kohlberg, *Essays on Moral Development*, 2 vols (San Francisco: Harper & Row, 1981 and 1984).

14 From *Fides et Ratio* in the *Catholic Philosophy Anthology*, 415.

Chapter 10

DARWINISM, MIND AND SOCIETY

Louis Caruana

It is one of the ironies of history that Charles Darwin was not the real founder of Social Darwinism. If one were pressed to pick out a single founder, it must be Herbert Spencer. This fact alone is enough to indicate the complex nature of the interaction between Darwin's empirical work and its application to human social and moral behaviour. Some years before the publication of Darwin's *Origin of Species*, Herbert Spencer, had argued that nature deals with the healthy by letting them survive and with the weak by letting them die. We should therefore do likewise in human society: 'If they are sufficiently complete to live, they *do* live, and it is well they should live; if they are not sufficiently complete to live, they die, and it is well they should die.'[1] Such an attitude towards nature and society was quite widespread before Darwin. The basic features of this attitude included the belief that nature produced inequalities. As a consequence, social phenomena must be explained in terms of competition, conflict and the equilibrium and adjustment that results from this.

Darwin's specific contribution came from his two core principles: first, that all species are descended from one progenitor; and second, that the mechanism how this descent occurs is natural selection. Biologists today may leave it as an open question whether one should assume just one progenitor or perhaps a very small number, and whether or not natural selection is the only mechanism involved. Nevertheless, we can say that Darwin's two core principles, which determine a unique research programme in the history of science, have withstood more than a hundred years of scrutiny. Is it possible to separate the scientific core of his theory from extrapolations of it to moral and social theory? Is it possible to separate the scientist Darwin from the ideological Darwin? Anyone who wants to answer in the affirmative would have to start with Darwin himself. Darwin saw his own work as extendable, without losing its continuity, from empirical observation of animal characteristics to questions related to morals and religion. As Spencer and others had done before him, Darwin considered it an essential part of his intellectual task to extrapolate his core principles to areas beyond the horizon of strictly empirical study. He worked out theories of the evolution of cognitive dispositions or habits, of ethics and even of religious behaviour. For instance, in his 1871 work *The Descent of Man, and Selection in Relation to Sex*, he asked: Are high moral standards advantageous? As regards the community, he answered in the affirmative. He observed that a tribe with self-sacrificing individuals would have survival advantage over another tribe without such individuals. In the long run, this results in natural selection. And hence, what he called 'standards of morality' tend to rise, in the sense that tribes with individuals open to the possibility of self-sacrifice tend to outlive other kinds of tribes.[2] Since then, many other thinkers took up Darwin's project of extrapolating evolutionary explanation so as to engage with philosophy of mind, ethics, and social and political philosophy. Not all of them agree on the extent to which such an extrapolation is legitimate. At one extreme we find some who insist that philosophy and natural science do not mix, and should therefore be kept apart. For these, natural selection in the evolution of hominids is completely irrelevant for the resolution of problems in these areas. At the other extreme, we find other thinkers insisting that philosophical problems we have been facing since time immemorial have been, and are being, resolved steadily as natural science pushes ahead.

The area represented by the middle ground between these two extremes is not easy to navigate. The issues as they stand today are multifaceted and compound, branching out into various areas of philosophy and theology. It is one of the aims of this chapter to add some clarity into this complex area of enquiry. I intend to do this with special attention to two traditions: the secular and the religious. In Part One, I will concentrate on purely philosophical issues, tracing the development of the idea of social Darwinism, from its origins to the present day. At the end of this first part, I will be in a position to determine one major root problem that is blocking further progress in the current state of things. In Part Two, I will shift into the religious mode of enquiry. I will give a sketch of the main features of the reaction to social Darwinism that arose from Catholic scholarship. I will then proceed by determining, from within this Catholic tradition, the main root problem of Social Darwinism as perceived from the religious viewpoint. These two lines of enquiry will enable us then to appreciate the extent to which the root problems determinable from secular, philosophical enquiry correspond to the root problems determinable from the Catholic tradition.[3]

1. Social Darwinism: The Philosophical Perspective

Darwin's attempts at explaining moral and social behaviour illustrate a social theory in the making, itself situated within a wider paradigm. This wider world-view had various characteristics. It included, for instance, an overall slant towards materialist explanation of human psychological and social affairs. It included also, as a consequence, a suspicion as regards any supernatural forces. The view that human beings were somehow evolved from non-human organisms was already present before Darwin. Moreover, even before Darwin's time, the search had been on for biological laws that would explain the entire range of living organisms. Many authors had discussed the fact that population growth affects the way living things compete for resources. The historian Mike Hawkins describes this paradigm by mentioning four features:

> This world view [. . .] consisted of the following elements: (i) biological laws governed the whole of organic nature, including humans; (ii) the pressure of population growth on resources generated a struggle for existence among organisms; (iii) physical and mental traits conferring an advantage on their possessors in the struggle (or in sexual competition), could, through inheritance, spread through the population; (iv) the cumulative effects of selection and inheritance over time accounted for the emergence of new species and the elimination of others.[4]

What Darwin added to this paradigm was a robust empirical basis. After the publication of the *Origin of Species*, supernatural and teleological accounts of species formation lost much of their previous plausibility. The urge to extend the natural-selection mode of explanation beyond the physical properties of humans became stronger and stronger. Social Darwinism, from that period onwards, can therefore be described as follows. It is the research programme in which what Darwin did for physical and biological features is assumed extendible to human social existence and also to human psychological attributes that determine the modalities of this social existence, especially morality and religion.[5]

   This programme, of course, didn't proceed without its share of opposition. To obtain some idea of the various kinds of challenges it had to face, the first thing one needs to keep in mind is that Social Darwinism was 'a broad church'.[6] On the one hand we have people like Thomas Robert Malthus who had prepared the background by highlighting the mutual dependence between population growth and conditions for survival. He argued that the less deprived will face more demanding conditions, because population grows at a geometric rate while food resources can only grow at an arithmetic rate. This preliminary trace of Social Darwinism can therefore be seen as that paradigm's pessimistic trend. On the other hand, we find Herbert Spencer, who was transforming biological thinking, albeit in its Lamarckian form, into a robust social philosophy with implications for economics, this time in an optimistic way. He emphasized a *laissez-faire* attitude that, according to him, guarantees progress. Both flanks had to face opposition. Malthusian thinking had to respond to the objection that an increase in population does not only mean an increase in need for resources but also an increase in productivity. Spencer's writings had to respond to objections related to the foundations of ethics. G. E. Moore argued in his *Principia Ethica* that Spencer had committed the naturalistic fallacy. According to Moore, Spencer errs because he allegedly substituted a non-natural property, namely goodness in itself, by a natural property, namely survivability.[7] The wider ramifications of this 'broad church' gave rise to controversies that had international significance and survived all through the twentieth century. Social Darwinism was linked to the eugenic movements in the USA and in Nazi Germany, and was also implicated within the nature-nurture debate in the development of human anthropology. On the one hand, anthropological studies in the first decades of the twentieth century, for instance those carried out by Margaret Mead, suggested that most human action is a result of environmental conditioning and not of genetic constitution. These studies therefore tended to undermine Social Darwinism. On the other hand, more recent studies in molecular genetics, like those of W. D. Hamilton in 1964, and E. O. Wilson in 1975, started supplying empirical evidence on how a specific genetic constitution indeed determines, to some extent at least, what humans do.[8]

The unifying characteristic of all the variations of Social Darwinism seems to lie in their common assumption. They all assume that humans, like other animals, compete for existence and that this fundamental feature explains the most useful aspects of social and political reality. If this assumption is made stronger, a more radical position results. If, in other words, we assume that the competition for existence explains not just most aspects of social and political reality but all of that reality, we end up with sociobiology. This position involves the idea of reduction. It works with the assumption that disciplines that have been up to now considered non-empirical, like ethics, psychology, social and political theory, are indeed entirely empirical after all. They are branches of biology. Sociobiology therefore can be considered an extreme version of Social Darwinism: a naturalistic Social Darwinism.[9] Of course, naturalism is most often described with respect to physics: physics is taken to be the core, or the only, discipline that matters in all philosophical topics. Here we have naturalism with respect to biology. Society is assumed totally explainable just like flora or fauna. There are various levels of organization, and each is explainable in terms of evolution propagated by blind variation and natural selection alone. Moreover, human society, just like the rest of the organic world, is explainable in terms of purposes, goals and functions of systems situated within larger systems.[10]

With these general features of Social Darwinism in view, we can now appreciate some typical arguments in its favour in current literature. A good source is Michael Ruse's *Taking Darwin Seriously*. In this book, he

takes the most convincing justification for sociobiology to be the success
with which altruistic behaviour in animals has been explained by kin
selection and reciprocal action.[11] A group of organisms that includes
self-sacrificing individuals has a higher chance of survival than a group
that does not. Altruistic behaviour results when two principles are at work.
It happens when the individual is, first, more likely to help close kin rather
than distant ones, and, second, when that individual helps another with
the expectation of having the favour returned. Ruse argues that, for some
organisms, these conditions are indeed satisfied. Moreover, humans are
such animals. Therefore their altruistic behaviour is fully explainable in
this naturalistic way.

What are the hidden logical nuances of this argument? In line with the
sociobiology programme sketched above, Ruse is essentially explaining, in
purely naturalistic terms, one of the fundamental moral traits of human
behaviour. The suggestion is that what we can do as regards altruism may
be done also as regards other moral habits. So the outcome of such an
explanatory project seems to be inevitable: we are heading towards global
determinism as regards human culture, because every human act would be
seen as the outcome of biological mechanisms. Ruse is aware of this, and
he tries to avoid such a slippery slope by a simple claim. He insists that
arguments like the one about altruism are only about constraints our
evolutionary past has established – nothing else. So he writes: 'The question is not whether every last act of Western man or woman is governed
by kin selection or reciprocal altruism or some such thing. I am sure
it is not.'[12]

It is interesting to note that, in the very same book, he himself renders
such an excuse somewhat ineffective. At one point he tries to remain at the
level of broad, general principles allegedly touching only some constraints.
At other places, he presents his thesis as relevant for the entire spectrum
including both meta-ethics and normative ethics. In meta-ethics, we try to
explain why humans adopt the moral principles that they in fact adopt.
For instance, as regards altruism, we assume that humans show this
tendency, the habit of helping others via self-sacrifice, as a common
characteristic. Notice therefore that those engaged in a meta-ethical
enquiry are not concerned with questions dealing with specific applicability, such as: 'Should I be altruistic in this specific case?' The basic form
of the question they are interested in is: 'Why do we have this habit, most
of us, most of the time, when it seems, at face value, to go against the
survival of the fittest?' Habit and principle here merge into each other.
Ruse is right in claiming that sociobiology is relevant here. As regards
normative ethics, the relevance is less obvious. In normative ethics, the
major focus is on the action to be done, not on the habits of the agent. The
typical question here is of the form: 'Should I do action A in this specific
situation?' or 'What am I obliged to do in this specific situation?' At first

sight, it may appear that evolutionary explanation cannot be a useful resource for normative ethics, especially if we accept that an 'ought' cannot be derived from an 'is'. We may however make evolutionary explanation relevant by inserting an ethical bridge-principle. And this is precisely what evolutionary ethics sometimes purports to do. It introduces the idea that 'we ought to do what is in line with our normal biological functioning'. The plausibility of such an ethical bridge-principle makes Ruse's suggestion that sociobiology is relevant for both meta-ethics and normative ethics quite appealing. His caution as regards sliding towards global determinism does not stop him from supplying impressive arguments in support of Social Darwinism in its strongest form.

In spite of the attraction of extending evolutionary explanation beyond biology, there have been various arguments advanced against sociobiology.[13] I will concentrate on one major issue only, one which has been somewhat neglected. I will focus on the very nature of intentional states. My basic claim is that the application of evolutionary explanation to moral, social and political philosophy tends to work with a view of intentional states that is to some extent distorted. Because of this, it ends up leaving some essential properties of human society out of consideration.

In what follows, the crucial assumption is that, although our main focus is Social Darwinism, it is often useful to start from more basic considerations.[14] Take the human sciences in general. On close inspection, one realizes that a serious challenge arises because of the special character of mental states. Naturalists confront this challenge by adopting the methods of empirical science. For natural scientists, laws of nature in general are relations between some variables, and these variables are chosen in a specific way. The variables must, first of all of course, be useful in describing the phenomenon under study. They must also, however, be independent of each other. They must be both logically independent, in the sense that their meaning is accessible independently, and also methodologically independent, in the sense that they should be measurable separately. When this basic strategy is applied to ethics and social science, naturalists assume the existence of laws that express links between desires, beliefs and actions, and maybe some other elements of our normal way of behaviour. So here we have the set of variables for this kind of enquiry. A typical law would be: for any human individual x, if x desires q, and x believes that doing action A is the best means of attaining q, then x does A. This is practically saying that the relations between intentional states and actions are assumed to be explainable on the model of causation in physics.

Is this viable? The major problem lies with one of the underlying assumptions. When we assume that what works for science must work also for ethics and society, we are assuming that intentional states are independent variables, while in fact they are not. They are, in fact, logically inter-dependent because of their intentional content. To determine the content of a belief or a desire, you need to ask the person who has them what he or she really believes or desires. Likewise, to determine an action, observing the bodily movement is not enough. This fundamental point rules out physics as a model for social and ethical explanation. Does it rule out biology as well? Admittedly, biology differs from physics in various ways. Evolutionary biology, for instance, is interested not in the relation between variables associated with a particular individual agent, but in what happens to average values of traits within a group.[15] Could it be that, because of this shift in viewpoint from individual to group, the problematic mutual dependence between specific beliefs, desires and actions vanishes as we zoom out, as it were, from the scenario involving the individual? If it does vanish, or become negligible, then evolutionary explanation will indeed be applicable to social and ethical issues.

Only some further analysis, however, is needed to show that no such vanishing occurs. The problematic mutual dependence between beliefs, desires and actions resurfaces at all levels. At the level of the individual, this dependence is clear, as mentioned above. At the level of the group, mutual dependence between belief, desire and action takes the form of reflexivity. This term is used by critical theorists who are sensitive to the fact that knowledge and truth are dependent on human interests. For my purposes here, we can take the term reflexivity to refer to the fact that, in the human sciences, the objects under study (human beings) are not left undisturbed by the theories proposed to describe them. In concrete terms, this means that when a group is told about a theory proposed to explain its behaviour patterns, the group is not only capable of shifting its behaviour away from what is predicted, but very often does precisely that. The history of humanity gives ample evidence of this kind of reaction. And this shows how beliefs, desires and actions remain intertwined at the group level as well. The upshot is that evolutionary explanation of social and ethical behaviour needs some fundamental revision even to get off the ground.[16]

Could it be that Social Darwinism is still defensible in spite of this problem? The only way forward is to claim that Social Darwinism is good for *some* aspects, but not for *all* aspects of moral and social behaviour. Philip Kitcher seems to defend this middle-ground position. It is a position that corresponds very well, I think, to most people's pre-philosophical intuitions. His main point is that Darwinism, as an explanatory tool, has to be used with caution. When people appeal to natural selection in order to draw conclusions about psychological faculties and moral or social dispositions, their argument is always vulnerable. It is always open to the challenge that alternative explanations in these areas are possible. At best, a Darwinian explanation supplies us with an explanation not of how human morality and human social dispositions evolved but of how they *might* have evolved. To conclude his paper, Kitcher writes:

Darwin's great achievement doesn't make all other considerations and disciplines irrelevant, and, in particular, it shouldn't lead us to dismiss the potential insights of pre-Darwinian philosophizing. My recommendations for applying evolutionary ideas within philosophy are, I trust, obvious from my illustrative examples, and their prevailing character is one of cautious exploration. Darwin deserves his due, neither more nor less.[17]

In the terminology used above, Kitcher seems to be assuming, deep down, that intentionality can be divided into two layers. The lower layer corresponds to instinctive behaviour; the upper level to non-instinctive behaviour, where action is the result of conscious deliberation. For instinctive behaviour, beliefs, desires and actions are so simple that they are indeed independent variables. A Skinner-type stimulus-response scenario involves a person with a simple desire-belief-action sequence, such as when someone acts 'mechanically', as we often say. Are there *real* desires, beliefs and actions in these scenarios? Many of us would say yes. They are genuine desires, beliefs and actions, but they are not the object of our attention. They are not the object of attention either because the individual is alienated with something else, or because the individual is being carried along by the crowd. When, as it were, I don't look straight at my desires, beliefs or actions, I live in the mechanical mode. At any moment, however, I can stop and attend to them. When I do so, these intentional states become the object of my self-reflection. Up to now, I have been discussing the individual. But the argument applies also to a group. A group, or even the species taken as a whole, has beliefs, desires and is engaged in action. It is fully conscious of some of these beliefs, desires and actions. It may however be unaware of others. Hence, just as in the individual's case, the group can stop and attend to itself, in a moment of group self-reflection. In this way, its hitherto mechanical beliefs, desires and actions start becoming interdependent. It is therefore by attending to them, that the individual or group will detach itself from the picture supplied by the Darwinist account of social and ethical reality. Here we have the second layer of intentionality.

Kitcher's position seems balanced and plausible. Nevertheless, if I am right about this hidden assumption involving two levels, it starts showing worrying signs of over-simplification. The idea of a clear boundary between intentional states in the mechanical mode and intentional states in the non-mechanical, or free, mode looks too good to be true. I fear that the world is messier than we often wish it to be. If, in our understanding of mental properties and of practical reason, we follow the route of Aristotle, as reworked recently by D. Davidson and J. McDowell, we'll see that there cannot be any clear distinction between empirical content and conceptual scheme. This essentially means that what I have been calling *mechanical* beliefs, desires or actions are not beliefs, desires or actions at all. Once humans become aware of anything – once they become aware of cognitive dispositions, of basic wants or urges, or of possible control over bodily movement – their rationality is engaged, whether they like it or not. A mechanical action, after all, is, in so far as it is deprived of intention, not ethical. So what is the major issue in this entire debate? Even this very quick glance at mental properties and practical reason is enough to show that the major issue is human freedom. If Social Darwinism explains anything about humans, it explains what lies outside free deliberation. It explains what lies outside the specifically human.

Let me recapitulate: The aim of this section was to determine one of the root problems that is blocking further progress. I've structured my reasoning by listing some arguments in favour of Social Darwinism and some against. Concentrating only on intentional states, I've come to the conclusion that, when we apply evolutionary explanation to moral, social and political philosophy, we tend to ignore the basic fact that the content of human beliefs, desires and action are inter-dependent. We tend to disregard the human ability to react against constraints. The root problem is the stubborn fact of human freedom with respect to natural constraints.

2. Social Darwinism: The Religious Perspective

We shift now to the religious viewpoint. The interaction of Social Darwinism with Christianity has taken many forms. A quick historical glance shows that clashes occurred principally around the following four areas.[18] First, Christianity defends the idea of human nature or human essence, and considers this indispensable as a basis for freedom. Social Darwinists, on the contrary, work with the assumption that there is no such thing as a fixed human nature or essence. This clash was first explicitly pointed out as early as 1866 in the first French translation of Darwin's *Origin of Species*.[19] One needs to add here, however, that, since those early years, ideas on this point have evolved. Within the Darwinian camp, defenders of punctuated equilibrium have highlighted the fact that, although speciation is possible, species usually remain unchanged over long stretches of time; moreover, speciation occurs only within relatively brief intervals. Within the phylum that includes humans, significant biological changes have not occurred for thousands of years. It is plausible to consider this point a satisfactory justification for the idea that, although human nature or human essence may not be fixed, it is virtually timeless. The second area of dissonance occurred because Christianity considers universal brotherhood as possible, and in fact never ceases to encourage people to strive to achieve it. Social Darwinists, on the contrary, insisted that human divisions are perennial because they are founded on tribal conflict. Humans in fact can never escape their dual mentality of being locally friendly, but globally belligerent.[20] Thirdly, Christianity considers herself the channel of God's revelation to humanity, and, especially within the Catholic tradition, sees religion and science as necessarily harmonious with each other as they issue from the same source, God. On the contrary, influential, popular, Social Darwinists like Ernst Haeckel (1834–1919) argued that science and religion are in direct and eternal conflict and that what is valid in Christianity was taken from other cultures and what is specific to it is wrong.[21] Fourthly, Christian tradition, especially within Catholicism and the Orthodox traditions, sees a vital spiritual value in priestly celibacy and in the idea of belonging to a community of shared norms. Social Darwinists opposed this. They argued that priestly celibacy is an encumbrance to society because it reduces the best offspring, and that conformity and tolerance block the purity of the superior race.[22]

In spite of these areas of contention, the interaction of Social Darwinism with Christianity has enjoyed elements of constructive dialogue. For many centuries before Darwin's days, the Catholic intellectual tradition had been engaged in social and political philosophy in various ways. In spite of such a sustained effort, no complete, systematic theory of society has ever been formulated and officially sanctioned, even to this day. One sees rather a general attempt at highlighting a number of principles that must be respected at all costs. Social Darwinism has represented an opportunity for Catholic scholars to explore areas that had hitherto been neglected or simply ignored. I will proceed by examining three of these principles.

The first one deals with realism as regards the nature of all created things, including societies. Drawing from Aristotle and Augustine, official Catholic doctrine has always highlighted the idea of the autonomy of each aspect of reality: 'created things and societies themselves enjoy their own laws and values which must be gradually deciphered, put to use, and regulated by men.'[23] The basic tenet of faith that God is the creator of everything justifies the assumption that all processes unfold according to their own laws. This holds not only for physical reality but for biological and social reality as well. To avoid sliding towards the idea that the goodness of the Creator ensures an easy access to these laws, the acknowledgment of this realism needs to be counterbalanced. It is counterbalanced by recalling the enormous complexity of reality: not only of physical reality, but also of biological and especially human reality. Any trace of reductionism in social explanation should therefore be viewed with suspicion. A typical statement highlighting this caution is found in an official text that expresses concern about the straightforward application of Marxist doctrines to society: 'In the human and social sciences it is well to be aware above all of the plurality of methods and viewpoints, each of which reveals only one aspect of reality which is so complex that it defies simple and univocal explanation.'[24] This caution is valid not only for

Marxist explanation. It is valid also for Social Darwinism, for both explanations are practically always taken to be exhaustive.

This point leads naturally to the second principle highlighted within the Catholic tradition as regards social reality: the danger of having social theory hijacked by dangerous ideology. The usual victim of such hijacking is human freedom. That the application of Darwinism to social explanation is easy prey for ideology has been highlighted not only by religion-inspired scholars but also by others.[25] The possibility of distortion arises because, in explaining a given social aspect, one can often choose the variables deliberately to support a hidden agenda.[26] Social Darwinism has often been used in this way to support various forms of determinism that undermine moral responsibility.

Now, one needs to recall that the Catholic tradition does not say that human deliberation and choice are not determined in any way. The Augustinian and Thomistic heritage grapples with the question of freedom in relation to God's fore-knowledge and God's omnipotence. Aquinas had no problem with proposing that the human will is, in its very nature, strictly determined toward an object recognized intellectually as the *universal* good. For him, human freedom is only possible when humans deal with *particular* goods.[27] In such cases, deliberation and choice are indeed affected by the physical state of the individual. For instance, a person may be more emotional than another, or more impulsive than another, according to each person's temperament and prior conditioning. There may also be unconscious influences. Individuals are often not fully aware of all that is affecting their deliberation and choice. Nevertheless, it is legitimate in such cases to consider them free in the sense that they are deliberating and choosing consciously, while having the added commitment to uncover as many as possible of the hidden influences. When Social Darwinists therefore argue that moral choices are conditioned by habits hammered into human living in the course of hominid evolution, they are not out of line with the Catholic tradition. When they claim however that, because of such habits, moral choices are illusory, they are seen as contravening the basic principle of human freedom.

Not to remain too much on the abstract level, we may consider the particular example of economics and *laissez-faire*, or unrestricted, capitalism. As mentioned above, H. Spencer's writings on Social Darwinism had proposed that an economic system should allow businesses to operate with little or no government interference. With such an outlook, the role of society's deliberation and choice is reduced to a minimum. There is no trace of the fact that human beings are the sort of creature that, once a previously hidden influence on the run of things becomes visible, they become capable of deliberating about it. In the late nineteenth and early twentieth century, this kind of deliberation actually erupted in the United States, when state and federal governments came under pressure to regulate unrestricted capitalism via legislation on working conditions, wages and child labour.[28] In a recent official document, which offers a synthesis of much work from the Catholic tradition, one finds an explicit reference to this tension between, on the one hand, social forces that may be accounted for in terms of Darwinian principles and, on the other hand, human freedom and responsibility:

> *The free market cannot be judged apart from the ends that it seeks to accomplish and from the values that it transmits on a societal level.* Indeed, the market cannot find in itself the principles for its legitimization; it belongs to the consciences of individuals and to public responsibility to establish a just relationship between means and ends. The *individual profit* of an economic enterprise, although legitimate, must never become the sole objective. Together with this objective there is another, equally fundamental but of a higher order: *social usefulness*, which must be brought about not in contrast to but in keeping with the logic of the market. When the free market carries out the important functions mentioned above it becomes a service to the common good and to integral human development.[29]

The suggestion here is that the *laissez-faire* mentality is not wrong in itself but is to be judged according to its service to the common good. The element of freedom and responsibility remains: a good illustration of the second principle I wanted to highlight, a principle that emerges in a new light because of the interaction between Social Darwinism and Catholic thought.

The third principle concerns the dignity of the human person. For an explicit formulation of this principle, in relation to evolutionary explanation, one may refer to a section of Pope John Paul II's address to the Pontifical Academy of Sciences delivered in 1996: 'Theories of evolution which, in accordance with the philosophies inspiring them, consider the spirit as emerging from the forces of living matter or as a mere *epiphenomenon* of this matter, are incompatible with the truth about man. Nor are they able to ground the dignity of the person.'[30] The suggestion here is that, to be acceptable, any philosophy of evolutionary biology, and also any associated social theory, must consign to the human person absolute value. The theory must be able to ground the dignity of the person. This requirement is being presented as a constraint on the various possible uses of evolutionary explanation in understanding human reality. Hence, giving less importance to the individual person than to the genes that partially constitute him or her is unacceptable. Giving less importance to the individual person than to the aggregate (species or society), to which that person belongs, is likewise unacceptable. The person comes first. No person is to be considered merely an instrument for the survival of the species. No person is to be considered merely a carrier of an exotic gene.

On this particular point, the fiercest ideological battles were fought in debates concerning Eugenics. The advent of Darwinism encouraged the consideration of the human phenomenon from new perspectives. It encouraged the study of traits, over and above the consideration of human individuals. It encouraged the study of populations, again over and above the consideration of individuals. The systematic study of methods for hereditary improvement of human population by controlled selective breeding arose concurrently with Darwin's work. In spite of this however, eugenics is quite distinct from Social Darwinism. Eugenics represents a kind of 'reverse-engineered' version of Social Darwinism. Darwin had started from the model of goal-directed animal-husbandry, and then moved on to the elimination of purpose. In eugenics we find the opposite. Francis Galton uses Darwin's views on natural selection to return to goal-directed human intervention: hence the popular idea that eugenics is the self-direction of human evolution. Having said that, however, we need to recall that the *aim* behind eugenics is very often in line with Social Darwinism. The idea of a struggle for survival is always in the background. What we often see within the eugenics movement is an acknowledgement that the struggle for survival of one particular race needs to be carried out intelligently and methodically. The upshot is: eugenics and Social Darwinism are strange bedfellows.

There is a lot to say about the complex reaction of the Catholic Church to the eugenic movement, especially as regards the forms that movement adopted in Nazi Germany.[31] I will concentrate on one foundational point only, a point that illustrates the principle of the irreplaceable value of the individual person. This one foundational point is that, although there is much to condemn in the philosophy of eugenics, there are some elements that are in harmony with genuine human flourishing. Only if we highlight the value of the individual person, can we determine these positive elements in line with human flourishing. No one can deny that there is a moral obligation for one generation to ensure that the next generation enjoys a quality of life better than its own, or a quality of life at least as good as its own. For a correct judgment on how this can be achieved, one must respect the right priorities that determine the individual's deliberations. Hence, physical well-being cannot be taken to override moral and spiritual well-being. Such ideas were expressed by Catholic scholars not only in learned works but also in pamphlets directed to the masses. For instance, Thomas Gerrard in 1912 published a booklet entitled *The Church and Eugenics*. He explains how 'instinct shall be ministrant to intelligence, and intelligence ministrant to love'.[32] In the same vein he writes: 'the physical element in man must always be subordinate to the psychic and the psychic to the spiritual.'[33] His point is not that we should disregard or hinder the lower aspects. It is rather to care for them, but to do so in so far as they enhance the development of the higher aspects. The main question that emerges therefore is: what is the ideal that humans should seek? Gerrard argues that genuine Catholic doctrine brings out the best in eugenics. The Catholic 'ideal' is neither Nietzsche's *Über-Mensch*, nor the humanists' Ideal Scientist or Ideal Artist. It is rather the genius in morality and holiness, or, in other words, the saint. He concludes: 'Catholicism then, far from seeking to hinder eugenic reform, seeks rather to promote it by setting it on a lasting basis, the basis of the spirit.'[34] Gerrard's arguments are a good illustration of the Catholic trend to defend the dignity of the individual. The individual's freedom and responsibility explains why no one is to be considered merely an instrument for the survival or purification of the race.

Conclusion

In Part One, I concentrated on purely philosophical issues, especially those dealing with intentional states. I arrived at the conclusion that one of the major problems concerns human freedom with respect to natural constraints, whether these constraints arise from immediate physical limitations or from more long-term conditioning. In Part Two, I explored some aspects of the way Social Darwinism interacted with Christian thought, especially in the Catholic tradition. In this regard, the religious viewpoint has highlighted three principles: realism as regards social entities; the danger of having social theory hijacked by dangerous ideology; and the absolute value of the person. These two parts of this chapter represent two distinct lines of enquiry, one deriving its inspiration from reason and observation; the other from reason, observation and religious faith. It is interesting to see how both lines of enquiry converge onto the same area. They both indicate that there is something wrong when Social Darwinism or sociobiology is allowed to stifle human freedom and responsibility.

The basic insight therefore that emerges from the foregoing arguments is that even if Social Darwinism or sociobiology supply convincing evidence that social injustice, war or interpersonal aggression are *natural*, we are still obliged to exercise our freedom with respect to these aspects of human living and to do so responsibly.[35] Social Darwinism and sociobiology do not hinder the role of social policy, still less do they eliminate it. On the contrary, they are a help. They tell us where we really stand. They facilitate effective planning. Admittedly, it often happens that, when belief-desire-action sequences are left unattended, both at the level of the individual and at the level of society, they tend to become instinctive, ingrained or mechanical: a kind of second nature. When this happens, any unwanted consequences may surprise us. This element of surprise should trigger our concern. Darwinism therefore is indispensable, not because our freedom is illusory but because we need all the information we can get so as to exercise freedom responsibly.

Notes

1 Herbert Spencer, *Social Statics* (London: Routledge/Thoemmes Press, 1996). 414–5. As regards biology, Spencer was in line with Lamarck rather than with Darwin. So for Spencer, new species emerged as a result of modifications in existing species, brought about by exposure to new conditions. They did not emerge via natural selection. See his essay 'Progress: its Law and Cause', in: H. Spencer, *Essays: Scientific, Political and Speculative* (London: Williams & Norgate, 1890).

2 Recent work in this area shows that Darwin's reasoning is incorrect on this point. A group-selection mechanism like the one he had in mind will die out in the long run because of infiltration into that group of selfish individuals. The egoism of these individuals will be advantageous within the group, and will thus undermine its moral standards. See A. Rosenberg, 'The Biological Justification of Ethics: a best-case scenario', *Social Philosophy and Policy* 8 (1990): 86–101; reprinted in: A. Rosenberg, *Darwinism in Philosophy, Social Science and Policy* (Cambridge: Cambridge University Press, 2000), 118–36.

3 In line with this volume's overall line of enquiry, I will concentrate on the Catholic religious viewpoint, without negating that a study of other religious viewpoints is of course important as well.

4 Mike Hawkins, *Social Darwinism in European and American thought, 1860–1945: nature as model and nature as threat* (Cambridge: Cambridge University Press, 1997), 31. For a detailed treatment of how Darwin's theory depends on its historical context, see G. Radick, 'Independence, history and natural selection' in: J. Hodge & G. Radick, *The Cambridge Companion to Darwin* (Cambridge: Cambridge University Press, 2003), 143–67.

5 Through the past decades, Darwinian explanation has been extrapolated beyond its normal habitat not only in the directions indicated here but also in other directions as well. Lack of space forbids considering these other areas at any length in this chapter. They include, for instance, (1) the relatively new area of teleosemantics, where works like R. Millikan's *Language, thought, and other biological Categories: new foundations for realism* (Cambridge, MA: MIT Press, 1984) and D. Papineau's *Reality and representation* (Oxford: Basil Blackwell, 1987) try to develop an evolutionary explanation of meaning and intentionality; (2) the area of phylogenetic relationship. This second area involves the search for a 'family tree'. A great deal of work in evolutionary biology is devoted to determining what the family trees are for various taxonomic groups. The detailed working out of ancestry is a separate task from the identification of the adaptive significance, if any, of the traits that various species possess. To see how elements of culture, or how existing languages, or how various manuscripts (like the four Gospels), are sometimes related to each other genealogically is a question in which insights from evolutionary biology can play an important role.

6 See Robert M. Young, 'Darwinism *is* Social', in: David Konn (ed.), *The Darwinian Heritage* (Princeton: Princeton University Press, 1985), 609–38; the quote is from 623.

7 *Principia Ethica* (1903), Chapter 2.
8 Two fundamental recent studies showing how a specific genetic constitution can determine, to some extent at least, what humans do are: W. D. Hamilton's original 1964 paper 'The Genetic Evolution of Social Behaviour', in: R. Axelrod (ed.), *The Evolution of Cooperation* (Ann Arbor, MI: University of Michigan Press, 1984); E. O. Wilson, *Sociobiology: the New Synthesis* (Cambridge MA: Harvard University Press, 1975).
9 See also Richard Nelson, 'Universal Darwinism and evolutionary social science', *Biology and Philosophy*, 22 (2007): 73–94; Howard L. Kaye, *The social meaning of modern biology: from Social Darwinism to sociobiology* (New Haven (CT); London: Yale University Press, 1986).
10 It must be recalled that at present biologists are apparently divided on the question whether evolutionary biology *justifies* or *negates* functional explanation. Sociobiology shows the same split. Some conclude that the biological model illustrates how purpose and function is irrelevant within a society. Others conclude that the biological model illustrates the opposite.
11 *Taking Darwin Seriously: a naturalistic approach to philosophy* (Oxford, New York: Basil Blackwell, 1986; reprint with updates Prometheus Books, 1998).
12 Ibid., 230.
13 The major ones are: T. Nagel, 'Ethics as an autonomous subject', in: G. Stent (ed.), *Morality as a biological phenomenon* (Berkeley: University of California Press, 1980), 196–205, where sociobiology is deemed useless because moral philosophy is an autonomous discipline; O. Flanagan, 'Is morality epiphenomenal?' *Philosophical Forum*, 2/3 (1981): 207–25, where moral beliefs are shown to be too complex for sociobiology to handle; P. Kitcher, *Vaulting Ambition: Sociobiology and the Quest for Human Nature* (Cambridge, MA: MIT Press, 1985), where sociobiology is accused of taking humans for fundamentally selfish organisms; A. Flew, 'E.O. Wilson after Twenty Years: Is Human Sociobiology possible?' *Philosophy of the Social Sciences* 24/3 (1994): 320–35, where sociobiology is shown to entail genetic determinism that is incompatible with human freedom. For a reaction to these, see J. Lemos, 'A defence of Darwinian accounts of morality', *Philosophy of the Social Sciences* 31/3 (2001): 361–85.
14 For more details, see L. Caruana, 'A neglected difficulty with Social Darwinism', *Heythrop Journal* XLIX (2008): 652–58.
15 For more on how biology differs from physics, see Alex Rosenberg, 'Limits to biological knowledge' in his *Darwinism in Philosophy, Social Science and Economics* (Cambridge: Cambridge University Press, 2000), Chapter 3.
16 For a general and responsible attempt at incorporating beliefs, desires and action within social explanation, see Jon Elster, *Explaining Social Behavior* (Cambridge: Cambridge University Press, 2007). Because of the interdependence I talk about, he calls such variables *fragile*.
17 Philip Kitcher, 'Giving Darwin his due', in: J. Hodge and G. Radick (eds), *The Cambridge Companion to Darwin* (Cambridge University Press, 2003), 399–420.
18 I'm drawing here from Hawkins, *Social Darwinism in European and American thought*.
19 It was expressed by Clémence-Auguste Royer in her 'Avant Propos' to the second edition of her translation of Darwin's *De l'origine des espèces* (Paris: Guillaumin, 1866), and was then followed by a fuller, philosophical treatment by John Dewey, *The Influence of Darwinism on Philosophy and Other Essays* (New York: Henry Holt and Company, 1910).

20 For an example of this mentality, see Arthur Keith, *Essays in Human Evolution* (London Scientific Book Club, 1944).

21 See for instance his *Riddle of the Universe*, trans. by J. McCabe (London: Watts & Co., 1902).

22 For an early expression of this, see Georges Vacher de Lapouges (1854–1936), *L'Aryen: son rôle social* (Paris, 1899).

23 Vatican Council II, *Gaudium et Spes*, §36.

24 Congregation for the Doctrine of the Faith (1984), *Instruction on certain aspects of the 'Theology of Liberation'*, § 5. See http://www.newadvent.org/library/docs_df84lt.htm

25 For instance S. Rose, L. J. Kamin, and R. C. Lewontin, *Not in Our Genes: biology, ideology and human nature* (Harmondsworth: Penguin, 1984).

26 The issue here is quite distinct from the influence of values in the development of science. See Robert C. Richardson, 'Biology and ideology: the interpenetration of science and values', *Philosophy of Science*, 51 (1984): 396–420.

27 See for instance *Summa Theologiae* I–II, Q.10, a.2: 'if the will be offered an object which is good universally and from every point of view, the will tends to it of necessity, if it wills anything at all; since it cannot will the opposite. If, on the other hand, the will is offered an object that is not good from every point of view, it will not tend to it of necessity.' See *The Summa Theologica of St Thomas Aquinas*, trans. The Fathers of the English Dominican Province (Online Edition by Kevin Knight, 2008) http://www.newadvent.org/summa/

28 A significant early opponent of economic liberalism from within the Catholic tradition was Heinrich Pesch, S.J., who was based mainly in Köln and died in 1926. His major contribution is found in his five-volume *Manual on the National Economy* (published 1905–1923), in which he attempted to integrate economic theory with Aristotelian-Thomistic categories of thought. He is considered by many the link between the papal encyclical *Rerum Novarum* (1891) and the corresponding encyclical *Quadrogesimo Anno* (1931).

29 Pontifical Council for Justice and Peace, *Compendium of the Social Doctrine of the Church*, (USCCB Publishing, 2005), §348 (italics in the original).

30 *Truth Cannot Contradict Truth: Address of Pope John Paul II to the Pontifical Academy of Sciences* (October 22, 1996) (English version in: *L'Osservatore Romano*, English edition, Oct. 1996), (italics in the original).

31 A crucial figure in Germany was Joseph Mayer, a Catholic priest, scholar of Eugenics and Moral Theology, and assistant in the *Institut für Caritaswissenschaften* at Freiburg. He wanted to establish a society on the model of Francis Galton's Eugenics Society in England. See Ingrid Richter, *Katholizismus und Eugenik in der Weimar Republik und im Dritten Reich: zwischen Sittlichkeitsreform und Rassenhygiene* (Paderborn: F. Schöningh, 2001); Michael Burleigh, *Death and Deliverance: 'Euthanasia' in Germany 1900–1945* (Cambridge: Cambridge University Press 1994).

32 Thomas J. Gerrard, *The Church and Eugenics* (England-Catholic Social Guild, Catholic Studies in Social Reform No. 4, 1912; 2nd edn 1917), 20.

33 Ibid., 23.

34 Ibid., 57; see also Richard John Neuhaus (ed.), *Guaranteeing the good life: medicine and the return of eugenics* (Grand Rapids: Eerdmans, 1990).

35 A. Rosenberg makes this point against Kitcher in: 'Grievous Faults in Vaulting Ambitions?' *Ethics* 98 (1988): 827–37.

Chapter 11

DARWINISM AND ECONOMICS

ALBINO BARRERA

When it comes to economic life, Darwinism[1] and Catholicism diverge from each other on the notion of competitive selection. However, they partially concur in their views on the evolutionary nature of economic life and on the use of causality as a framework of analysis. Examining and understanding these points of divergence and partial convergence take on even greater importance in the face of contemporary globalization in which ever larger swaths of social life are governed by market rules. Each of these is discussed in what follows.[2]

1. Competitive Selection

The single most important, and controversial, legacy of Darwinism to economic thought is the use of natural selection in justifying competitive selection in the marketplace. Geoffrey Hodgson disagrees with this claim and argues that Darwinism is first and foremost about causality and not about the many other positions commonly, but mistakenly, ascribed to it.

> Darwinism does not [. . .] provide any moral justification for 'the survival of the fittest.' Furthermore, Darwinism does not imply that militant conflict is inevitable, that human inequalities or [in] power or wealth are inevitable, that cooperation or altruism are unimportant or unnatural, that evolution always leads to optimization or progress [. . .] that human intention is unimportant, or that human agency is blind or mechanistic.[3]

I will not dispute this characterization of what Darwinism is or is not given our severe space constraint in this chapter. All we have to do is to simply look at how Darwinism is understood and used in both academic and popular literature. Writing on his entry 'competition and selection' in the *New Palgrave Dictionary of Economics*, Sidney Winter notes that biological natural selection maintains its widespread influence among economists to this day by serving both as the analogue for business profit-maximizing behaviour and as the 'informal auxiliary defense' for optimization-equilibrium economic analyses.[4] Devoting an entire chapter to 'Social Darwinism' in his book on the ethics of pursuing economic efficiency, John Wright notes the influence of Herbert Spencer on Andrew Carnegie and John Rockefeller.[5] To this day, Darwinism in economic and business circles is used in the context of market competition.[6] That Hodgson himself feels compelled to disabuse readers of what Darwinism is not is indicative of the extent to which Darwinism is received in the literature in terms of all that he says it is not.[7] Thus, pace Hodgson, I will have to address Social Darwinism's competitive selection in this essay. I will deal with Darwinian causality in the last section of this chapter.

A. Allocative efficiency

To fully appreciate why biological natural selection has exerted such an enduring influence in economic thought and policy, it is important to understand first the nature and dynamics of a central concept in mainstream, neoclassical economics: allocative efficiency. Social Darwinism dovetails neoclassical economic thought so well because of the pivotal role of competition in reaching the latter's much sought allocative efficiency. This link is best explained in three steps.

First, the key concern of neoclassical economics is the employment of scarce resources to their optimum uses. This is more than just engineering efficiency in which output is maximized given a limited set of inputs. It entails manifold, independent economic agents simultaneously making the right decisions on the disposition of their resources. The right goods are provided in the right quantities and quality, produced with the most cost-effective means, and then brought to the right markets at the right time. There are no unsold inventories, all markets clear, and the community as a whole satisfies its preferences within the constraints of its available technology and finite resources.

Second, reaching this optimum point of allocative efficiency is obviously a tall order. We can only tend towards or approximate this point, at best, but we never fully attain it. As if this were not enough of a challenge, the economy is extremely fluid and produces a constant stream of new information that must be internalized by people as they adjust their decisions to suit ever-changing conditions. The market is the only social institution thus far that has come close to satisfying these stringent constraints. At the heart of the market is its price mechanism. Price is an effective vehicle for digesting large amounts of breaking information and conveying this simultaneously to economic agents spread over a wide geographic area. The market's price is an exceptionally timely and cost-efficient mechanism for gathering, synthesizing, disseminating, and then using valuable information. For example, note how commodity and stock markets are extremely responsive to geopolitical, social, and economic events.

Third, the market accomplishes what it does best (tending toward allocative efficiency) only to the degree that economic actors have the incentive to constantly adjust their decisions and reallocate their resources to their optimum uses as new information becomes available. It is market competition that compels economic agents to be vigilant and to embark on often painful and work-intensive changes. It is the competition that provides both the 'carrot' (new profit opportunities) and the 'stick' (potential economic losses) as incentives that keep market participants on their toes and attentive to shifting economic conditions. Indeed, competition is a necessary condition for allocative efficiency, both in theory and in practice. On the one hand, private initiative and freedom of entry or exit are necessary conditions of the model of perfectly competitive markets in economic theory. On the other hand, empirical studies conclusively show that the most vibrant nations are also the ones driven by market economies. Countries that temper their private sectors in the crucible of international markets are the ones that have prospered the most.[8] This all-important freedom of economic action has a mirror image: competition. It is the competition that produces seasoned entrepreneurs and disciplined economic behaviour.

But all this is only half the story. There is a big downside to the single-minded pursuit of allocative efficiency. The price changes and adjustments that are critical to attaining economic efficiency is a *de facto* redistribution of burdens and benefits among economic agents. Thus, the manufacturing and white-collar jobs that have been outsourced in the name of allocative efficiency benefit workers overseas at the expense of their counterparts in the developed countries. Cheaper foreign imports of goods and services are a boon for local consumers who see an increase in their real incomes, but a real threat to the job security of domestic providers and workers. Free market advocates note that international trade (and competition, by extension) is not a zero-sum phenomenon because all trading partners can potentially benefit. This may be true in the long-term. But in the meantime, we can be sure that during this painful period of adjustment, there will be losers, some of whom may never even recover at all from their dislocation. Competition can inflict enormous collateral costs that can either be ameliorated or simply ignored. Unfortunately, in many cases, we choose the latter path. And Social Darwinism's natural selection provides a convenient, and even acceptable, rationalization for taking the latter path of least resistance.

B. Natural selection and competitive selection

Natural selection is to biological processes as competitive selection is to economic dynamics. There are two important similarities between the preceding description of allocative efficiency via market competition, on the one hand, and Darwin's theory of natural selection, on the other hand. In the first place, both natural selection and competitive selection are the endogenous, spontaneous outcomes of 'natural processes'. No exogenous interventions (e.g. government action) are involved; nature simply takes its course. This is particularly attractive and important for people who believe that what is natural is good.

Second, both cases of selection ultimately lead to a much desired improvement in the state of affairs. In the case of natural selection, 'inferior' organisms eventually make room for an improved species. In the case of markets, competitive selection sets aside weaker players in favour of the stronger players. By putting weaker economic agents in areas in which they have better comparative advantage, competitive selection's 'survival of the fittest' enhances the entire economy and even sets the stage for even more vibrant growth for subsequent rounds of economic activity. In both cases, whether for biological organisms or the economy, culling is a necessary condition for progress and improvement.

C. Normative implications

Using natural selection as a conceptual anchor for competitive selection in economic life carries significant normative risks. In the first place, it desensitizes people to the plight of those who bear the cost of competitive selection in terms of lost livelihoods and disrupted lifestyles in the wake of the market's pecuniary externalities (unintended consequences arising from price adjustments). At best, the notion of competitive selection minimizes obligations we may have towards those who have been hurt by market competition and are unable to fend for themselves. There is the danger of simply resigning ourselves to the reality that there will always be losers and winners in the marketplace. There will always be beneficial and harmful pecuniary externalities by the nature of market operations. Adverse pecuniary externalities are accepted as an unavoidable rite of passage to economic growth and development, a necessary path to progress.[9] At its worst, such insensitivity can end up in indifference and a willingness to sacrifice the weak for the sake of the strong, who are believed to be much better poised to contribute more to the community. We can even turn the moral obligation of assistance on its head by reasoning that our duty may in fact be to let the chips fall where they do for the sake of the good of the whole and the good of subsequent generations.

Second, using natural selection to justify competitive selection can be harmful for policy. The Reverend Thomas Malthus frowned on poor relief because the human lot is inevitably one of subsistence living.[10] Recall his principle of population in which food production grows arithmetically even while population increases geometrically. Improvements in living conditions are only dissipated in further population growth, thereby bringing the wages back down to subsistence levels. Consequently, ameliorative social programmes are futile and even counterproductive in slowing down an unavoidable natural process of correction.

Similarly, proponents of a Darwinian biological metaphor for market competition may be prone to view ameliorative extra-market forms of assistance to those severely affected by market competition as futile and perhaps even counterproductive. After all, the whole point of market competition is to compel the community to adjust the disposition of its scarce resources to their best uses. This includes putting people in roles within the economy according to their constantly shifting comparative advantage. The sooner market participants are placed where they ought to be and the quicker we are able to make the necessary adjustments in the economy, the sooner we can approximate allocative efficiency and the better it is for the entire community. There is danger of simply leaving people to fend for themselves for their own long-term good. Ameliorative extra-market assistance only slows down the unavoidable painful process of adjustment by enabling economic agents to delay making the necessary, often traumatic, changes in their behaviour or lifestyles. And indeed, there is ample empirical evidence to confirm such a dynamic. For example, scholars and policymakers have repeatedly argued that unemployment rates have been consistently much higher in the European Union than in the USA partly because of the more generous unemployment and welfare benefits in the former. There is less urgency in Europe for the unemployed or underemployed to make drastic or painful adjustments.[11]

Third, using natural selection to justify competitive selection is harmful for normative economics because it entrenches economic thinking further in its utilitarian mindset and in mistaking allocative efficiency as the end of economic life rather than merely as a means to a much greater goal. The consequence of this for social policy is predictable: leaving the displaced from market competition to fend for themselves or, worse, treating people as factors of production in our single-minded pursuit of economic efficiency without paying attention to the means we employ. Outcomes matter, but so does the process by which we reach these end states.

The preceding are not far-fetched normative concerns. To my mind, Joseph Schumpeter's famous association of capitalism with its 'gale of creative destruction' illustrates not only the good conceptual fit between natural selection and competitive selection but also its ill effects on normative economics.[12] There is no denying that the dynamism of the modern market economy since the Industrial Revolution has been due to the major technological leaps that have transformed and energized socioeconomic life. This was true two hundred years ago and we find it unfolding again today in our information economy. We owe these technological advances to the private initiative unleashed by market competition. Thus, Schumpeter was correct in highlighting the creativity of capitalism. However, he was also accurate in noting that there is a concomitant destructive process to this creativity. In other words, 'creative destruction' already alerts us that there will always be winners and losers as part of capitalism. Unfortunately, it is often easier to focus on the capitalism's creativity alone (especially with its spectacular accomplishments) but not on its attendant costs (especially since these are often borne disproportionately by the powerless and the voiceless).

Take the case of the current debates on international trade and offshore outsourcing. Advocates of free trade argue that dislocation and disequilibria are accepted as necessary paths to creativity, renewal and progress. In fact, one can even make an even stronger statement that such dislocation and disequilibria are not a matter of choice but of necessity. Globalization's fierce market competition will bring these about whether or not we accept them voluntarily and whether or not we are ready. Moreover, it is easier to accept the costs and, in fact, even forget about those who bear such costs because of the conviction that the market is robust enough to reabsorb these displaced workers. The market is dynamic and creative enough to be able to create new jobs, and even better ones, to replace those that had been lost overseas, so goes the argument. This is true, but only in the long-run and only after a painful period of adjustment. Moreover, the new jobs created go to the new, younger, and better trained entrants to the job market, not to those who had been displaced to begin with.[13] Indeed, competitive selection means that many laid-off middle-aged workers will most likely have to accept lower-paying jobs. It is largely through the efforts of critics of unfettered market operations that some form of extra-market assistance has been provided of late (e.g., trade-related adjustment assistance programmes).

It is important to note that there is nothing in Darwin's theory of natural selection that necessarily calls for the aforesaid behaviour or attitude of minimal assistance or indifference when it comes to competitive selection. Instead, it is Social Darwinism that seems to foster such a disposition.

D. Catholic social thought

The recent Catholic social documents have been much more appreciative of the value of free enterprise and competitive markets, especially in the wake of the collapse of the Soviet-style economies in 1989. Nonetheless, the Catholic Church continues to be highly critical of the market economy on account of the latter's manifold, unaddressed ill effects.[14] Just as Marxism is incompatible with Catholic social teachings because of the former's materialistic philosophy and flawed anthropology, Social Darwinism's competitive selection is likewise irreconcilable with Catholic thought because of (1) its implicit defective or malign Divine Providence and (2) its abnegation of human accountability for critical market outcomes and processes.

D.1 Defective or malign Divine Providence

To accept competitive selection as an intrinsic, natural economic process is to say that the God created economic life with a Hobbesian twist to it by design. Competitive selection means that the marketplace is a battle zone by the nature of things: everyone is at war against everybody else; economic agents are fighting for positional advantage, if not their own survival; no one can be trusted and seemingly cooperative ventures are in fact pursued out of mere expediency or fear; self-interested, even predatory, behaviour is a must in the face of an unforgiving, hostile and zero-sum environment; finite resources are for the taking, as much as one can in order to be even more competitive in the next rounds of economic activity. Life is harsh and brutish because ceaseless conflict and insecurity are the defining characteristics of an economic order driven by competitive selection.[15] Such a view of socioeconomic life is hugely problematic for Catholic theology for a number of reasons.

First, it implies that Divine Providence is flawed or even malicious. A bedrock theological claim of Catholicism is that human beings have been created by God for their own sake to share in divine life, happiness and love.[16] To accept competitive selection as a natural process is to have a severely broken, indeed inhospitable, order of creation. Far from putting human beings in a setting that provides the best chance of flourishing in God's proffered love, happiness and peace, competitive selection sets the stage for a lifetime of mutual rivalry and acrimony. Reason alone (without the use of Revelation) tells us that there is a much better existence than this. If competitive selection were indeed a constitutive element of the created order, then it must be that God's plans are either flawed in their conception, or defective in their execution, or malign in their intentions, or a combination of these. If so, then such imperfection or malice in God means that God cannot be God at all! After all, God is, by definition, all-perfect, almighty and all-good. There is a logical inconsistency between the existence of an almighty, provident sovereign God and the claim of competitive selection by design in the order of this God's creation.

Second, the Hobbesian condition characteristic of competitive selection is completely inconsistent with scriptural witness. The two *Genesis* accounts of creation both point to the collaborative nature of economic life, by design, as seen in the divine mandate to man and woman to exercise dominion over the earth. In fact, observe that in the primal history

(Gn 1–11), competition is consistently the immediate occasion for sin: Adam and Eve goaded by the serpent to be god unto themselves in knowing as much as God does (Gn 3:5), Cain resenting God's favor upon Abel (Gn 4:1–7), and the residents of Babel overstepping their bounds in their presumption (Gn 11:1–9).

In the rest of the Old Testament, the Chosen People of God were called to be a nation different from all the other nations around them partly because theirs was going to be an economy of mutual solicitude. Far from competing with each other, they were to take responsibility for each other's welfare and share in each other's travails. Thus, unlike their Ancient Near Eastern neighbours, they were morally bound to lend money or grain to their fellow Hebrews who had fallen on hard times and not charge any interest at all or even secure a pledge from destitute borrowers. Moreover, such debts were to be forgiven after six years. Land was never supposed to be sold in perpetuity but returned to their original owners at the Jubilee together with the manumission of all slaves and the release of all debts. They were to treat the poor, the orphans, the widows, and the aliens with special care. The Hebrews were constantly reminded to extend to each other the same favours extended to them by YHWH in their own moment of slavery and need. Indeed, cooperation and solidarity, rather than competition, were the hallmarks of Israel's election as God's Chosen People.[17]

This is an economic ethos echoed in the New Testament. The Gospels, especially *Luke*, clearly and repeatedly emphasize the need to use wealth in assisting the poor and in building up the community. The *Acts of the Apostles* describes an early Church in which goods were held in common and distributed according to need.[18] Indeed, in the view of Sacred Scripture, economic life is meant to be a vehicle for harmony and not for a competition that is ruinous of the community. The importance accorded to such solidarity in socioeconomic life is affirmed in Patristic, Scholastic, and modern Catholic social teachings.[19]

Third, in line with aforementioned values of trust and familial collaboration, Catholic theology maintains that union with God is the ultimate end of human life. The friendship that is characteristic of this union is partly actualized in the here and now to the degree that such friendship spills over into our interpersonal relationships. Love of God and love of neighbour are distinct but inseparable. For this reason, even as many social issues suggest that there seems to be an intrinsic conflict in interpersonal relations by the nature of things, Catholic thought has always argued that far from being in competition with each other, the good of the person and the good of the community are in fact necessary conditions to each other.[20] Competitive selection is antithetical to Catholic social thought's overarching framework, that is, the common good. The end of this common good is the union of hearts and minds. The adversarial tenor of competitive selection is a jarring contrast to the Catholic self-understanding of who we are as a human community: members of the one Body of Christ. There is simply no room for the notion of competitive selection in the building of the Kingdom of God.

In sum, both Sacred Scripture and tradition are incompatible with the Hobbesian state implicit in competitive selection as a natural process. Moreover, as I will argue in the last section, the cut-and-thrust of economic life is not the result of an embedded competitive selection by God's design, but the outcome of human sinfulness.

D.2 Abnegation of human accountability

Competitive selection minimizes human accountability for some of the most egregious market failures. Just like natural selection, competitive selection, if left on its own, will spontaneously lead to a much better state of affairs. There is an automatic, steady trajectory of improvement and progress if we simply allow such selection to take its 'natural' course. Such claims are unacceptable to Catholic moral thinking.

Humans are individually and collectively responsible for both market outcomes and processes. I will discuss the reasons for this at greater length in the next section, but it is sufficient to note at this point that we cannot excuse ourselves from attending to the ill effects of market competition. The demise of aging industries, the overnight obsolescence of skills and the inability of small- and medium-scale enterprises to match the price and the quality of much better financed and technologically advanced transnational corporations have a human dimension in the loss of livelihoods and disrupted lives. As already mentioned earlier in this chapter, the market is excellent at allocating scarce resources to their most valued uses because of the discipline imposed by the price mechanism on all market participants. However, this allocative dimension comes with unintended consequences, both good and bad. Price adjustments are a de facto redistribution of burdens and benefits across economic agents, and it is the poor and the ill-prepared who often bear the brunt of the market's harmful ripple effects.

In his book *Everything for Sale: The Virtues and Limits of Markets*, Robert Kuttner observes that the Church is the 'longest-running counterweight to the dogmas of a pure market'.[21] This is an accurate claim. In response to the tectonic changes in economic life inaugurated by the Industrial Revolution in both the nineteenth and twentieth centuries, the Roman Catholic tradition has vigorously urged correcting the market's flaws. It has advanced various principles to guide this effort, namely: the principles of human dignity, the universal destination of the goods of the earth, socialization, solidarity, subsidiarity, the primacy of labour, preferential option for the poor and the common good.[22] These provide a clear-eyed method for correcting the deficiencies of market operations.

Moreover, these principles affirm our mutual responsibility for each other's economic well-being, concretely actualized in the care and assistance we extend to the helpless in proportion to their needs. In other words, Catholic social thought will not allow us to simply walk away from the *chronic* ill effects of market operations because we are bound to each other by a tight web of obligations.

2. *Newtonian Mechanics versus Darwinian Evolution*

Besides the notion of competitive selection, there is a second reason why human accountability is minimized in neoclassical economic thinking, namely: the belief that the economic order operates in much the same way as the physical world, subject to an immutable set of laws. In the nineteenth century, the field of economics faced the proverbial fork in the road in having to choose a conceptual paradigm with which to extend the work of the Classical economists. On the one hand, there was a Newtonian mechanistic view of the world governed by a fixed set of laws that were discoverable. Such a world-view readily lent itself to Cartesian mathematics and prediction. On the other hand, Darwin's evolutionary theory provided a biological metaphor of natural selection. The discipline took the first route and the political economy of Adam Smith and David Ricardo gave way to the marginalist revolution of Walras, Jevons and Menger.[23] Equilibrium analysis rather than evolutionary economics became the mainstream in the discipline.

Darwin's theory of evolution has of late been a conceptual catalyst for re-energizing the school of economic thought that views economic life as evolving rather than fixed. Much work has been done to improve economic analysis with the use of biological metaphors.[24] This turn away from a mechanistic view of the economic order provides a conceptual basis for Catholic economic thinking on the value and place of extra-market interventions in social ethics.

A normative implication of a mechanistic view of economic life is the futility of engineering changes in economic processes. The market is subject to its own set of autonomous laws that cannot be repealed or amended. One can ignore these laws only at one's own peril. And, indeed, the conclusive failure of the command economies in the twentieth century provides empirical validation for the claim that there are certain aspects of the market that cannot be legislated. This provides the conceptual basis for discouraging extra-market interventions that mitigate the deleterious ripple effects of market operations. Not only is it ineffectual, but it may even cause more harm in the long-run by preventing the market to do what it does best. Humans are thus left off the hook with respect to responsibility for market outcomes and processes.

The alternative evolutionary account of economic life is more amenable to Catholic economic ethics. The market is a human construct; it is a human institution. It evolves. The market does indeed partly operate on its own set of autonomous laws that cannot be changed by legislation.[25] However, one must also remember that the market's operations and processes have been largely shaped by formal and informal conventions accumulated over generations and passed down and modified through time. For example, the medieval practice of handing down crafts from parent to child in the guild system has given way to the value attached by modern economic agents to making their own occupational choices. We have come to expect social and geographic mobility as a constitutive part of our inalienable rights. In other words, many critical aspects of market operations are not predetermined for us by natural design. We are responsible for them. Our continuously evolving economy is largely a product of our moral choices. Darwin's theory of evolution is, thus, a much better conceptual paradigm than Newtonian mechanics when it comes to describing the economic order. Nonetheless, there is still a major difference between Catholic thinking and this evolutionary description of economic life. It is to this that we now turn our attention.

3. Causality

As I have noted earlier, Hodgson laments that many people mistakenly believe that Darwinism in the social sciences is about inevitable conflict, inequality in power and wealth, spontaneous evolutionary progress, or the 'survival of the fittest'.[26] Instead, he claims that the more significant contribution of Darwinism is its use of causality as an analytical framework. This is a substantial overlap with Catholic moral theology in light of the latter's extensive use of Aristotelean-Thomistic causality earlier in its tradition. However, this overlap is more apparent than real. Hodgson himself is keen to point out that Darwinian causality has no teleology.

> Above all, Darwinism means causal explanation, where a cause is understood as necessarily involving transfers of matter or energy. *Divine, spiritual, miraculous, or uncaused causes are ruled out. Explanations of outcomes are in terms of connected causal sequences.*[27]

This is a significant divergence from Catholic thought.

Despite the absolute freedom of God, Catholic theology believes that God never acts in a random, whimsical fashion. There is a purpose to everything God does. There is an objective, intelligible order to divine creation and providence, including economic life. There is a *telos* (an end) to all of God's creation. Consequently, economic agency can be and ought to be evaluated in terms of its *telos*. Economics cannot be separated from morality, from questions of right or wrong, good or evil.

Despite the almighty nature of God, Catholic theology believes that God nonetheless works through nature. Creatures are used as instruments in the ongoing divine act of creation. However, unlike other creatures, human beings are more than just instrumental causes; they are secondary causes.[28] In contrast to an instrumental cause (such as a chisel in the hands of a sculptor), a secondary cause adds something substantive and distinctively its own (such as moral agency) to the final outcome.

So, what difference does Catholic thought's richer notion of causality (material, efficient, formal and final) make? What does it add to the underlying causality of Darwin's theory of evolution? Without an underlying teleology to Darwinism's causality, the most that competitive selection accomplishes in the allocative efficiency that it brings about is the satisfaction of whatever preferences individual economic agents bring to the marketplace. Whose competing preferences are satisfied is dependent on who has the larger purchasing power. Not surprisingly, this sets the stage for a Hobbesian state of intense, adversarial competition for economic power and resources.

In contrast, the manifold dimensions of causality (efficient, formal and final) in Catholic thought imbue our evolving economic order with an unfolding purpose.[29] Since God is the Final, Formal, and Efficient Cause in the order of creation, humanity is provisioned with material sufficiency. However, this sufficiency is conditional on the proper exercise of moral agency. Because of moral evil (e.g., greed and exploitation) and the chance and contingencies of economic life (e.g., natural disasters), these material provisions will be allocated in such a manner that some will enjoy great abundance even as others wallow in destitution. Since human beings are the only creatures capable of acting by choice rather than by necessity, they are the only ones capable of ameliorating the economic consequences of moral evil and the chance and contingencies of life. They are the only ones capable of effecting economic transfers from those with abundance to those with very little. And in doing so, human beings bring about God's envisioned material sufficiency for all. It goes against the noble qualities and the higher calling of human nature to leave the more severe consequences of market operations unattended. Chronic poverty, permanent unemployment or underemployment, stifled creativity and marginalization from economic life are not natural at all as part of the process of competitive selection, but are the result of our failure to live up to our obligations to God and to each other. In other words, the economic order serves as a venue for the satisfaction of human needs, for mutual caring, for generous self-sacrifice, for growth in moral agency – constitutive elements of human flourishing (the *telos* of economic life). Economic agency provides the occasion to participate in divine providence (secondary causality).

Thus, compared to the atomistic, self-absorbed economic actors of Social Darwinism's competitive selection, market participants in Catholic thought are bound to each other in mutual solicitude. Unlike the steady, spontaneous improvement believed to be the result of competitive selection, genuine economic progress from the Catholic perspective comes about only through deliberate effort and mutual sacrifice. The high point of competitive selection is the satisfaction of individual preferences, whatever these may be for as long as people are able to pay for them. In contrast, integral human development for every person is the crown of economic life in God's envisioned order of creation.

Summary

Darwinism has shaped economic thought and policy in at least three ways. First, Darwin's natural selection is the biological analogue for the all-important competitive selection that brings about economic efficiency. Competitive selection has an implicit Hobbesian view of economic life and also minimizes human accountability for market processes and outcomes. This implies a flawed or malign Divine Providence. Second, Darwin's theory of evolution provides an alternative conceptual paradigm to Newton's mechanics. Its view of an evolutionary economy in place of one that is governed by fixed, immutable laws is more amenable to Catholic economic ethics that calls for extra-market interventions in correcting the deficiencies of market operations. Finally, Darwinism's deeper contribution to the social sciences is said to be its use of causality as a framework of analysis. Unfortunately, it falls far short of the Catholic Aristotelean-Thomistic understanding of causality because Darwinism has no room for teleology.

Notes

1 There is a difference between Darwinism and what Darwin had written. Darwinism pertains to the school of thought that interpreted, further expanded, and applied Darwin's works to other questions not originally addressed by Darwin. For example, market competition has been likened to, indeed, even justified by its most avid advocates on the basis of Darwin's theory of natural selection; see Charles Darwin, *On the Origin of Species: a Variorum Text*, Morse Peckham (ed.) (Pennsylvania: University of Pennsylvania Press, [1859] 1959). And yet, there is no discussion of humans at all in the *Origin of Species* except in a single paragraph at the end of the work. The link between Darwin and economics is founded entirely on analogy from subsequent commentators; see: John Laurent, 'Darwin, Economics and Contemporary Economists', in: John Laurent and John Nightingale (eds), *Darwinism and Evolutionary Economics* (Northampton, MA: Edward Elgar, 2001), 17.

2 Much of the literature on Darwinism and economics revolves around the use of biological metaphors in enhancing the explanatory-predictive power of economic analysis, particularly in bioeconomics and evolutionary economics. For example, Darwinism has been used to account for the evolution of preferences (e.g. altruism) and socioeconomic institutions. This essay will not evaluate the impact of these Darwinian metaphors in economic modelling. That is a task beyond the scope of Catholic moral theology. Instead, in what follows, I will only examine the normative implications of the use of these biological metaphors inspired by Darwin's *Origin of Species* for economic policy and behaviour.

3 Geoffrey Hodgson, 'Darwinism and Institutional Economics', *Journal of Economic Issues* 37 (2003): 85–97; the quote is from 85–6.

4 Sidney Winter, 'Competition and Selection', in: J. Eatwell, M. Milgate and P. Newman (eds), *The New Palgrave Dictionary of Economics* (London, Macmillan, 1998), Vol. I, 545.

5 John Wright, *The Ethics of Economic Rationalism* (Sydney, Australia: University of New South Wales Press, 2003), 123–37. It was Spencer who coined what turned out to be Darwinism's most enduring description 'survival of the fittest' seven years before Darwin's *Origin of Species*; see Wright (2003), 125.

6 See, for example, Justin Fox, 'Profits, Darwinism, and the Internet', *Fortune* 141 (March 6, 2000): 5; Karmal Dean Parhizgar, 'Is There Any Ethical and Moral Consideration in the Theory and Practice of Global Business Social Darwinism?' *Journal of Transactional Management Development* 6 (2001): 123–43; and Richard Weikart, 'Laissez-Faire Social Darwinism and Individualist Competition in Darwin and Huxley', *The European Legacy* 3 (1998): 17–30.

7 Hodgson (2003), 85–6.

8 The empirical evidence on this is extensive. See, for example, the World Bank publications.

9 And this is not mere idle academic talk. As it is, neoclassical economic theory and policy view technological externalities (such as pollution) as market failures that have to be addressed because they prevent us from reaching allocative efficiency. In contrast, there is no urgency or interest in mitigating adverse pecuniary externalities because these are the mechanisms that bring us closer to allocative efficiency.

10 Thomas Robert Malthus, *On Population (An Essay on the Principle of Population, as it affects the Future Improvement of Society with Remarks on the speculations of Mr. Godwin, M. Condorcet, and other writers)*, edited and introduced by Gertrude Himmelfarb (New York: Modern Library, [1798] 1960).

11 Another example, an infamous one, is agricultural subsidies. It has long been known and understood that most countries lose their comparative advantage in agriculture as a normal part of economic growth; see Simon Kuznets, *Modern Economic Growth: Rate, Structure and Spread* (New Haven: Yale, 1966). The European Union, Japan, the USA and Switzerland, however, have employed tariffs, quotas and outright subsidies to protect their agricultural sectors from making the necessary adjustments either in moving out of the sector altogether or in shifting towards more specialized, high-value agricultural goods.

12 Joseph Schumpeter, *Capitalism, Socialism and Democracy* (New York: Harper, 1942), 81–6.

13 Martin Carnoy, *Sustaining the New Economy: Work, Family, and Community in the Information Age* (New York: Russell Sage and Cambridge, MA: Harvard University Press, 2000), 39.
14 See, for example, John Paul II, *Centesimus Annus* (Vatican, 1991); Pontifical Council for Justice and Peace, *Compendium of the Social Doctrine of the Church* (Vatican, 2004).
15 There is nothing in Social Darwinism's theory of competitive selection that requires such a process to be so fierce and unforgiving. In fact, one may even claim that the theory is compatible with mild or even friendly competition. Such a contention is problematic. By its logic and dynamic, rivalry in competitive selection can only escalate. The contest that is at the heart of competitive selection can only heat up in the absence of any institutional constraints. But imposing such exogenous limits is completely contrary to the endogenous, spontaneous nature of nature selection. Thus, one either operates in a competitive environment or one does not. There is no middle ground.
16 See *Catechism of the Catholic Church* (Vatican, 1994), §356.
17 Enrique Nardoni, *Rise Up, O Judge: A Study of Justice in the Biblical World*, trans. Seán Charles Martin (Peabody, MA: Hendrickson, 2004); H. Eberhard von Waldow, 'Social Responsibility and Social Structure in Early Israel', *Catholic Biblical Quarterly* 32 (1970): 182–204.
18 Allen Verhey, *The Great Reversal: Ethics and the New Testament* (Grand Rapids, MI: Eerdmans, 1984).
19 Again, see, for example, the Pontifical Council for Justice and Peace (2004).
20 E.g,, Jacques Maritain, *Person and the Common Good*, trans. J. J. Fitzgerald (New York: Charles Scribner's Sons, 1947).
21 Robert Kuttner, *Everything for Sale: The Virtues and Limits of Markets* (New York: Alfred A. Knopf, 1997), 54.
22 See Pontifical Council for Justice and Peace (2004) for a lengthier discussion of these principles.
23 See Philip Mirowski, *More Heat than Light: Economics as Social Physics, Physics as Nature's Economics* (Cambridge, UK: Cambridge University Press, 1989) for an account and assessment of this 'physics-envy' on the part of mainstream, neo-classical economics.
24 See, for example, Geoffrey Hodgson, 'Darwinism, Causality and the Social Sciences', *Journal of Economic Methodology* 11 (2004): 175–94; John Laurent and John Nightingale, 'Darwinism and Evolutionary Economics', in: John Laurent and John Nightingale (eds), *Darwinism and Evolutionary Economics* (Northampton, MA: Edward Elgar, 2001); R. C. O. Matthews, 'Darwinism and Economic Change', in: D. A. Collard *et al.* (eds.), *Economic Theory and Hicksian Themes* (Oxford, UK: Clarendon, 1984); Ulrich Witt, 'Bioeconomics as Economics from a Darwinian perspective', *Journal of Bioeconomics* 1 (1999): 19–34; Ulrich Witt, 'Economics and Darwinism', in: *Evolutionary Controversies in Economics: A New Transdisciplinary Approach*, edited by Japan Association for Evolutionary Economics/Y. Aruka (New York: Springer, 2001).
25 For example, we have the downward sloping demand curve for normal goods. An increase in price leads to a decline in the quantity demanded for such goods.
26 Hodgson (2003), 85–6.
27 Hodgson (2003), 86, emphasis added. See also Hodgson (2004), 182–4.
28 God is the First Cause.

29 Given the space constraints, I can only briefly sketch the implications of the use of Aristotelean-Thomistic causality in economic life. For an extended discussion, see Albino Barrera, *God and the Evil of Scarcity: Moral Foundations of Economic Agency* (Notre Dame, IN: University of Notre Dame Press, 2005), 28–40, 209–37.

Part Three

THEOLOGICAL THEMES

Chapter 12

INTELLIGENT DESIGN: SCIENCE OR FAITH?

Louis Dupré

In what follows, I intend to show that the arguments for the thesis of intelligent design as proposed by Michael Behe and William Dembski fail to prove the scientific necessity of a 'designer' of the process of biological evolution, though they may expose some insufficiencies in the current state of the theory. Equally unwarranted, however, are the conclusions of Richard Dawkins and Daniel Dennett that evolutionary theory excludes the notion of creation. The theory, scientifically the only satisfactory one, must not be regarded as a full, philosophically complete justification of the nature of biological processes. It assumes certain principles, which it does not explain, such as the dynamic tendency of matter towards increasing complexity, or the very presence of a DNA code, which regulates the process and is responsible for the changes that occur in it. These factors, without which there would be no evolutionary process, are *given*: presupposed by the theory, not deduced from it.

Both the theist and the atheist interpretations assume that God is a being separate from the being of the universe and that creation consists in a purely efficient causal act. To these assumptions, the author opposes the idea of God's total immanence within creation, as advanced by Eckhart and Nicolas of Cusa, as well as the ancient interpretation of causality (still present in Aquinas), according to which a cause may remain immanent in its effect. At the end I argue for the philosophical irreducibility of mind to a biological process.

1. A New Strategy

Quite a bit of confusion exists concerning the notion of intelligent design. Many regard it as a masked attempt to revive creationism, although with some concessions to modern science. The biblical account of creation is not interpreted as if all species had 'from the beginning' been in their present state, as creationism claims. Intelligent design accepts an evolution of all forms of life, but postulates that a divine designer supervises and controls the process at each stage. This recent attempt to reconcile faith in creation with the findings of modern science conflicts with the Darwinian theory that random mutations and natural selection determine the entire process. Mutations occur without purpose. They may have harmful consequences for the species, but they may also increase its chances of survival. The so-called 'survival of the fittest' does not mean that the *best* survive in this game of chance, but the *toughest*. Less complex organisms, like cockroaches and spiders, thereby stand a better chance than mammals.

Contemporary biologists' main objection to the theory of intelligent design is that it presents itself as a scientific alternative to be taught in schools alongside, or sometimes even in place of, the Neo-Darwinian theory of evolution. Although it has a few scientists of standing on its side, experts have almost unanimously decided that it rests on a fundamental misconception of the notion of science, which requires that conclusions be based on testable data through generally accepted methods. The 2001 Nobel Prize winner Eric Cornell wrote: 'Science isn't about knowing the mind of God; it's about understanding nature and the reasons for things [. . .] If you want to recruit the future generation of scientists, you don't draw a box around all our scientific understanding to date and say, "Everything outside this box we can explain only by invoking God's will." ' [1]

Two American scholars have tried to give the thesis of intelligent design certain plausibility. Michael Behe, a microbiologist, asserts in *Darwin's Black Box* that Neo-Darwinism does not suffice to explain the enormous complexity of cells. He admits that random mutations occur on the macro-biological level, but he discounts that randomness in the biochemical processes in the cells, which determine this evolution. He reasons as follows. All of our cells contain the same DNA, and each of them is able to mutate. When a mutation takes place in a reproductive cell – sperm or ovum – it becomes hereditary. Each mutation only has consequences in the place and time in which it occurs. It is not directed to any future purpose. Natural selection happens exclusively on the basis of functions that exist during that period of time in which the mutations take place. Complex alterations in biochemical processes, however, presuppose the *simultaneous* presence of a considerable number of factors. Thus to explain the presence of sight in more developed animals, many mutations are required, both at the site where the eye has to come into existence and in the brain, which was previously unequipped to interpret new impulses from the nerves as visual images. When a photon on the retina of the eye activates the optical nerve and thus allows the animal organism to see, one cannot but wonder: What causes the many mutations necessary to achieve this complex result, to occur together? Each mutation happens separately and can only perpetuate itself if it brings about certain advantages for survival. To make sight possible many factors have to be present simultaneously. The probability that such an accumulation of mutations occurs by chance is, according to Behe, extremely low.

Supporters of pure Darwinism, like Richard Dawkins, reply to this that a complex of conditions can in fact be achieved by a gradual process. It suffices that every phase of that process brings about a small improvement (or at least a change that does not decrease the viability of the organism), which, together with equally random mutations over a long period of time, creates the conditions that make the end result possible. Behe himself has admitted that his argument does not logically exclude Darwinism, but he considers the Darwinian explanation of the development of complex organisms by pure coincidence highly improbable. Dawkins, on the contrary, argues that over an enormous period of time, the probability of an accumulation of changes reaching the kind of molecular complexity to make life possible is considerable. Hence the evolutionary process is self-explanatory and justifies no introduction of an external agent.

Still the process presupposes the presence of certain conditions, which the process itself does not account for. Mutations occur in the cell's genetic material where they become capable of self-replication. What accounts for them? To this question, the evolution theory as yet offers no adequate answer. It would be illogical, however, to attribute them to a divine designer. What do we gain by projecting our ignorance to a factor outside the biological process, instead of leaving it inside that process until some day science might come up with an answer? Contrary to Behe, Dawkins recognizes no residual mystery after the scientific information is complete. He expects from biology an exhaustive understanding of life on all levels from the wing of the butterfly to the mind of the genius. The very idea of a designing God is a 'delusion' as the title of his recent book loudly proclaims.[2]

Behe avoids naming the designer. But his theory raises the question: What kind of designer would the evolutionary process require? Already in the eighteenth century, David Hume asked himself what kind of being would be necessary to bring about a world such as the one we know. Does it necessarily have to be a God? If it is, the thorny question remains why such divinely guided creation had to pass through so many detours and dead ends, so much pain and destruction, during millions of years to end up with a result that, to most, appears less than perfect. Moreover, does the idea of an external designer not rob life of its most distinctive feature, namely, vital creativity? Behe's questions suggest that the theory of natural selection may need to be supplemented. But they do not warrant the introduction of an external factor into the science of biology.

William Dembski, a mathematician with a doctorate in philosophy, differs from Behe in that he rejects the entire theory of natural selection, whereas Behe only does so for complex biochemical processes. Dembski

denies that it is mathematically possible within the bounds of a finite
process to arrive by chance at a *specific* complexity – that is, at a complex
of factors which render a determinate result (such as the construction of
the eye) possible. The words of a lengthy novel like *Moby Dick* could never
have come together by mere chance. Darwinists admit this, but argue that
he unnecessarily introduces the notion of 'purposiveness' into his argument. The theory of evolution recognizes no *determinate ends*. An extraordinary coordination of elements, such as the one which made vision
possible, is not the result of an attempt to reach a particular goal. No plan,
no design whatsoever guides the process. Evolutionary theory does not
recognize the term *end* (i.e. outcome) as *purpose*. *Purpose* is no more than a
retrojective interpretation of what preceded the end. The randomness,
according to a pioneer of Neo-Darwinism, Stephen Jay Gould, is essential
to evolutionary theory, even though Darwin himself may not have given
due attention to it. It does not allow us to conclude that chances of survival improve as the process develops. The process remains unpredictable.

Dembski's argument about the improbability of life emerging from a
chance evolution is not new. Half a century ago, the French biologist
Pierre Lecomte du Nouy, attached to the Rockefeller Institute and later to
the Pasteur Institute in Paris, calculated in *L'Homme devant la Science*
(1939) and again in his popular *Human Destiny* (1947) the chances of life.
He concluded that they were so small as to be negligible without the
interference of an agent extrinsic to the process. After an initial success,
the impact of this work rapidly decreased, because his conclusion led
him to accept the existence of a designing Creator. Darwinians have
attempted to defeat the idea of an overwhelming improbability in a
number of ways. The most effective one so far is that the initial explosion
(the *big bang*) resulted in an incalculable multiplicity of universes – which,
of course, enormously increased the probability that the right combination
might turn up. Yet this solution rests on the admission of a number of
unproven theses. Was there ever an initial explosion or had the universe or
a succession of universes always existed? Do we have any evidence of a
plurality of universes? As long as these questions cannot be answered,
the decisive argument against intelligent design should not be that no
intelligent design ever existed, but that a non-scientific hypothesis ought
not to be introduced into a scientific argument as long as not all other
explanations have been excluded. Since we shall never be able to conclude
that such is indeed the case, the methodological argument against the
acceptance of an intelligent design in biology will never lose its force.

Despite these strong counter-arguments, the proponents of intelligent
design do not relent. On 7 July 2005, Christoph Cardinal Schönborn,
archbishop of Vienna, published an article in the New York Times, in
which he claimed that Darwinism is irreconcilable with faith in God's
providential plan for creation.[3] This conflicts with the statement of John

Paul II to the Pontifical Academy of Sciences in 1996, that the concept of evolution can no longer be called a hypothesis, but is a proven theory.[4] Science and theology follow different paths. Biology neither affirms nor denies the existence of God. The scientist must recognize the limits of his science and in so doing he encounters questions of a different nature concerning the totality within which his scientific investigations take place. He or she may detect intimations of a transcendent presence, but those have no merit as scientific proofs. But neither can the scientist, on the basis of his scientific work, exclude a transcendent significance in the evolutionary process. As Cardinal Ratzinger asserted in a series of homilies he delivered in 1986 in Vienna: 'The theory of evolution seeks to understand and describe biological developments. But in doing so it cannot explain where the "project" of human persons comes from, not their inner origin nor their particular nature. To that extent, we are faced here with two complementary rather than exclusive realities.'[5] He added at a later place that living beings 'are not the products of chance and error, but point to a creating Reason'.[6] This addition was directed against the theory of pure chance advocated by the French biologist Jacques Monod, according to which even the existence of mind is entirely the outcome of a random biological process.[7] The question is whether this restriction does not undo his earlier assertion.

2. The Fertility of Nature

Before considering this question, I would like to introduce another factor seldom mentioned in contemporary theories of evolution, yet prominently present in the ones of earlier thinkers. Henri Bergson and Pierre Teilhard de Chardin speak in different ways of the internal dynamism of matter. This factor again appears in the sharp critique George Coyne, S.J., director of the Vatican Observatory, wrote on Schönborn's article. According to him, Schönborn's thesis is inspired by an unfounded fear that the theory of genetic mutation would render God's care for creation completely superfluous, a remnant, I suspect, of the seventeenth-century thesis that faith rests on scientific conclusions. To the two constituent principles of the theory of evolution, random mutations and natural selection, Coyne adds the 'fertility' of the universe, a somewhat different version of Bergson's *élan* and Teilhard's *radiation*. Darwin himself may have assumed something of this nature. But the assumption is absent from his followers today.[8]

Without an internal dynamic of matter, it seems indeed hard to see how life could have overcome the negative effect of the force of entropy constantly decreasing the amount of utilizable energy or the catastrophic events, which periodically threaten its continued existence. Nor do I see how nature could have reached the chemical conditions needed for life without a *drive* to greater complexity. The proponents of this dynamic fertility are not assuming that nature is predestined to make human life possible. Science has nothing to say about such teleological dispositions. Those who assert its presence merely conclude that without being dynamic and creative, matter would be unable to build and preserve the chemical complexification needed for life and to resist the cosmic catastrophes and biological dangers which continually threaten this process.

I therefore also believe that some 'effort to be', what Spinoza called a *conatus essendi*, is required to explain how nature succeeds in attaining ever more complex and stable biological constructions. Only in accepting some inherently dynamic quality in matter can we hope to propose a viable alternative to the thesis that an intelligent designer has guided each step of the evolutionary process. The existence of such a quality also suggests that a scientific theory of evolution need not coincide with Monod's senseless chaos of emerging and perishing. Nor is the admission of such a dynamic quality yet another theological presupposition. In the eighteenth century, Diderot, unacquainted with the idea of the transformation of species, used it as an argument against the need to appeal to an external cause of nature's development.

And still, the question returns, can self-conscious beings be the mere result of a physiological evolution? Obviously, the order of mind surpasses the biological order. Even the non-believer suspects some truth in the words Benedict XVI spoke at the entrance of his pontificate: 'We are not some casual and meaningless product of evolution. Each of us is the result of a thought of God. Each of us is willed, each of us is loved, each of us is necessary.'[9] To be sure, the conditions that render a psycho-somatic being possible belong to the biological order. Thousands of centuries of chemical and physiological development preceded the human species. Throughout a lengthy succession of mutations and natural selections, organic beings have succeeded in overcoming destructive powers and in building the awesomely complex molecular structures of human life.

The brain is obviously a necessary condition for thinking, feeling and willing. Yet these activities are not mere 'products' of the brain. We may be inclined to reduce consciousness to a physiological state. But self-consciousness or reflection belongs to a different order of reality. To be sure, we relate our experiences to the various physiological conditions that make them possible. But physiology in no way accounts for self-knowledge. Roberto Unger describes the difference as follows: 'The power of mind may be inseparable from the precise constitution of the brain. Its historical roots may lie in the natural history of the brain [. . .] as a problem-solving device. Nevertheless, once established, this faculty of representing the scene of action as structured wholes and bundles of relations outreaches the natural occasions for its emergence. It becomes a revolutionary principle of seeing the world as a whole.'[10]

When the biological infrastructure was finally ready and the giant step to animal consciousness had been made, self-conscious life emerged. Biologically it caused no disruption in the chain of life: the strange new mammals seamlessly developed out of other animal life. Nor did the transition occur as a sudden leap. It might be compared to the mental progress we observe in an infant. At which point is it conscious of being an 'I' different from other beings? Psychology informs us at which age it appears to possess some rudimentary idea of selfhood. But between that stage and the beginning of life lies a considerable stretch of gradual development. Once self-consciousness is established, the evolutionary process undergoes a major change. It is, as Teilhard de Chardin memorably described it, an entering into a new interior space, a mode of self-concentration, which at some time concentrates the known world around that self.

To the mind reflecting on its own prehistory, a totally new chapter begins. Mind somehow possesses an internal necessity, in this sense that it cannot be deduced from anything else. Small wonder, then, that humans seek a higher intervention in a transforming event, which turns the evolutionary process in an entirely new direction. Here, I believe, lies the grain of truth in the intelligent design thesis, however inappropriate it may be in a biological theory. From a biological point of view, hominization is an accident, the outcome of random mutations. But philosophically and theologically speaking, a spiritual being arrives with a necessity of its own that cannot be explained as a mere effect of a biological cause. Though mind comes at the end of the evolutionary process, it is the factor that conveys meaning to all previous stages. Philosophers, beginning with Plato and Aristotle, and concluding in our age with Whitehead and Heidegger, consider mind or spirit as coming first in the order of meaning. Few have been materialist and, since Democritus, none of the best. To reduce the mind, then, to an accident of evolution, may be appealing to a physiologist, but is philosophically simplistic. Still it does not follow that we must ascribe the transition to an outside intervention. To do so would be biologically simplistic and philosophically unnecessary.

The transition to mind affects not only the individual consciousness; it transforms the entire relation of individuals to the phylum. Without self-consciousness animals are hardly differentiated from others of the same species. What counts is the species itself. With self-consciousness, the significance of the individual *vis-à-vis* the group increases enormously. Only reflection leads to full individualization. Human individuals are *persons*, each one of whom possesses a life of his or her own. One might even consider the evolution of the human race from its primitive beginnings a unique case of transmission of acquired qualities. Through education, humans transfer to the next generation what they have learned themselves. This evolutionary process may be indefinitely extended by means of writing. With it originates a new sphere of reality that surpasses the biosphere and even the human species as a whole: culture, or the sphere of spirit. Henceforth, the individual's task no longer consists only in physical reproduction but also, and more importantly, in the production and advancement of this spiritual realm.

3. *The God Question*

After the discovery of genetic mutations, the temptation of a reductionist interpretation of mind became even stronger than it was in Darwin's time. To reductionist scientists, religion irrationally resists the science of evolution. The philosopher Thomas Nagel writes in an article on Dawkins' *The God Delusion*: 'Dawkins like many of his contemporaries is hobbled by the assumption that the only alternative to religion is to insist that the ultimate explanation of everything must lie in particle physics, string theory, or whatever purely extensional laws govern the elements of which the material world is composed.'[11] H. Allen Orr, a biologist himself, in a devastating review of that same work claims that Dawkins is still undergoing the influence of Darwin's first run-in with religion. 'What Dawkins never seems to consider is that this incident might have been, in an important way, local and contingent'.[12]

Indeed, some of Darwin's predecessors, friends and followers held quite different positions on the relation between evolutionary theory and religion. In the first place, the man who in 1858, before the publication of *The Origin of Species* and independently of it, proposed a theory of evolution by natural selection, the mostly self-educated zoologist Alfred Russel Wallace, spent years at the Amazon River, in Singapore, and on the island Ternate, where he discovered the theory of evolution complete with the idea that new species would originate out of unpredictable variations in some individuals, of which the fittest would survive. When Darwin received the paper in which Wallace described his hypothesis in June 1858, he feared that his own 'originality, whatever it may amount to, will be smashed'. He need not have feared; the unambitious Wallace always took second place to his better-connected friend. In a later writing, Wallace, formerly an atheist, presented the process of evolution by natural selection as controlled by a Power, 'which has guided the action of those laws in definite directions and for special ends'. I mention this early case of 'intelligent design' only to show that the relations between Darwinism and religion were by no means always as hostile as they seem to have become in Dawkins' book.

Problems with religion were not all of the scientists' making. Theologians have, of course, been unanimous in attributing a unique, irreducible significance to the existence of the human person. But as long as they continue to assume an absolute separation between God's being and creation's own, their presentation of creation remains incompatible with the Darwinian theory on at least one crucial issue, namely, that a divine election of man must control the evolutionary process. But there exists a different way of conceiving the relation between God and nature. The whole situation changes if we regard the Being of nature *as* God's own Being. In creation, God expresses Himself. He constitutes the creature's Being. What distinguishes the two (without separating them) is the *limitation* inherent in all finite beings.

This hypothesis is actually not as revolutionary as it may appear. I even think that its foundation may be found in the theology of Thomas Aquinas, who writes that God as Being is innermost in all created being. In the *Summa Theologiae* (I, art. 8, 1), he poses the question whether God is present in all beings. He answers: 'Being is innermost in all things and most fundamentally present within all things, since Being is formal in respect of everything found in a thing. Hence God must be in all things and innermostly.' He further explains that God is intimately present in all things by being their *cause*. But the term *cause*, as we shall see, possesses a different meaning than the narrowly extrinsic one it has in modern thought. For Aquinas, the cause may be most intimately present in the effect. A similar ideal of the intimate union between creature and Creator, though based on a different kind of ontology, may be found in Eckhart and, most radically expressed, in Nicolas of Cusa. For Cusanus, the nature of divine causality in the act of creation implies that the creature participates in God and is the *explicatio* of God's own Being.[13]

If the creature partakes of God's Being, the sharp separation between Creator and creature, typical of much later theology, disappears. That separation stems from an impoverished notion of causality. Such early modern thinkers as Descartes, Spinoza and Newton, reduced causality to mere efficiency, for which the mechanical contact between bodies was the model. For ancient and medieval thinkers, the notion of cause had possessed a richer content: causality had been formal and final as well as efficient. The difference is crucial for the understanding of creation. Whereas a cause that is merely efficient remains separate from its effect, as appears in mechanistic theory, a cause in the older, comprehensive sense may remain united to its effect. The medieval idea of creation still assumed the quasi-formal presence of God in creation. In modern times, only a few spiritual writers dare to do so.

A return to the more comprehensive meaning of divine causality should make a friendlier relation between religion and evolutionary biology possible. If the evolutionary theorist remains aware of the limits of his method and if the theologian adopts a more immanent presence of God in creation than that of a merely efficient cause, no conflict ought to occur. Viewed from that perspective, terms such as natural selection and random mutation assume a different, theologically less threatening significance. If

God is the Being of all that is, nature preserves its own autonomy and develops in accordance with its own order. In this more intimate presence, even the blind determinism and undirected power of the evolutionary process has a spiritual significance.

From a biological point of view, humanity is the outcome of a biological process. The fact that there is human life must be considered a remarkable accident. Yet spiritually, human beings belong to a different order altogether. They are the ones who convey meaning and sense to the universe. Without intelligence capable of unifying the multiplicity of the real into a structured whole, there would be no 'world', that is, no totality of which all beings form integral parts. From that perspective, a being endowed with mind must be considered a *necessity* in the world we know. But this is not a biological statement. No biological evidence confirms that the human race is more than the fortuitous result of a random process.

Are there at least indications that the process of evolution moves towards that spiritual end, without constituting a necessary conclusion? I mentioned the creative power of matter, which played such an important role in Diderot's view of nature and which reappears among some recent scientists, such as Coyne and Teilhard de Chardin. The phenomenon of increasing complexity, admitted by all, is obviously a move towards interiorization. It shows the organism's tendency to turn back upon itself. Eventually it reaches some kind of conscious life, very advanced in primates. We may feel inclined, then, to view the reflective consciousness of humans to be the natural end of the evolutionary process. There is, however, no scientific evidence that the interiorization process necessarily *had* to reach this point, nor that, if it did, this end was the built-in 'purpose' of the process. Still, philosophically we cannot consider this outcome to be an accident. Even Kant, who so thoroughly criticized the use of teleological speculations in natural science, claimed in his *Critique of Judgment* that the existence of a certain teleology in nature is a necessary precondition of any science. The presence of such a natural teleology, however, would still not prove that the transition to self-consciousness requires a divine intervention.

But does the transition to self-consciousness, this unique break in the process of evolution, this *metabasis eis allo genos*, as Aristotle would call it, not prove that at least at this stage of evolution an extrinsic intervention is necessary? Again, I am afraid the answer must be negative. Kant affirmed the necessity for the scientific mind to assume the presence of teleology in nature as strongly as he denied the validity of the teleological argument for the existence of God. Philosophy cannot prove the existence of God any more than biology can prove that mind, whatever it is in itself, results from a *natural* evolution of the animal consciousness.

That a fundamental change occurs cannot be denied. Whereas a biological event remains *intrinsically* dependent on the factors that brought it about, mind, once it appears, belongs to a different order than the chemical and biological processes that made it possible. But does human nature's intrinsic surpassing of its biological conditions require a transcendent intervention? I suspect that the *origin* of the fundamental change in the process may be less decisive in determining the difference between a biological event and a state of reflection than we have assumed. Is it not possible that, as in the relation between quantity and quality, at a certain point one becomes transformed into the other? Is it excluded that animal consciousness, when it becomes even more interiorized, becomes self-conscious? I think not.

But, of course, in this discussion the strongest arguments in favour of a divine intervention have come from theology. The concept of a soul distinct from the body became soon the basis for the Christian belief in a life after death. At least the form of this argument was heavily influenced by Plato's idea of the independent soul. Once incorporated within the Christian theology of creation, this came to be interpreted as meaning that the soul was created separately from the body. Interestingly enough, Christianity inherited its belief in life after death from late Judaism, which made no such distinction between soul and body: the whole person would rise to new life. Still despite the pre-Christian origins of the theory of the soul, I would hesitate to touch on a subject that has received such a long, continuous acceptance and such careful philosophical reflection.[14]

Nevertheless, I am not convinced that theology ought to close this subject to further discussion. Our question is not: Is the soul distinct from the body in such a manner that it possesses an independent existence? But rather: Does the nature of the incarnated mind necessarily require a special divine intervention? As long as the belief in life after death is not jeopardized, I do not believe that either natural development or divine intervention is excluded.

Conclusion

What can we conclude from a discussion in which so much uncertainty remains? The following theses seem well enough established. (1) The notion of intelligent design as formulated today has no place in a scientific theory of evolution. It conflicts with the method proper to science by introducing a non-scientific factor. (2) For reasons exposed in this chapter, the arguments in favour of divine intervention are not persuasive. (3) Intelligent design should form no part of the scientific curriculum of school or college.

On the other hand: (1) The scientists who have proposed the argument of intelligent design have drawn attention to the fact that the principles of natural selection and random mutation are not sufficient to explain *all* elements of the evolutionary process. Some factors are assumed to be given, not justified. Among them, the dynamic quality of nature, the existence of DNA. (2) The argument of some contemporary biologists that the scientific theory of evolution replaces the mystery of creation is not based on scientific evidence. (3) The theology of the modern age is co-responsible for the existing tension between religion and science. It presents creation as a form of efficient causality wherein cause and effect remain separated. In the older, richer concept of causality, the Creator remains united with the creature and most of the tension vanishes.

Notes

1 Eric A. Cornell, 'What was God thinking? Science can't tell', *Time* (Nov. 6, 2005).
2 Richard Dawkins, *The God Delusion* (New York: Houghton Mifflin, 2006). See also: Daniel C. Dennett, *Breaking the Spell: Religion as a Natural Phenomenon* (New York: Viking Penguin, 2006).
3 Christoph Cardinal Schönborn, 'Finding Design in Nature', *New York Times* (July, 2005); for the ensuing debate, see Stephen M. Barr, 'The Design of Evolution', *First Things* (October, 2005); Christoph Cardinal Schönborn, 'The Designs of Science', *First Things* (January 2006).
4 *Truth Cannot Contradict Truth: Address of Pope John Paul II to the Pontifical Academy of Sciences* (22 October 1996) (English version in: *L'Osservatore Romano*, English edition, Oct. 1996).
5 Joseph Ratzinger, *In the Beginning. A Catholic Understanding of Creation and the Fall*, trans. Boniface Ramsey (Grand Rapids: Eerdmans, 1995), 50.
6 Ibid., 56.
7 Jacques Monod, *Le hasard et la nécessité* (Paris: Seuil, 1970).
8 George Coyne, 'God's chance creation', *The Tablet* (6 August 2005).
9 *Homily of Pope Benedict XVI for the Inauguration Mass of his Pontificate*, St Peter's Square (Sunday, 24 April 2005).
10 Roberto Mangabeira Unger, *The Self Awakened. Pragmatism Unbound* (Cambridge: Harvard University Press, 2007), 98.
11 Thomas Nagel, 'The Fear of Religion', *The New Republic* (23 October 2006).
12 H. Allen Orr, 'A Mission to Convert', *The New York Review of Books* 54, I (11 January 2007).
13 Louis Dupré, 'Nature and Grace in Nicholas of Cusa's Mystical Philosophy', *American Catholic Philosophical Quarterly LXIV* (1990, 1), 153–70.
14 For instance, St Thomas' definition of the soul as forma *substantialis subsistens*, that is, as informing the body, while at the same time possessing a separate existence.

Chapter 13

EVOLUTION AND THE DOCTRINE OF CREATION

Joseph M. Życiński

The argument for the creation of the universe provided by Stephen Hawking in his combination of sophisticated mathematics with naive metaphysics, according to Quentin Smith, can be regarded as 'the worst atheistic argument in the history of Western thought'.[1] Conversely, combining the Christian doctrine of creation with a total rejection of the theory of biological evolution provides, in my opinion, the worst version of theism ever met in the Western intellectual tradition.

At the time of Darwin, only a few authors claimed that there must be an inevitable opposition between evolution and creation. Most of the adherents of evolutionary ideas argued that there is no real opposition between the Creator and the laws of biological evolution because God acts through these laws and discloses His divine immanence in evolutionary processes. There was no need for 'creation science' when 'creation', 'evolution' and 'science' referred to various forms of the expression of God's creative wisdom.[2] The situation changed radically when the understanding of the very term 'evolution' itself evolved. At the end of the nineteenth century, as a result of the positivist critique of classical metaphysics, any reference to extra-natural factor was consistently eliminated from scientific theories, whereas some methodological principles were transformed into a substitute for metaphysics. According to new epistemological patterns, propagated by August Comte and Karl Pearson, the only valuable knowledge was supposed to be provided by the natural sciences. Accordingly, there was no reason to explore additional aspects of the evolutionary problems theologically. Even today, the expression of this mentality leads to more controversies than does the fundamentalist denial of Christian evolutionism.

1. The Rise and Growth of Methodological Naturalism

The necessity of a methodological distinction between the scientific and the theological approach was already suggested in some texts by Galileo and Newton. In pre-Galilean science, both natural and extra-natural elements were referred to in order to explain the well-known physical and astronomical phenomena. For instance, angels were supposed to take care of the orbits of planets to explain regularities in planets' motion. Although Galileo never questioned the value of theological explanations, he understood that one cannot critically develop new astronomy when replacing empirical evidence by substantive theses of metaphysics or theology. If, in the spirit of medieval astronomy, the hypothesis of the role of angels is ever introduced into the explanation of the motion of the planets, astronomy could easily be transformed into applied angelology, because the hypothesis of angels can be freely accepted to justify any set of empirical data.[3]

In the methodology accepted by Galileo, there is a fundamental role played by the principle of methodological naturalism, also called methodological positivism or scientific naturalism. This principle claims that, in scientific theories, the particular state of a physical system must be explained by reference to other physical states of the same system. Any attempt to appeal to non-physical factors would be inconsistent with the methodology of the natural sciences. The accepted research procedure does not exclude the existence of non-physical factors. Only for methodological reasons does it restrict the attention of research to physical objects.

There is no opposition between methodological naturalism and the Christian doctrine of creation. On the level of philosophical views, the supporters of methodological naturalism not only accepted God's continuous presence in His creation but also criticized deistic explanations in which God was supposed to act mainly in special interventions.

Darwin himself consciously avoided metaphysical questions, concentrating on physical–biological aspects of the explored evolutionary changes. However, when in post-Darwinian debates some scientists resigned from key concepts that for a long time had played a key role in the philosophical understanding of creation, their critics immediately declared that, in such a world, blind chance and deterministic necessity must reign in the realm of evolutionary changes. What was supposed to be a result of the divine *Logos*, was later identified either with irrational chaos or with a mysterious form of physical necessity that can be ascribed to deterministically understood laws of nature.[4] At the beginning of the twentieth century, the positivist critique of classical philosophy resulted in the abandonment of profound philosophical interpretations in which evolutionary theism seemed both well-grounded and consistent with the natural sciences.

One finds similar interpretations, for example, in the papers of A. L. Moore, Oxford botanist and Anglican clergyman. In his article of 1888, he emphasized that Darwinism makes it easier for us to see the oversimplifications of deism and, at the same time, provides an opportunity to critically rethink God's immanence in nature:

Either God is everywhere present in nature, or He is nowhere [. . .] He cannot delegate His power to demigods called 'secondary causes'. In nature everything must be His work, or nothing. We must frankly return to the Christian view of direct Divine agency, the immanence of Divine power in nature from end to end, the belief in a God in Whom not only we, but all things have their being.[5]

In the suggested explanatory perspective, there is no opposition between God and physical laws. God acts through the laws and His creative activity is discovered in these laws. 'For the Christian theologian, the facts of nature are the acts of God'.[6] Similar explanations were also accepted at that time by the rector of the Rochester Theological Seminary, A. H. Strong. In his attempt to formulate the fundamental theses of a theistic evolutionism, he argued that the principle of scientific evolution is the fundamental manifestation of Divine wisdom, revealing God's presence in the order of nature and specifically in the laws of nature. If that approach had found a consistent development, contemporary fundamentalism would be generally recognized as inconsistent with the principles of theology.

2. Between Darwin and Carnot

In the context of classical thermodynamics, Darwin's scientific explanation seemed to be in conflict with principles of Carnot's thermodynamics. According to the latter, the evolution of physical systems was to bring an increase of entropy and suggested that the thermodynamic death of the universe should be the final state of evolving physical systems. According to the Darwinian theory, natural selection brings about the self-organization of biological systems resulting in the emergence of new sophisticated structures. In classical thermodynamics, when perturbations affect the equilibrium of the evolving system, the principle of the minimum entropy growth determines its further evolution. New aspects of the thermodynamic evolution in the so called non-linear systems were discovered in the twentieth century. They indicate that there is no physical law which would guarantee the relative stability of the further evolution in these systems; accordingly, the system can reach the state of bifurcation in which small statistical perturbations play a much more important role than the deterministic laws. This bifurcation can be a breakthrough state after which there follows a relatively stable evolution subjected to new physical principles.

New conceptual schemes worked out in non-linear thermodynamics facilitated the disclosure of an order hidden in biological systems, atmospheric phenomena and physical chaos. What previously seemed irrational or even paradoxical became rational when the new cognitive framework was adopted. The dynamic systems in a far-to-equilibrium state are subject to physical laws. These thermodynamic laws, however, are much more sophisticated than they seemed to be within the framework of the nineteenth-century physics. The alleged opposition between Darwin and Carnot disappeared as a result of new discoveries in non-equilibrium thermodynamics.[7]

An important confirmation of the evolutionary paradigm was also provided by genetics when Gregor Mendel, an Augustinian monk of Brün, discovered the principles of biological inheritance after performing a series of experiments with peas in his monastery garden. Mendel's results became generally known circa 1900, but fifty years later genetics was still being criticized as a reactionary pseudo-science on the basis of ideological premises. In the early 1950s, its Marxists critics accentuated, for ideological reasons, the role of environment, and argued that the existence of genes is inconsistent with the spirit of empirical evidence because genes, as invisible objects, cannot be accepted by serious scientists.

3. No Longer a Mere Hypothesis

New discoveries in palaeontology, biochemistry, molecular biology and relativistic cosmology justified the statement formulated in 1973 by the renowned geneticist Theodosius Dobzhansky: 'nothing in biology makes sense except in the light of evolution.' A milder version of this conclusion was contained in John Paul II's *Message to the Pontifical Academy of Sciences* of 22 October 1996. Describing the development in the Church's attitude towards the theory of evolution, the Pope referred to the contemporary scientific evidence: 'new knowledge has led us to realize that the theory of evolution is no longer a mere hypothesis. It is indeed remarkable that this theory has been progressively accepted by researchers, following a series of discoveries in various fields of knowledge. The convergence, neither sought nor fabricated, of the results of work that was conducted independently is in itself a significant argument in favor of this theory'.[8]

When commenting on the important changes in the Church's view of science, George V. Coyne claims that these changes passed through four stages in which science was regarded respectively as Trojan horse, antagonist, enlightened teacher, and a partner in dialogue.[9] Nowadays, in places where some version of fundamentalism dominates, the theory of evolution is still being regarded as an antagonist. For many reasons, this fundamentalist critique resembles the Marxist critique of genetics; for the same reasons, it seems more interesting for the history of pseudoscience than for the development of scientific ideas.

In the context of contemporary evolutionary debates, the real problem lies with the cognitive importance of metaphysical aspects of evolution.

There are authors who argue that any reference to God's immanence in nature or to His role in cosmic evolution is inconsistent with the principle of explanatory economy. In other words, introducing God's role goes against Ockham's razor. For them, science and religious faith can never be partners in dialogue, because a monologue is enough to discover certain elementary truths. Consequently, some supporters of Richard Dawkins or of Daniel C. Dennett see no reason to refer to God, or to the Divine Absolute. They prefer different explanatory patterns in which God is replaced by 'the blind watchmaker', 'the river of genes' or 'the virus of religious faith'. Such metaphors could be suggestive, but their semantic content remains ambiguous. Even when one avoids poetic terminology, any reference to 'chance,' 'necessity' or 'evolutionary discontinuities' raises the question of what precise meaning should be ascribed to such terms. It is easier to forego using Ockham's razor than to avoid semantic fuzziness in the use of terms that had quite different meaning in classical philosophy and in the natural sciences.

4. Methodology or Doctrine?

Ockham's razor is a methodological principle, not a doctrinal one. It can inspire effective research procedures. One cannot apply it, however, in the search for simple answers to complicated metaphysical questions. Even at the level of scientific research, the principle has sometimes played a negative heuristic role. Its critics point out the numerous examples of the negative consequences of its application in the natural sciences. It is a fact that the appeal to Ockham's razor in the nineteenth century delayed the development of extragalactic astronomy by nearly a century. Uncritical adherents to the principle of Ockham's razor maintained at that time that there were no extragalactic objects, because all observed astronomical phenomena could be explained much more efficiently by referring exclusively to the objects of our galaxy. That search for simplicity led to the emergence of false astronomical theories. As a consequence, in contemporary philosophy of science there emerged a special project of de-Ockhamization, in which the principle is given a purely relative value, and not an absolute one.

To illustrate the unjustified praxis of regarding Ockham's razor, an effective means of eliminating any reference to God in philosophical comments about new scientific theories, it is enough to mention research in quantum cosmology, and specifically the paper on the wave function of the universe published by Hawking and Hartle in 1983.[10] In their famous paper, these authors presented a concept of the universe which created itself. Hawking presented his very interesting ideas in the presence of John Paul II during an academic meeting in the Vatican. According to many of his own statements, he had expected to be condemned by the Pope just as

Galileo had been many centuries before. John Paul II disappointed him, because, without a word of condemnation, he listened to the account of the creation of the universe in which there is no mention of God the Creator.

A few years later, when attending an academic meeting in Castel Gandolfo, I mentioned to John Paul II a paper by John Gibbins in which he wrote how disappointed Hawking had been due to the lack of papal condemnation. John Paul II smiled and asked, 'Why should I have argued with him? A physicist does not have to speak about a creator-God; that is the task of the theologian. However, the physicist cannot prevent the theologian from asking such questions as: "Why are there certain laws which rule the universe and why is it possible to use the language of mathematics?" I don't think that Hawking would be opposed to such questions. Because of that, I do not see any reason for a conflict.'

The wisdom of these words is confirmed by the fact that many theologians have published inspiring papers in which they develop the theology of creation using Hawking's model. In interdisciplinary dialogue, creative cooperation develops precisely in the areas where positivist critics of classical philosophy suggested an inevitable conflict.

5. More than Design

At the end of the twentieth century, various versions of creation, including creation of the universe *ex nihilo*, were proposed in physical theories.[11] In the initial state of the debates, the dominant opinions were that the new physics of creation leaves no place for the traditional metaphysics of creation since new cosmological models ultimately explain how the Universe created itself, emerging from nothingness. Consequently, the metaphysicians were supposed to be 'out of a job' because the key metaphysical problem can now be explained in physics.[12] In the present discussions, there prevails Chris J. Isham's opinion that some important and cognitively intriguing problems related to the creation and evolution of the universe should be explored beyond the cognitive perspective of physics. In particular, one must go beyond this perspective to satisfactorily explain the nature of creation *ex nihilo*.[13]

When discussing this issue, Isham suggests that, from an aesthetic point of view, the Hartle-Hawking proposal seems more attractive for the theist than the classical models that involve an impersonal dependence of the universe on God. Isham's approach suggests the concept of the world being held in the palm of God's hand.[14] As a result, one has to notice that the ideas of quantum cosmology that were originally proposed to eliminate any reference to God the Creator are today being developed to illustrate the classical doctrine of creation. Consequently, metaphors so often met in Dawkins' publications can also be used to defend theistic evolutionism. Although they do not replace philosophical arguments, one can use them to illustrate the controversial issues discussed in long-lasting philosophical controversies.

One of the risky metaphors dealing with God's role in the process of creation was introduced by William Paley in 1802. He compared God the Creator to a designer. The metaphor was impressive in the epoch of Comte when the social prestige of engineers was very high. From the theological point of view, however, it is not enough to reduce the role of God to the executor of an initial act of creation, to the designer of the structure of the cosmos or to a specialist in extraordinary interventions. In the dynamic conception of an evolving nature, God creates the universe, sustains its being and is subtly present not only in its universal laws of evolution but also in local events specific for our daily existence. In this perspective, God could be conceived of not as a Paleyan designer but as a composer unfolding the possibilities hidden within His creation. His role can be compared to that of the improvizing artist who demonstrates his unsurpassed ingenuity in disclosing a new beauty contained in the initial composition. In this aesthetic model of evolution, God appears simultaneously as a composer as well as a conductor. He not only determines the patterns of harmony that can be actualized in human life but also helps us to actualize them.

Thanks to God's non-deterministic mode of operation, evolution has not been the ordinary actualization of necessary links, but a creative process, in which diverse factors cooperate to actualize the large spectrum of natural possibilities. The God hidden in evolution directs that process towards a transcendent reality which is not yet physically realized, but, in a sense, pre-exists in possible physical structures. Consequently, to describe metaphorically the history of the evolving world, one should not refer to a recording played from a cosmic compact disk. One should refer rather to the completion of a great symphony in which human persons can aim at Divine patterns of order, but can also express their freedom.

To avoid the risk of new anthropomorphisms, one may use the analogies of non-linear thermodynamics and conceive of God as an evolutionary attractor. The state to which the non-linear thermodynamic evolution of physical systems tends is called an 'attractor' because, in the entire evolution of the system, it behaves as if it would attract the other stages of the dynamical growth.[15] Such a form of cosmic directedness is much more sophisticated than that suggested in the traditional argument from design. In the non-Paleyan versions of Christian evolutionism, God is understood as an evolutionary attractor and shares with all creatures their own openness to a future that is not fully determined.[16] Into evolving nature, He introduces His own canons of cosmic growth, but does not impose these canons deterministically. God's action should be conceived of as expressed in a persuasive rather than in a coercive manner. His creativity, expressed in divine 'persuasion', recognizes the autonomy of created beings and brings proposals of evolutionary growth that need not be necessarily followed in the process of human evolution.

The future of evolution is not the result of cosmic determinism. One should not formulate it in terms of a fatalistic necessity, in which the future of our race is understood by looking back at the extinction of the dinosaurs. The future of our species depends to a large extent on correlating our activity and creative cooperation with the action of the Divine Creator.

Notes

1 Quentin Smith, 'The Wave Function of a Godless Universe', in: W. L. Craig & Q. Smith, *Theism, Atheism and Big Bang Cosmology* (Oxford: Clarendon Press, 1995), 322.

2 See Ernan McMullin (ed.), *Evolution and Creation* (Notre Dame, Indiana: University of Notre Dame Press, 1985).

3 A. Favaro (ed.), *Le opere di Galileo Galilei* (Florence: G. Barbera, 1890), VII, 263; VII, 325 and V, 316.

4 J. Życiński, *God and Evolution: Fundamental Questions of Christian Evolutionism* (Washington, D.C.: Catholic Press of America, 2006), 138f.

5 A. L. Moore, 'The Christian Doctrine of God', in: Charles Gore (ed.), *Lux Mundi: A Series of Studies in the Religion of the Incarnation*, 10th ed. (London: Murray, 1890), 99f.

6 A. L. Moore, 'Recent Advances in Natural Science in their Relation to the Christian Faith', in: *Science and the Faith: Essays on Apologetic Subjects* (London: Kegan Paul, Trench, Trübner, 1889), 226.

7 See I. Prigogine & I. Stengers, *Order out of Chaos: Man's New Dialogue with Nature* (New York: Bantam, 1980).

8 John Paul II, 'Message to the Pontifical Academy of Sciences', in: *Evolutionary and Molecular Biology: Scientific Perspectives on Divine Action*, edited by. R. J. Russell W. R. Stoeger and F. J. Ayala (Vatican Observatory Publications, 1998; University of Notre Dame Press, 1999), 4.

9 George V. Coyne, 'Evolution and the Human Person: the Pope in Dialogue', in: *Evolutionary and Molecular Biology*, 11.

10 James Hartle, Stephen W. Hawking, 'The Wave Function of the Universe', *Physical Review* D 28 (1983), 2960.

11 They are described, for instance, in: Michael Heller, 'On Theological Interpretations of Physical Creation Theories', in: *Quantum Cosmology and the Laws of Nature*, edited by R. J. Russell *et al.* (Vatican Observatory Publications, 1999), 93–104.

12 J. Gribbin, *In Search of the Big Bang: Quantum Physics and Cosmology* (New York: Bantam Books, 1986), 392.

13 C. I. Isham, 'Creation of the Universe as a Quantum Process', in: *Physics, Philosophy and Theology*, edited by R. Russell *et al.* (Vatican Observatory Publications, 1988), 405.

14 Ibid.
15 J. Życiński, 'God, Freedom, and Evil: Perspectives from Religion and Science', *Zygon* 35 (2000), 653–64.
16 J. Haught, *God after Darwin. A Theology of Evolution* (Oxford: Westview Press 2000).

Chapter 14

DARWINISM AND MORAL THEOLOGY

Stephen J. Pope

This chapter offers a brief introduction to how Darwinism can be related to Catholic moral theology.[1] Rather than develop an historical survey of the various ways in which Catholic philosophers and theologians have responded to Darwinism over the course of the last century and a half, this contribution attempts only modestly to assess the significance of Darwinism, and particularly approaches to human evolution, for contemporary moral reflection in the Roman Catholic community.[2]

The potential range of connections is vast but the topic has been generally neglected by moral theologians, in large part because of disciplinary specialization, the practical bent of the discipline and moral objections to some versions of Darwinism itself. This chapter focuses on three major aspects of fundamental moral theology: the Catholic view of human nature, the virtues and natural law. Catholic moral theology stands to gain from the complex, ambiguous and dynamic view of human nature developed by Darwinism. It maintains that Catholic moral theology can appropriate important insights of Darwinism while correcting its tendency to engage in misplaced reductionism.

1. Darwinism, Evolution and Human Nature

The Catholic tradition has held that morality is an essential part of human nature, and that moral theology has to be informed by the best available accounts of human nature. Scientific information and theories have been less important for moral theology than the discipline of philosophy, but the general affirmation of the harmony of faith and reason provides an important vantage point from which one can see the relevance of Darwinian theory for moral theology.

'Darwinism' is sometimes regarded as equivalent to 'evolution', of which it is the major theoretical paradigm. Both terms have been used in multiple ways. The term 'evolution' tends to be used in one of at least four ways: (a) a fact (i.e., it is the case that species have evolved), (b) a course of natural history (i.e., how this or that species actually evolved), (c) a scientific theory (involving common descent, the evolutionary history of particular organisms and the mechanisms of evolutionary change) and (d) a worldview based on 'scientific materialism' (also known as 'ontological naturalism' or 'ontological reductionism').

'Darwinism' has also been subject to multiple interpretations. Creationists regard 'Darwinism' as a global scientific materialism that necessarily implies atheism. Palaeontologist Stephen Jay Gould criticized the common conviction of 'ultra-Darwinists' that 'natural selection regulates everything of any importance in evolution, and that adaptation emerges as a universal result and ultimate test of selection's ubiquity'.[3] It is important to distinguish (a) Darwin's theory of evolution in terms of natural selection and differential reproduction, (b) theories of evolution that have developed in light of Darwin's theory (including the 'modern synthesis') and (c) social and moral theories that claimed to be justified in an account of what Herbert Spencer called the 'survival of the fittest'. Moral theologians do well sharply to distinguish the first two uses of Darwinism from the third.

Pope John Paul II taught that the basic discoveries of evolutionary biology and its allied disciplines have to be taken seriously by anyone wanting to understand the natural world.[4] Yet three major obstacles present themselves to anyone who would strive to appropriate Darwinism into moral theology. One concerns human dignity, a second is the apparently anti-religious nature of Darwinism and a third focuses on improper reductionism.

First, Darwinism from its inception was taken to present a major challenge to human dignity. Christian polemicists regarded Darwinism as implying that the person is but a 'civilized, dressed up, educated monkey, who has lost his tail'.[5] Darwin himself saw no inherent conflict between common descent and human dignity. The closing observations of *The Descent of Man* argued that, 'As love, sympathy and self-command become strengthened by habit, and as the power of reasoning becomes clearer, so that man can value justly the judgments of his fellows, he will feel himself impelled, apart from any transitory pleasure or pain, to certain lines of conduct. He might then declare . . . in the words of Kant, I will not in my own person violate the dignity of humanity'.[6]

Darwin himself did not construct an ethical theory on the basis of nature; some of his peers, notably Herbert Spencer, were less hesitant. As noted above, it is important to keep the Darwinian theory of evolution separate from the social and political use of natural selection by social Darwinism, including *laissez-faire* capitalism, colonialism and Nazi ideology. The Catholic affirmation of the human person as created in the image of God implies that we are much more than biological beings, and points up the moral danger of reducing us to mere members of a species. Darwinian scientific accounts of the evolution of the human species are necessary but not sufficient for understanding the true dignity and inviolability of each human person. The church understands that our affirmation of human dignity requires a proper interpretation of evolution, not its repudiation.

Second, moral theologians can be put off by the explicit and sometimes fanatical rejection of religion by many evolutionists, and particularly by neo-Darwinians like Richard Dawkins and others known as the 'new atheists'.[7] Darwin's own struggle with the 'problem of evil' led him to harbour serious reservations about theism.[8] Other chapters in this volume take up this important issue. Suffice it to say here that evolutionary theism regards evolution as the means by which God creates and governs the world. God's will works in and through the natural dynamics of chance and necessity, contingency and law. Evolution is inherently opposed to fundamentalism but not to theologies informed by the principle that truth cannot be opposed to truth and faith cannot be opposed to science.[9]

Third, moral theologians are alert to the highly reductionistic character of a great deal of popular Darwinism, particularly sociobiology and evolutionary psychology. Yet it is important to note that reductionism comes in several forms, some proper and others not.[10] Francisco Ayala urges that we distinguish the unjustified epistemological and ontological forms of reductionism from the legitimate and necessary methodological reductionism employed by the natural sciences. Moral theology is consistent with the latter but not with the former.

First, methodological reductionism holds that the natural sciences can explain the physical, chemical and biological processes without recourse to non-scientific ways of thinking. It proceeds on the assumption that the world is intelligible and amenable to scientific investigation. Some historians hold that this conviction originated in the Judeo–Christian tradition.[11] Methodology is 'reductionistic' when it attempts to break down complex wholes into their component parts, for example, the attempt to understand the mechanics of the heart in terms of its pumps and valves. Though common to all forms of scientific enquiry, methodological reductionism has intrinsic limits that make it unsuitable as the sole means of finding answers to every important human question. Disciplinary pluralism more adequately reflects the diversity of questions generated by the human desire to know.

Second, epistemological reductionism maintains that traits found in higher levels of complexity can be explained entirely in terms of what is discovered on lower levels of complexity, for example, that biological events can be fully accounted for in terms of less complex chemical reactions, biochemistry in terms of chemistry and chemistry in terms of physics. This 'theory reduction' attempts to explain events studied by biology as special cases of the laws of chemistry, and events studied by chemistry as special cases of the laws of physics. Epistemological reductionism proceeds from the essentially unprovable presupposition that all phenomena of life, society and mind are explicable in terms of a unified set of physical laws. The presupposition of epistemological reductionism commits sociobiologists to attempting to explain social and cultural phenomena in terms of the 'inclusive fitness' of individuals.

It is the case that lower-level entities impose constraints on characteristics that can exist in the higher-level entities of which they are constituent parts. The functioning of living systems abides by fundamental physical and chemical laws, yet it must also be noted that these laws represent necessary but not sufficient conditions for the functioning of higher-level entities. Relatively more complex entities are characterized by capacities that cannot be derived simply from the capacities of their constituent parts – they are thus beneficiaries of 'emergent' capacities. Moral theologians devote considerable attention to examining the nature of human agency – the nature of freedom, moral knowledge, conscience, etc. – that epistemological reductionism seeks to explain away in evolutionary terms.[12]

Third, ontological reductionism holds that more complex, higher-level traits or entities are nothing more than a particular way in which simpler traits or entities are organized. It insists that the character of wholes is determined entirely by the traits of their constituent parts. Ontological reductionism entails 'ontological naturalism', the unproven assumption that only entities or processes found in nature are real. It rejects the 'vitalistic' claim that entities are influenced by souls or what are taken to be other non-natural metaphysical forces. Neo-Darwinians often erroneously assume that methodological reductionism entails ontological reductionism.

Evolutionary ontological reductionism ironically shares with 'scientific creationists' a failure to distinguish properly scientific from philosophical and theological claims. Moral theologians allow that science should be given as room to operate as possible to seek explanation for natural phenomena (methodological reductionism). However, they accept neither the premise that science alone has the ability fully to explain all phenomena (epistemological reductionism) nor that the material world alone is real (ontological naturalism or ontological reductionism).

2. Human Evolution in Darwinian Perspective

The Catholic tradition holds that that what is 'natural' to human beings is ultimately rooted in the distinctive traits that make each member of the species. The notion of Darwinian evolution suggests that nature is neither inevitably progressive nor structured in a linear hierarchy, only that, over long periods of time, evolution tends to increase the complexity of structures and to move from homogeneity to heterogeneity. Evolution is a 'branching' process whose pace is slow, irregular, haphazard and unpredictable, but it does – at least sometimes – move life towards higher and higher levels of organization.

Evolution is a process that gives rise to the emergence of kinds of wholes that are accompanied by new kinds of capacities, processes, and traits. Ian Barbour describes 'emergence' as 'the claim that in evolutionary history and in the development of the individual organism, there occur forms of order and levels of activity that are genuinely new and qualitatively different. A stronger version of emergence is the thesis that events at the higher levels are not determined by events at lower levels and are themselves causally effective'.[13] Barbour helpfully describes the meaning of emergence: 'A living organism is a many-leveled hierarchy of systems and subsystems: particle, atom, molecule, macromolecule, organelle, cell, organ, organism, and ecosystem. The brain is hierarchically organized: molecule, neuron, neural network, and brain, which is in turn part of the body and its wider environment.'[14] The complex structure of human nature bears the imprint of our evolutionary past.

Human nature has evolved to possess sets of emergent cognitive, emotional and social capacities. First, the evolution of cognitive symbolic capacities led to the existence of personal beings possessing unified, self-conscious centres. The development of consciousness and self-consciousness makes possible unprecedented degrees of behavioural flexibility that allow us to be less restricted by the limits of our local environments than many other species. Self-reflective awareness and new degrees of self-possession made it possible for a person to direct his or her energies and capacities to goals on behalf of the whole organism.

Our enormous capacity for information processing and for forming symbolic representations of things in the world empowers us for kinds of agency that are impossible for other animals. It provides the context for memory, choice and planning, and therefore for moral responsibility. Emerging cognitive capacities make it possible for us to engage our imaginations, to speculate about various courses of action and to interpret the mental and emotional states of our interlocutors with subtlety and nuance. Intelligence is extended not only to behaviour involving hunting and gathering, but also to modes of personal and group living. Integral to personal and group living is the social institution known as 'morality'.

Second, human emotional capacities and needs are also the product of a long evolutionary process. Emotions constitute states of pleasure or pain that take place within the deeper context of underlying behavioural proclivities that are known as 'drives' and 'motivations'. Emotions evolved as ways to help our evolutionary ancestors cope with their environments.

They play two key regulative roles in the biological life of an organism. First, they allow the organism to react to an object that causes the emotion, for example, to flee danger, recognize the presence of food or drink, etc. Second, they shape the internal condition of the animal so that it is able to react in the right way when called upon to do so. Primary emotions recognized across cultures include fear, anger, happiness, sadness, disgust and surprise. 'Secondary' or 'social' emotions – emotions generated in relation to other people – include embarrassment, pride, jealousy and guilt.

Behavioural plasticity and flexibility is one of the most important features of human nature, and emotions can affect actions in ways that are either beneficent or malfeasant. Unlike all other animals, we are not bequeathed with a strong set of instincts but rather need to be taught how to live. Moral training brings a more or less settled set of patterns to how the agent acts upon natural emotional capacities, and specifically empowers the mature adult to transcend the appeal of immediate gratification of desire in pursuit of more worthwhile ends. It allows one, for example, to resist the emotional appeal of quick retaliation as a response to aggression or betrayal. Reason guides the expression of emotions rather than vice versa, but it does not suppress or destroy them. The recent focus in moral theology on the virtues attends to the ways various communities shape character. Evolutionary analysis similarly underscores the importance of the habituation of mind and heart.

Third, we inherit from our precursors a strong social capacity – a tendency to live and thrive in groups, to depend upon networks of cooperation, reciprocity and commitment to one another. The emotional and cognitive capacities already mentioned make possible unprecedented psychological complexity, forms of communication and cognitive depth and symbolically-based reasoning – all of which are played out in social life. Moral theologians increasingly emphasize not only the social nature of the person but also the significance of the social dimension of all ethical concerns.

We are bequeathed with social emotions; pity, empathy, and other prosocial feelings are not simply laid on top of a substrate that is essentially antisocial. Whereas 'ultra-Darwinism' regards every person as fundamentally self-centred and not genuinely altruistic, the Catholic moral vision regards our first-person experience of caring for others is neither illusory nor derivative from self-concern. In this case, social institutions have more to build on than atomistic individualism recognizes. Society is a network of communities that make a positive contribution to human well-being. Social ethics takes its bearings from an account of what contributes to the common good, and politics ought to work for its promotion through laws and public policy.[15] Certain kinds of social conditions can increase the likelihood of aggression and others decrease it. Recent primatological research on affiliative and reconciliatory behaviours indicate the evolutionary roots of our social nature.[16]

Moral theologians ought to appreciate the attention given by Darwin to the pro-social capacity for sympathy. Darwin held that we have evolved to possess an innate emotional preference for family members and those who are friendly with us, but he also held that we can be taught to extend our natural sympathies from loved ones 'to the men of all nations and races'.[17] Neo-Darwinians, though, have tended to see the scope of this sympathy as restricted to one's circle of kin and 'reciprocators'. Richard Alexander, for example, maintains that we evolved to be strongly inclined to 'in-group amity' but 'out-group enmity'.[18] While drawing the line between in-group and out-group too sharply, the evolutionists suggest that there are natural conditions that present obstacles to universal charity.

All three dimensions of human nature – cognitive, emotional and social – underscore our complexity. Human motivations are mixed, ambiguous and wide-ranging. They are made possible by the evolution of the 'limbic system' and neurotransmitters but also deeply shaped by particular cultures. The kinds of complex reasoning usually associated exclusively with the recently evolved neo-cortex of the higher brain does not just 'ride on top of' the much older and more primitive lower brain associated with the emotions and physical states. Both parts of the brain are intimately involved in processes that involve reasoning and emotional experience.[19]

The persistence, power and complexity of human emotional inclinations mean that the process of habituation often has results that are unstable, uneven and incomplete. The language of virtue can be interpreted to suggest that once habits have been formed, characters are set. An evolutionary view of human nature, however, suggests that habituation can only go so far, and that is accomplished with a great deal of effort. A permanent disposition to certain kinds of goods, morally appropriate or not, is an ineliminable part of human nature. There may always be a human tendency to want to cheat to gain an advantage or to counter what one perceives as an unfair advantage held by others. This obdurate part of human nature seems to be especially the case when it comes to our appetites, particularly for food and sex.

The juxtaposition of various kinds of adaptations and motivations leaves the human psyche fraught with moral complexity, ambiguity and tension. Moral theologians regard sin as amplifying our conflicts and impairing our attempts to negotiate them. But we also affirm the power of grace to transform us so that we can become more decent, just and morally integrated human beings. The process of being made more Christ-like involves the graced perfection of nature, including our evolutionary nature. The primary human expression of this growth lies in the theological virtues.

3. The Theological Virtues

The human acceptance of the offer of divine grace inspires the three theological virtues – faith, hope and charity – in the minds and hearts of believers. 'Faith' is primarily a matter of trustfully believing God and, secondarily, believing in the truth about God and humanity given in revelation.[20] 'Hope' is the theological virtue in which the believer moves towards a goal that is difficult but (because of grace) not impossible to attain, namely, eternal union with God. 'Charity' is the grace-infused love of God and love of neighbour 'in God'.

First, the theological virtue of faith involves a deep personal response to a personal God. Faith affirms the existence of God as an intellectual conviction, but it also, and more profoundly, constitutes a complete and profound personal response to God in contemplation and in action. Faith is nurtured, expressed and challenged to develop within the faith community. The faith of the individual Christian is always shared with fellow believers and with the whole church, understood as past (the 'apostolic tradition'), present (the tangible 'Body of Christ' in the world) and future (the coming 'Kingdom of God'). It thrives within the living church despite its flaws, weaknesses and sins.

Second, theological virtue of hope yearns for complete union with God in the future, but the experience of the love of God anticipates this union here and now. As a theological virtue, hope is grounded not in reasonable optimism but in a trusting affirmation that God will fulfil the promises of a future reconciliation of all things. Whereas the 'new atheists' regard hope in the face of suffering as naively escapist, Christians regard hope as the basis for the courage to respond to evil and to accept suffering as the cost of fighting it.

Finally, the theological virtue of charity constitutes the grace-inspired love of God and love of neighbour 'in God'. Love in its most basic sense is an affirmative response to the good, an affective affirmation of what we recognize as good (what Thomas Aquinas called 'complacency in good').[21] Love in this mode issues in one of two directions, either as desire for the good that is absent, or joy in the good that is present. The term 'care' refers to the response of love to the beloved's need. The Catholic tradition distinguishes various meanings of the term 'love' that include the natural human emotion or 'passion' (*amor*), the product of deliberate human choices (*dilectio*), the mutual love of friendship (*amicitia*) and the theological virtue of charity (*caritas*).

The Catholic moral tradition has spoken of charity first of all as the love of God, not as an optional caring for the needy.[22] Charity cannot be reduced to altruism, but its most characteristic effect and expression lies in the love of one person for another. It constitutes a love for the highest good that transcends love for oneself, for pleasurable activities and good

things and even for those near and dear to us. Theocentric love decisively
re-centres the self towards the common good.[23] Love of neighbour flows
from a prior and more fundamental re-orientation of the agent's entire life
from a disordered and wrong-headed egocentric love to an all encompass-
ing love for God. The test of love for God lies in love for neighbour
(1 John 4:20; also Mt 25:31–46). Since the greatest and unsurpassable
revelation of God's love was manifested in Jesus' self-surrender on the
Cross, the Christian life is shaped in the form of the Cross. The ultimate
significance of the emergence of distinctively human capacities lies in their
capacity to be drawn by grace into a pattern of life that echoes the eternal
inner self-giving mutuality of God's own Trinitarian love.

Just as grace perfects nature, so charity perfects our natural capacity to
love. Charity retains the natural tendency of the person to love most those
to whom he or she is most closely bound by marriage, family or any other
kinds of particular connections or friendships – relations supported by the
evolution of what neo-Darwinians call 'kin altruism' and 'reciprocal altruism'. At the same time, grace also restores, purifies and heals our natural
ability to recognize in every person the goodness, worth and dignity that he
or she possesses simply in virtue of being human. At the very minimum,
this love means good will (Thomas' 'love of benevolence') regardless of
any other features of the other person's moral worthiness, attractiveness
and the like. This moral universalism contrasts with the limits imposed on
concern for others predicted by most Darwinians. Christian transformation is ordered to allowing God to become the effective centre of one's
existence, the greatest good, and the ultimate end of action. As a result,
relations to self, kin and reciprocators are all relativized. The claims of kin
and reciprocators do not always override all other concerns, and help is
directed to those who have no ability to reciprocate.

The love of God carries an important implication for the moral worth
of human beings. As purely biological entities, human beings have the
same status as other 'sentient beings'. It appears that, from a *purely
biological* standpoint, individuals belonging to a global population of
six billion human beings are less valuable than members of endangered
species. In sharp contrast, the Catholic moral tradition regards the human
person as bearing a special intrinsic worth because made in God's image
(Gen 1:26).

This dignity grounds the legitimacy of self-love, rightly understood.
Moral theologians in different respects both reject and encourage self-love.
The former is more familiar: disciples are commanded to forget themselves and pick up the Cross (Mt 10:37–9; Lk 14:26, 17:33; Mk 8:34–5).
Yet the *imago Dei*, and more generally the doctrines of creation and
redemption, provide strong warrants for the moral legitimacy and even
the duty of proper self-love. Concern for others is supported by balanced
self-care.

The rather pessimistic Darwinian view of human nature can in some respects be taken as confirming the destructive tendencies of what has been symbolically referred to by Christians as our 'fallen humanity', as distinct from the original innocence of the 'integral human nature' intended by the Creator. Yet the Catholic tradition maintains that our deeply ingrained tendency to prefer ourselves to others is corrected not by ceasing to love ourselves altogether but rather by loving ourselves in the right way. Instead of completely abolishing self-love, then, we ought to love the self in proper relation to the love of God and neighbour, strive to live virtuously and in spirit of generosity towards others and the common good.

Neighbour-love of course is much more emphasized in moral theology than is self-love. The most frequently cited formula for love of neighbour is the golden rule: 'do to others as you would have them do to you' (Mt 7:12; Lk 6:31). Darwin regarded the golden rule as the foundation of morality, but he thought that its support comes from its contribution to the struggle for survival rather than from its moral rationality or religious backing.[24] This formula is often confused with an injunction to reciprocity – to treat others the way they treat you – and as a religiously-backed version of 'Tit-for-Tat' reciprocity based on enlightened self-interest. The unilateral nature of the golden rule is in fact neutral with regard to reciprocity: regardless of how others treat you, do to others as you would like to be treated. It places no conditions of reciprocity on the action of the agent and it makes no mention of limits to what the agent does. Moral theologians regard the virtue of prudence as the human capacity to discern the right way in which to enact the golden rule in concrete circumstances.[25]

Evolutionists claim that 'good Samaritanism' helps to build the altruist's good reputation within a community and thereby indirectly contributes to his or her reproductive fitness. Richard Alexander believes that, 'whether or not we know it when we speak favorably to our children about good Samaritanism, we are telling them about a behavior that has strong likelihood of being reproductively profitable'.[26] This claim, however, misses the point of the story of the good Samaritan (Luke 10:29–37), who, while travelling along the road to Jericho, shows what it means 'to be neighbour' when going out of his way to care for a stranger who had been beaten and left for dead by robbers. The term 'neighbour' during Jesus' time meant 'near one' but the story stretches the term to include the enemy. The Samaritan is not an 'altruist' who helps a member of his own community, but a traveller moved by heartfelt compassion to come to the aid of an historic enemy. 'Being neighbour' means overcoming boundaries that mark webs of indirect reciprocity. It means extending care to all who are needy, whether they are members of one's own in-group or not. This universality is 'perverse'[27] from a sociobiological standpoint, but ideal for the Christian ethic. Moral theologians would regard evolutionary reductionism as leading both to a diminished view of our natural moral capacities and to its dismissal of the power of divine grace to transform moral agents. The significance of human moral capacities is further highlighted in the analysis of the natural law.

4. Natural Law

The Christian moral life is structured by the pursuit of the human good. Human flourishing in this life involves not only grace but also a human nature that has been shaped by millions of years of evolutionary history. At the same time, the Christian understanding of human life as a journey to God relativizes the merely biological good. The letters of Paul and other New Testament texts (and Hebrew Bible texts as well) presume that 'general human standards' are normative. As William Spohn explained, 'The gospel is not the only norm, as shown in Paul's frequent appeals to human values, practical logic, common secular wisdom, and the like'.[28] At the same time, Spohn emphasized, 'The life of Jesus as related in the Gospels . . . is the fundamental norm for Christians'.[29] This means that the human good in its deepest meaning is pursued through following Christ. Christian identity is shaped by the virtues, taught by communities, displayed in the acts of moral exemplars, and communicated in paradigmatic narratives upheld by the Christian tradition.

Christian life is also shaped by the 'moral law' – by norms, rules, principles or standards that inform decision-making, the formation of intentions, and moral judgments regarding what to do in concrete situations. Moral law and virtues thus ideally exist in spiral relation to one another.[30] Moral laws reinforce virtues, and virtues extend our understanding of moral laws. The moral law is comprised of the principles and rules of action authoritatively articulated in the gospel and in the Christian tradition, developed by the contemporary church and taught by the hierarchical magisterium. It includes not only distinctively Christian teachings, but also the moral insight discovered by reason, philosophy, and human experience broadly construed. This array of teachings includes what the tradition calls the 'natural law'.

The natural law is ordered to human flourishing, and its standards are intended to shape human action in ways that allow the agent to live the good life as it is understood in Christian terms. The natural law tradition, in other words, understands moral claims to be warranted by their contribution to human flourishing. Moral theologians ought to consult scientific knowledge of evolution, then, precisely because it provides a new and very important source for understanding human nature, human flourishing, the natural law and the virtues. Natural law orders our actions to the proximate human good – the good that accords with our nature as

God created it. Natural law is complemented by the virtues. Living a good life as a Christian does not simply occur spontaneously. As Nicholas Lash notes, the Christian tradition has long recognized the need for 'discipline, *ascesis*, the taming of the violence of the human heart, lifelong education into patterns of attentiveness, and peacefulness, and trust. Humanity, we might almost say, does not come naturally to us'.[31]

The evolutionary view of what is 'natural' to human beings is based on what occurs with some frequency under various ecological conditions. In this sense of the word it is entirely 'natural' for some male animals to practice infanticide, to kill conspecifics from other groups and to engage in forced copulation with fertile females.[32] Acts like these were probably also placed by natural selection on our own evolved menu of behavioural options in the course of our evolutionary past because they were in the distant past 'fitness enhancing' under certain conditions. At the same time, empathy, parental caring, familial cooperation, reciprocity and other forms of pro-social behaviour are now widespread because, in a multitude of ways and over the long run, they promoted rather than undermined reproductive fitness.

Darwinians hold that, under other circumstances, egocentrism, lying, self-deception, out-group bias and aggression can promote 'fitness', but that under other circumstances the opposite strategies are 'fitness maximizing'. These behaviours are 'natural' in the sense that they are favoured by selection under certain circumstances. Thus 'kin altruism' is adaptive over a wide range of environmental contexts, yet conditions of scarcity may be so severe than natural parental solicitude is jettisoned in favour of infanticide.[33] In some conditions, similarly, polygamy rather than monogamy would be considered the most natural arrangement between the sexes, at least in the sense that it might be the most effective 'mating strategy'.[34]

Natural law, on the other hand, holds that what is 'natural' includes biology but also our more distinctively human capacities. A right way of acting is not ethically obligatory or legitimate simply because it is 'natural', in the scientific sense, as 'evolved' or 'genetically based'; it is obligatory because it accords with what is good for human beings, considered comprehensively. The obligatory character of morality – the 'law' – binds the person to moral standards that promote the well-being, or flourishing, of the person and his or her community. It is wrong to murder, to be sexually unfaithful, to steal, to lie and to cheat because doing so undermines the good of both self and others. General norms are not matters of arbitrary taste or idiosyncratic preferences, but reflect judgments about structures of living that promote human flourishing. Our basic orientation to the good is not extinguished by wrong-doing: even liars resent being lied to, and victims of theft get morally outraged despite the fact that they themselves steal from others.

The normative ideal of natural law identifies certain human capacities from within the larger conglomeration of traits that constitute our evolved human nature, but it is selected on theological and moral rather than on biological grounds. Natural law promotes the activation of our created potentialities for loving the good and knowing the truth. The natural law promotes human flourishing comprehensively considered. Since God is eternal love and pure wisdom, and human beings are created in the image of God, the natural law lies in our capacity to know what is true and to love what is good. This means first of all to know and love God, and secondly to know and love ourselves and our neighbours. This is the deepest meaning of Thomas' description of the natural law as 'the rational creature's participation in the eternal law'.[35]

The core of the natural law does not lie in a detailed moral code, or defined set of moral rules, or specific 'action-guides' but in the virtues that shape and perfect our capacities for knowing and loving. The desire to know and to love are not merely two tendencies among others, but our central and most definitively human inclinations. The Catholic moral tradition holds that our activities of knowing and loving are brought to their highest level in the exercise of wisdom and charity. Charity as the 'form of the virtues' shapes and inspires the cardinal virtues of prudence, justice, temperance and fortitude. Virtues of knowing and loving provide the proper basis for ordering all our other acts, habits, attitudes and desires. They are what help to make human sense of the elementary inclinations that we share with other animals. This capacity moves well beyond the narrow orientation to genetic fitness but cannot take place without adequate functioning of the biological aspects of human nature. The emergent human cognitive and emotional capacities that give us the ability to pursue what is good and know the truth regardless of its impact on self-interest depend upon but transcend the lower-level biological operations.

The natural law tradition has historically tended to downplay the existence of conflict between goods, but some important forms of conflict are built into our nature. We find internal conflict over various goods (e.g., the need for security and the need for food), as well as external conflicts between different individuals over the same goods (e.g., two males and one female). In the human context, sin no doubt significantly intensifies the factor of conflict in human life, and it introduces new kinds of conflicts (e.g., over prestige, status, possessions, etc.) whose ferocity and ill effects extend very significantly beyond what is found in nature. Yet it remains the case that human beings have been 'set up' by evolution to experience multiple inclinations that sometimes reinforce and at other times conflict with one another and it is the case that communities are the scene of competition and conflict among and between both individuals and groups.

A view of natural law more attuned to the possibility of conflict of goods and responsibilities might be more willing to concede that at times the pursuit of one good, judged to be higher or otherwise more important, might require the direct negation of another good. This also implies that on occasion the exercise of one virtue (say, mercy) might not only be neutral with regard to another (e.g., justice) but actually works against it. This point raises the spectre of consequentialism, the moral logic according to which the ends justifies the means, and the 'slippery slope' of situation ethics. One extreme reaction against moral deterioration is absolutism, unwavering and rigid adherence to the letter of the law that allows for no exceptions, but absolutism has been known to lead to moral absurdities that do not need to be illustrated here.

In natural law ethics, true moral objectivity is achieved in concrete acts through the exercise of the virtue of prudence. What is objectively binding in a particular situation, in other words, is what is most in keeping with the first principle of practical reason: do good and avoid evil. General moral knowledge includes various beliefs about which aspects of our inherited behavioural repertoire ought to be approved of, acted upon and promoted, and which ought to be inhibited, sublimated or closely monitored. It also includes general knowledge of which kinds of acts tend to undermine the human good and which kinds of acts promote it, but moral decision-making only succeeds when attention is focused on concrete goods and evils at stake in particular situations.

The virtue of prudence allows the agent to perceive the morally salient factors at stake in concrete human experiences. It is in and through concrete experience that people discover, appropriate and deepen their understanding of what constitutes true human flourishing. Interpretations of these experiences are influenced by membership in communities shaped by particular stories. Discovery of the natural law, Pamela Hall notes, 'takes place within a life, within the narrative context of experiences that engage a person's intellect and will in the making of concrete choices'.[36] The virtue of prudence avoids applying moral rules in a way that, in concrete situations, damage human lives. Rather than prescribing a universal and exhaustive moral code proper for all times and all people, natural law must be understood in a way that is dynamic, flexible and open to new developments as a result of changing human circumstances.[37]

Natural law is necessary but not sufficient for moral theology. The human good requires the transformation of our motivations, attitudes and intentions, and in a way to a degree that surpasses our natural human capacities. The Christian moral life strives to shape the evolved 'matter' of our inherited human nature so that it is more in keeping with the 'form' of the good life revealed in Jesus. The 'matter' includes but is not exhausted by our biologically evolved natures. The church attempts to inform our natural sense of fairness by shaping the Christian imagination according to the key narratives, parables, injunctions, etc., present in Scripture. Jesus concludes the parable of the Good Samaritan with 'go and do likewise'

(Luke 10:37). Christian ethics expands justice beyond our natural satisfaction with family and friends to include strangers and enemies. Indeed, Christian ethics inclines us to regard the good of others as in some sense also our own good; this of course is where a vision of the good that is more than biological offers a radically more humane ethic than anything envisioned by sociobiology or evolutionary psychology.

Christian natural law theory identifies which actions comport with moral goodness and which do not. They are concerned not only with *selecting* which capacities, desires and needs are part of the good life, but also what *shape* they are going to take in the moral life as well as how they are to be *ordered* to one another and to the common good. When it comes to the standard for Christian ethics, then, the central focus is not 'naturalness' per se but transformation 'in Christ', not in biological evolution but spiritual and moral growth. Saints continue to be human beings with same natural constitution as other human beings, but they face the challenge of habituation in the good and they learn to order their affections so that they accord with the Christian vision. Christian ethics, then, regards human nature as properly developed in the virtues, and above all in faith, hope and charity.

Conclusion

This chapter has traced the relevance of Darwinism to Catholic notions of human nature, the virtues and natural law. It argues that moral theologians have legitimate concerns about Darwinian, or Darwinian-based, forms of social morality that undercut human dignity, indiscriminately reject all forms of religion and advance without justification a naturalistic ontology under the guise of natural science. Yet it also maintains that a critical appropriation of legitimate scientific methodological reductionism that recognizes the limits of scientific discourse is no threat to moral theology. Indeed, it argues that a properly interpreted theory of Darwinian evolution supports a view of human nature as constituted by capacities that can be incorporated into and trained within the Christian moral life. The virtues shape these capacities when ordered to the authentic human good, and the 'natural law' constitutes the ordering of human acts to human flourishing. The Christian moral life, then, can be seen as proceeding through the work of grace as it builds upon, corrects and enhances the moral capacities that have been given to us by the evolutionary process. In this vision, the work of the Creator and the work of the Redeemer converge in the life of grace perfecting nature.

Notes

1 For a general overview, see Don O'Leary, *Roman Catholicism and Modern Science: A History* (New York and London: Continuum, 2006).

2 For a more extended treatment, see Stephen J. Pope, *Human Evolution and Christian Ethics* (New York: Cambridge University Press, 2007).

3 Stephen Jay Gould, 'Darwinian Fundamentalism', *The New York Review of Books* 44.10 (12 June 1997):34–7, at 37.

4 See Pope John Paul II, 'Message to the Pontifical Academy of Sciences on Evolution', *Origins* (14 Nov. 1996), pp. 350–2. See more recently the July 2004 Vatican Statement on Creation and Evolution, 'Communion and Stewardship: Human Persons Created in the Image of God', *Origins*, CNS Documentary Service, 34.15 (23 September 2004), 233–48.

5 P. R. Russel, 'Darwinism Examined', *Advent Review and Sabbath Herald* 47 (1876):153, cited in Numbers, *The Creationists*, 5.

6 'Descent of Man', in: Philip Appleman (ed.), *Darwin: A Norton Critical edition*, second edn, (New York: W. W. Norton, 1979), 310.

7 See Richard Dawkins, *The God Delusion* (Boston: Mariner, 2006) and Daniel C. Dennett, *Breaking the Spell: Religion as a Natural Phenomenon* (New York: Penguin, 2006).

8 See Darwin, 'Autobiography', in: Gavin de Beer (ed.), *Charles Darwin and Thomas Henry Huxley: Autobiographies*, (London: Oxford University Press, 1974).

9 See John Paul II, 'Letter to the Rev. George V. Coyne, S.J.', *Origins* 18 (17 November 1988), p. 377; *idem*, 'Lessons of the Galileo Case', *Address to the Pontifical Academy of Sciences*, 31 October 1992, *Origins*, 22 (1992), 371–73; *idem, The Splendor of Truth: Veritatis Splendor* (Washington, D.C.: United States Catholic Conference, 1993); and *idem, Fides et Ratio: On the Relationship between Faith and Reason* (Boston: Daughters of St Paul, 1998).

10 See Francisco J. Ayala, 'Introduction', in: Francisco J. Ayala and Theodosius Dobzhansky (eds), *Studies in the Philosophy of Biology: Reduction and Related Problems* (Berkeley: University of California Press, 1974); *idem*, 'Reduction in Biology: A Recent Challenge', in: D. Depew and B. Weber (eds.), *Evolution at the Crossroads* (Cambridge: MIT Press, 1985); and *idem*, 'Biological Reductionism: The Problems and Some Answers', in: F. E. Yates (ed.), *Self-Organizing Systems: The Emergence of Order* (New York: Plenum Press, 1987), 315–24.

11 See Stanley Jaki, *The Road of Science and the Ways to God* (Chicago: University of Chicago Press, 1978), vii.

12 See Richard M. Gula, S. S., *Reason Informed by Faith: Foundations of Catholic Morality* (Mahwah, N.Y.: Paulist, 1989), and Josef Fuchs, S.J., *Personal Responsibility and Christian Morality*, trans. William Cleves (Washington, D.C.: Georgetown University Press and Dublin: Gill and MacMillan, 1983).

13 Ian Barbour, 'Neuroscience, Artificial Intelligence, Human Nature', in: R. J. Russell, N. Murphy, T. C. Meyering and M. A. Arbib (eds), *Neuroscience and the Person: Scientific Perspectives on Divine Action* (Vatican City: Vatican Observatory/Berkeley, CA: Center for Theology and the Natural Sciences, 2002), 271.

14 Ibid., p. 269.

15 See David Hollenbach, S.J., *The Common Good and Christian Ethics* (New York: Cambridge University Press, 2002).

16 See Robert W. Sussman and Audrey R. Chapman, (eds), *The Origins and Nature of Sociality* (New York: Aldine de Gruyter, 2004).
17 Cited from *The Descent of Man*, in ibid., 173.
18 R. D. Alexander, *Biology of Moral Systems* (New York: Aldine de Gruyter, 1987), 95.
19 See Antonio Damasio, *Descartes' Error: Emotion, Reason, and the Human Brain* (New York: Avon Books, 1994), 128. See also *idem, The Feeling of What Happens: Body and Emotion in the Making of Consciousness* (New York: Harcourt Brace and Co, 1999).
20 See *Summa Theologiae* II-II, 1, 2 ad 2.
21 See *Summa Theologiae* I–II, 26,1, 2; I–II, 28, 2.
22 *Summa Theologiae* II-II, 26, 1; E. C. Vacek, S.J., *Love, Human and Divine* (Washington, DC: Georgetown University Press, 1996).
23 See David Hollenbach, S.J., *The Common Good and Christian Ethics* (New York: Cambridge University Press, 2002).
24 *Descent*, 319.
25 See James F. Keenan, S.J., 'The Virtue of Prudence (IIa IIae, qq. 47–56)', in: Stephen J. Pope, (ed.), *The Ethics of Aquinas* (Georgetown University Press, Washington, D.C., 2002), 259–71.
26 Alexander, *Biology of Moral Systems*, 102.
27 Michael Ruse, 'Evolutionary Theory and Christian Ethics', *Zygon: Journal of Religion and Science* 29 (1994), 5–24; the quote is from p. 19.
28 William C. Spohn, *Go and Do Likewise: Jesus and Ethics* (New York: Continuum, 1999), 11.
29 Ibid.
30 See James F. Keenan, *Moral Wisdom: Lessons and Texts from the Catholic Tradition* (Kansas City: Sheed and Ward, 2004).
31 Nicholas Lash, *The Beginning and the End of 'Religion'* (New York: Cambridge University Press, 1996), 208.
32 For this approach, see Martin Daly and Margo Wilson, *Sex, Evolution, and Behavior* (North Scituate, MA: Duxbury Press, 1978) and *idem, Homicide* (New York: Aldine de Gruyter, 1988).
33 See ibid., Chapters 3–4.
34 For a response from within the moral theology, see Lisa Sowle Cahill, *Sex, Gender, and Christian Ethics* (New York: Cambridge University Press, 1996).
35 See Craig A. Boyd, 'Participation Metaphysics in Aquinas's Theory of the Natural Law', *American Catholic Philosophical Quarterly* 79.3 (2005):169–85.
36 Pamela M. Hall, *Narrative and the Natural Law: An Interpretation of Thomistic Ethics* (Notre Dame and London: University of Notre Dame Press, 1994), 94.
37 See Keenan, 'The Virtue of Prudence', 259–71.

Chapter 15

DARWIN, DIVINE PROVIDENCE AND THE SUFFERING
OF SENTIENT LIFE

JOHN F. HAUGHT

After Darwin, Catholic thought has been slow to integrate into its theologies the four-billion-year evolutionary story of life's struggling, striving
and suffering. Even though Catholic theologians renounce scriptural
literalism, the cosmological assumptions underlying their Christologies,
soteriologies and spiritualities still generally reflect a pre-evolutionary
chronological literalism in the narration and proclamation of God's creative and saving acts. Theologians, along with homilists and catechists,
continue, at least unconsciously, to imagine the created universe as having
been virtually completed by an almighty Creator *in principio*. They are
notionally aware, of course, that the traditional idea of *creatio continua*
(ongoing creation) is consistent with the fact that the universe is still
unfinished, still becoming 'more', but this aspect of creation has yet to
penetrate fully the sensibilities of many theologians, some of whom still picture the world as a static, vertical hierarchy of levels presently in progressive
decline from an integral initial state of being.

Moreover, theological anthropology has also failed to keep pace with
new scientific information about the gradualness of *human* evolution.[1]
Even though Catholic theologians do not formally contest this evidence, as
do creationists and 'intelligent design' opponents of evolution, their con-
ceptualization of sin, suffering and salvation still generally ignores scientific accounts of human emergence. Even in the face of palaeontological
evidence of the incremental arrival of modern humans out of a primate
and hominid ancestry, theologians habitually write about the creation of
human beings in the image of God as having occurred instantaneously in a
chronologically foundational event. It is not surprising then that *The Catechism of the Catholic Church* reflects this same literalism.[2] Even though
verbal scriptural literalism may have been formally abandoned, an *imaginative* literalism still provides the pictorial backdrop not only of Catholic
proclamation and religious education, where it may have pedagogical suit-
ability, but also of Catholic theological reflection, where it is confusing at
best. For many educated people, therefore, embracing Catholic faith still

seems to require an ignoring, if not suppression, of some of the most important truths they have learned from the natural sciences.

The all too frequent perception by non-Catholics that Catholic faith requires a *sacrificium intellectus* on the part of educated people is a pastoral as well as catechetical scandal that Catholic seminaries and departments of theology still fail to address adequately in the formation of students, priests and religious educators. In my own experience, the closest most Catholic pastors and clergy come to paying attention to evolutionary science is in their granting permission to lay adult religious educators to hold lectures or sponsor adult study groups on topics related to science and faith. Having delivered numerous lectures and workshops on evolution and theology at Catholic parishes in the United States over the past 35 years, I can now recall only a handful of occasions where priests in these parishes showed up as participants.

Furthermore, the theological mindset of most Catholic bishops in the world remains largely untouched by science except for issues relating to human fertility, genetics, technological advances and (occasionally) environmental abuse.[3] Even though Catholic tradition includes episodes of expansive openness to lively intellectual conversation, a high quality of exchange in ecclesiastical conversations with science is still rare. As a result, many scientifically educated Catholics now struggle unnecessarily to hold onto their faith in the age of science.[4] As long as theology, catechesis, preaching and official church documents (such as *The Catechism of the Catholic Church*) fail to connect the promises of Jesus, or the Church's sacramental life, with the fascinating new portraits of life evolving, humanity emerging and a universe still coming into being, Catholicism will fail to provide an inviting intellectual and spiritual home for many educated seekers.[5]

The reluctance of modern and contemporary Catholic thought, broadly speaking, to engage science in depth shows up most painfully in its failure to recognize that, for thoughtful people, evolution now raises serious questions about the meaning of creation, suffering, sin, redemption and especially the doctrine of providence.[6] Taking 'providence' in its most general sense, therefore, I want to ask here how Catholic thought might link Darwin's puzzling portrait of life-evolving, and especially his laying open the long and previously unknown epochs of suffering in sentient organisms, with the constant teaching that God cares for the world intimately and everlastingly.

In his recent encyclical *Spe Salvi*, Pope Benedict XVI asserts that the Christian belief in the personal providence of God contradicts the ancient assumption that nature is at the mercy of impersonal forces. Commenting on a text from Saint Gregory Nazianzen, he writes:

[. . .] at the very moment when the Magi, guided by the star, adored Christ the new king, astrology came to an end, because the stars were now moving in the orbit determined by Christ. This scene, in fact, overturns the world-view of that time, which in a different way has become fashionable once again today. It is not the elemental spirits of the universe, the laws of matter, which ultimately govern the world and mankind, but a personal God governs the stars, that is, the universe; it is not the laws of matter and of evolution that have the final say, but reason, will, love – a Person. And if we know this Person and he knows us, then truly the inexorable power of material elements no longer has the last word; we are not slaves of the universe and of its laws, we are free. In ancient times, honest enquiring minds were aware of this. Heaven is not empty. Life is not a simple product of laws and the randomness of matter, but within everything and at the same time above everything, there is a personal will, there is a Spirit who in Jesus has revealed himself as Love.[7]

This confession of faith is foundational to any Christian theology of nature. However, to many if not most scientists and philosophers today, Pope Benedict's providential vision will, quite frankly, seem unbelievable. Inspiring though his profession of faith may be to those of us who embrace Catholic faith, Benedict does not discuss in *Spe Salvi*, or any-where else that I can recall, how it is that the idea of divine 'governance' of nature does not stand in contradiction to evolutionary science. Nor does *The Catechism of the Catholic Church*, which states that 'Divine providence consists of the dispositions by which God guides all his crea-tures with wisdom and love to their ultimate end' (§ 321). Catholics may personally see no difficulties here, but the fact is that countless scientists and philosophers, as well as an increasing number of other educated people, are convinced that after Darwin the idea of a personal God who 'governs' and 'guides' the cosmos is less believable than ever. And even though Albert Einstein and other physicists may have dimly discerned an 'intelligence' behind the laws of physics, for many biologically informed scientific thinkers such an intelligence disappears altogether in the fog of evolutionary accidents, waste and wild experiments. For many, Darwin has now made the natural world look antithetical to any notion of divine providence.

To cite only one of many possible examples of such scepticism, the esteemed philosopher Philip Kitcher, in his readable new book *Living with Darwin*, declares that 'a history of life dominated by natural selection is extremely hard to understand in providentialist terms'. Highlighting the struggle, suffering and long duration of evolution, Kitcher concludes that 'there is nothing kindly or providential about any of this, and it seems breathtakingly wasteful and inefficient. Indeed if we imagine a human observer presiding over a miniaturized version of the whole show, peering down on his "creation" it is extremely hard to equip the face with a kindly expression'.[8]

The question of evolution's compatibility with trust in divine providence has been central to the conversation of theology and science ever since Darwin's own day,[9] but in my opinion Catholic theology is still, generally speaking, reluctant to face this issue head-on. Even Pope John Paul II's 1996 public approval of evolutionary biology did not address the difficulty so many scientists and philosophers have especially in reconciling the high degree of contingency in evolution with divine providence.[10] The 2004 International Theological Commission, working under the supervision of Joseph Cardinal Ratzinger, later Pope Benedict XVI, acknowledged that 'according to the Catholic understanding of divine causality, true contingency in the created order is not incompatible with a purposeful divine providence'. But the document does not speak directly to Kitcher's complaints. It simply asserts that:

> [. . .] even the outcome of a truly contingent natural process can nonetheless fall within God's providential plan for creation. According to St Thomas Aquinas, 'the effect of divine providence is not only that things should happen somehow, but that they should happen either by necessity or by contingency. Therefore, whatsoever divine providence ordains to happen infallibly and of necessity happens infallibly and of necessity; and that happens from contingency, which the divine providence conceives to happen from contingency (*Summa Theologiae*, I, 22, 4 ad 1)'. In the Catholic perspective, neo-Darwinians who adduce random genetic variation and natural selection as evidence that the process of evolution is absolutely unguided are straying beyond what can be demonstrated by science. Divine causality can be active in a process that is both contingent and guided.[11]

There is at least a willingness here on the part of theologians to face the fact of accidents in nature, but from the point of view of critics such as Kitcher the notion of providential 'guidance' makes no sense at all in the light of the high degree of chance in evolution. Kitcher cites St Basil the Great's reference to non-Christian thinkers 'who deceived by the atheism they bore within them, imagined that the universe lacked guidance and order, as if it were at the mercy of chance'.[12] But then he goes on to argue in effect that Darwin has once again restored to respectability the pre-Christian (atheistic) view that nature and life are indeed at 'the mercy of chance' and other impersonal influences.[13] The International Theological Commission states that 'an unguided evolutionary process – one that falls outside the bounds of divine providence – simply cannot exist because . . . [according to Thomas Aquinas] 'all things, inasmuch as they participate in existence, must likewise be subject to divine providence (*Summa Theologiae* I, 22, 2)'. But Kitcher's criticism still leaves theology with the important project of specifying how it is that a process can be both contingent and 'governed', to use Pope Benedict's term, or 'guided' as the International Theological Commission states. *The Catechism* (§ 302) teaches that 'by his providence God protects and governs all things which he has made, 'reaching mightily from one end of the earth to the other, and ordering all things well'. But what can 'govern', and 'guide', and 'order' mean when we try to understand how providence relates to the meandering, experimental, awkward and accident-driven ways of evolution? With respect to evolution, after all, the idea of providential governance or guidance even seems to exacerbate the question of how God's capacity to 'order' events could also be consistent with an infinite love. Moreover, if providence entails a divine 'plan' (*The Catechism* § 306) or 'design', critics of Catholic teaching rightly wonder how God's capacity to oversee everything protects providence from the accusation of complicity in the excessive suffering of sentient life.

Theologically speaking, three features of evolution seem particularly difficult to square with the understanding of divine governance as expressed, for example, in *The Catechism* and in the citation given above from Pope Benedict's recent encyclical *Spe Salvi*. First, there is the enormously *high amount* of accidents in evolution. As we now realize, random genetic mutations provide the raw material of evolutionary change, but they also bring about extravagant loss, death and extinctions, not just opportunities for creative new evolutionary outcomes. How do undirected genetic mutations and other contingencies in natural history that shape the trajectory of life – events such as asteroid impacts, earthquakes and sudden climatic changes – fall within a theologically acceptable vision of divine 'governance' or providential 'guidance' of the world?

Second, what sense can theology make, providentially speaking, of the *impersonality* of natural selection, the Darwinian mechanism that ruthlessly discards most instances of life while preserving, at least temporarily, only a few adaptive versions? If selection is a 'secondary cause' through which providence orders nature, what is the nature of the 'primary' providential guidance that it fails to prevent the excessive degree of loss and apparent unfairness in the creation of living diversity?

And, third, if evolutionary science and contemporary theology are telling us the truth about nature, what is the providential meaning of the fact that our Big Bang universe takes nine billion years to give rise to the first living cells, and then labours, blindly it would seem, through four billion more years of striving, struggling and suffering before producing conscious organisms that now spend an inordinate amount of their brief life-spans asking why suffering needs to happen at all?

In view of Darwin's three-part recipe for evolutionary diversity – chance, selection and deep time – is there any plausible place left for a theologically illuminating understanding of divine providence? Before attempting a response, theologians must also take into account the fact that, at least as far as scientific naturalists like Kitcher are concerned, Darwinian biology at last offers a fully satisfying answer to the question of why innocent living beings, including humans, have to put up with suffering. According to the naturalistic account, were it not for the irritation of pain, living beings could not adapt to a dangerous world. According to Darwin, 'all sentient beings have been formed so as to enjoy, as a general rule, happiness', but pain or suffering is 'well adapted to make a creature guard against any great or sudden evil'.[14] If they lacked the capacity for pain or suffering, whose function is to signal the presence of danger or the prospect of death, many living beings would perish before having the opportunity to mate and reproduce. To the scientific naturalist, this evolutionary account of suffering seems sufficient. And even if the nervous systems of some organisms tend at times to be hyper-sensitive, thus making their torment excessive, this is just further evidence to the scientific naturalist that providence has no role whatsoever to play in 'guiding' the story of life.

In contemporary biology, Darwinians account for the suffering of sentient life more specifically in terms of the migration of populations of genes from one generation to the next. Genes have a better chance of surviving into future generations if they occupy organisms that are able to tell when danger or death is imminent. Survivable populations of genes do well, therefore, to jump aboard 'vehicles' whose sensitive nervous systems increase the probability of their being passed on to future generations. In evolutionary history, after life had become enormously complex, organisms whose genes had by accident programmed them for the experience of pain had a higher probability of surviving than those that did not. Reflecting on the adaptive role of suffering, many scientifically informed people today wonder, then, why there is any need to look for a providential meaning to life's suffering at all, including our own.

1. Order and Expiation

Complicating our theological inquiry further is the fact that the notion of a providential design or plan for creation provides a necessary presupposition for the idea of an original ancestral transgression and for the expiatory interpretation of evil and suffering that has accompanied it. As Pierre Teilhard de Chardin observed in 1933:

> In spite of the subtle distinctions of the theologians, it is a matter *of fact* that Christianity has developed under the over-riding impression that all the evil round us was born from an initial transgression. So far as dogma is concerned we are still living in the atmosphere of a universe in which what matters most is reparation and expiation. The vital problem, both

for Christ and us, is to get rid of a stain. This accounts for the importance, at least in theory, of the idea of sacrifice, and for the interpretation almost exclusively in terms of purification. It explains, too, the pre-eminence in Christology of the idea of redemption and the shedding of blood.[15]

The theological assumptions to which Teilhard is pointing still underlie the general understanding of evil and suffering in Catholic seminaries, schools of theology and official ecclesiastical documents. These assumptions also persist in the spiritual sensibilities of countless lay people. The recent film *The Passion of the Christ*, produced by actor Mel Gibson, is a vivid portrayal of an approach to the problem of evil and suffering that many Catholics still appreciate: the worse the offence against a divinely established order, the more intense the suffering needed to expiate it. So by portraying in the most graphic terms the sufferings of Jesus, the innocent victim, the faithful can be assured that atonement for their sins has been more than fully supplied.

Of course, at times Catholic theology has experimented with other ways of thinking about the suffering of Christ. Emphasis on redemption for sins in terms of expiation by the shedding of Christ's blood is not the only way of understanding what God is doing in the Incarnation, public ministry, crucifixion and Resurrection of Jesus. Recently, some Catholic theologians, perhaps influenced by Teilhard as well as by the much earlier writings of St Irenaeus and Duns Scotus, have linked Christ's salvific significance more tightly to the doctrine of creation than had been customary in Western theology.[16] And some Catholic theologians are beginning to pay closer attention to Eastern Christianity's theme of divinization as central to the work of Christ.[17] Nevertheless, as Teilhard rightly points out, the mythic idea that a primordially perfect order was disturbed long ago by a sinful human act of rebellion against God continues to provide the temporal coordinates of Catholic religious instruction about evil, suffering and redemption.

Such a schema implies that the work of Christ is essentially an expiatory sacrifice for the *initial* transgression along with the history of sin pursuant to it. The Cross is a necessary condition of *restoring* the created cosmic perfection that had become unsettled in the beginning. Most Catholics are still comfortable with this way of narrating the story of salvation. However, if taken literally – as the imaginative framework of Christology, soteriology and eschatology – it has the inevitable effect of bending our ethical and religious aspirations more deliberately towards repairing (reparation of) a lost perfection and less towards participating actively in the breaking in of a truly new and unprecedented future of creation up ahead. Nostalgia for a state of initial perfection easily becomes a substitute for real hope, in which case, as Teilhard emphasizes, ethical existence loses the 'zest for living' that might connect human obligation to the creative bringing about of *more being*.[18] The supplanting of hope by nostalgia may also gain support from the Church's liturgical life and even its Eucharistic theology whenever exponents of the latter interpret the Mass exclusively as a re-enactment of Christ's expiatory sacrifice rather than (also) as a foretaste of eschatological communion with God, or as an incentive for all of us to participate enthusiastically in the ongoing creation of the cosmos as essential to the coming of God's reign.

An exclusively expiatory understanding of suffering and evil tends inherently to support religious opposition to evolution. Its emphasis on human suffering prevents theology from arriving at an understanding of divine providence that would take into account the undeniable fact of life's passage through a long history of innocent suffering to which any notion of expiation would be inapplicable. To the extent that faith and worship continue to be shaped dominantly in accordance with the themes of expiation and reparation instead of the motif of new creation, contemporary Catholic theology will persist in evading objections such as Kitcher's concerning the doctrine of providence after Darwin.

The belief that God 'provides' or cares intimately for the creation is central to the Abrahamic faiths. Indeed, these traditions stand or fall with the believability of the doctrine that God is involved, active and 'interested' in the creation. The general notion of providence functions for the Abrahamic faiths comparably to the way in which a theoretical core functions in science. Following loosely the terminology of philosopher Imre Lakatos (1922–74), we note that in science, a theory – for example, the geocentric theory of celestial motion – inevitably comes under attack sooner or later. So, as more precise observations begin to accumulate, a belt of 'auxiliary hypotheses', is invented to protect the core of the theory.[19] In order to save the geocentric theory, once it became evident that planets in the solar system fail to follow the predicted paths, astronomers contrived the idea that planets revolve in epicycles around imaginary points on their main orbit of Earth. A protective belt of auxiliary hypotheses, especially the idea of epicycles, helped to save the theoretical core of Ptolemaic cosmology for centuries. Nevertheless, eventually the whole system collapsed when the auxiliary hypotheses were shown to be groundless and could no longer protect the theoretical core.

Let us suppose then that the claim that 'the universe is in the hands of a providential God who is faithful and deserves our trust' is something like the 'theoretical core' of biblically-based faith traditions; then allow the classic doctrine of expiation to stand in relation to this core analogously to the way in which an auxiliary hypothesis functions to protect the central content of a scientific theory. The point of this comparison is to suggest that the theology of expiation is not the main point of biblical faith, and that it is tied in a subordinate, rather than definitional way, to trust in divine providence.

If the core teaching of biblical faith is that God is faithful and deserves our trust, then every other theological claim must support that claim whenever it is challenged. For example, in the midst of suffering, as the experience of Job, the prophets and Jesus all testify, the challenging question arises: 'Why, God, have you abandoned me (or us)?' A frequent response has been that God has *not* abandoned us at all but is transforming our sufferings into expiation so that, along with those of Christ, they can be redemptive and thus endowed with an eternal meaning.[20] In classical soteriology, the auxiliary hypothesis of expiation has served to save the more fundamental theme that God is faithful and will not allow suffering and death to be devoid of meaning. After Darwin, however, the expiatory theme appears, in the light of sentient life's long history of suffering and perishing, to have become as problematic as epicycles in modern astronomy.

Another 'auxiliary hypothesis', related to but still distinguishable from that of expiation, proposes that suffering is divine pedagogy. Our own suffering makes sense if we can learn to appreciate it as educational, as challenging us to practice virtue, or as training us to trust in God. This is why God 'chastises' those whom God loves (see, for example, Hebrews 12:5ff). Here, the meaning of suffering consists of its providing a *school* for the development of virtue, character, or 'soul'.[21] Our sufferings, when viewed as pedagogical, do not constitute evidence contrary to the central 'theory' that God cares for us. Instead, our sufferings are a sign that providence is watching over us even *in extremis*.

Once again, however, after Darwin one has to ask how applicable this auxiliary hypothesis is in view of the suffering of nonhuman life. Why, we might ask, do all the other living species have to go to school with us? The idea that evolution is theologically justifiable as divine pedagogy seems especially crude. Kitcher refers to this kind of theodicy as an 'ambitious providentialism'. It is unable to justify all the suffering of nonhuman life without making God seem monstrous:

> When you consider the millions of years in which sentient creatures have suffered, the uncountable number of extended and agonizing deaths, it simply rings hollow to suppose that all this is needed so that, at the very tail end of history, our species can manifest the allegedly transcendent good of free will and virtuous action. There is every reason to think that alternative processes for unfolding the history of life could have eliminated much of the agony, that the goal could have been achieved without so long and bloody a prelude.[22]

So in the wake of the evolutionary picture of life, not to mention the horrors of the Holocaust, both expiation and education now seem to have spent much of their theological utility. If they still have explanatory power it is only because they point to a wider and deeper truth. To scientifically informed sceptics such as Kitcher, they clearly fail to protect the idea of providence from the charge of incoherence. So Catholic theology after Darwin must also ask whether theodicies based on the themes of expiation and divine pedagogy can any longer bolster our trust that a beneficent providence is deeply involved and interested in our universe. Are they perhaps like the epicycles of ancient and medieval astronomy that eventually became stressed to the point of collapse by the accumulation of fresh astronomical data pointing to a heliocentric system of the skies that had at one time been inconceivable? Is the new evolutionary portrayal of life's long and wide expanse of innocent suffering now providing data that may require a similarly drastic reconfiguration of the Catholic theological heavens?

Moreover, instead of offering a good reason to trust in God, is it not the case that fixation on the 'auxiliary' ideas of expiation and education may even serve to justify suffering rather than provide the motivation to destroy it?[23] Whenever our theologies tie providence too closely to order, expiation, and pedagogy, they may open up a lawful space for suffering in the whole scheme of things. The theodicies of expiation and education, of course, are part of the perennial religious quest for an always deeper coherence. However, limited auxiliary hypotheses must be held to tentatively, not frozen into timeless truths around which everything else in theology must then revolve. Once the auxiliary explanations themselves are turned into indispensable components of a theological system they may begin to function – like epicycles in the history of astronomy – to suppress the appropriation of relevant new information that may at times require a *radical* renewal of faith and theology.

The expiatory vision still functions in Catholic and other Christian presentations of the mystery of redemption to forestall a fully open embrace of evolution and its implications. In its own way so also does the theodicy of divine pedagogy, but for simplicity's sake I shall concentrate here only on the theme of expiation. Is it conceivable, I want to ask, that over the course of time expiatory theology has shifted away from the status of being a tentative auxiliary satellite helping to centralize the doctrine of divine fidelity, and has at least at times become the centre around which a diminished idea of providence is itself now forced to orbit?

The conviction that providence is an ordering principle can easily support the human obsession with expiation. The philosopher Paul Ricoeur has argued persuasively that there is a close tie-in between the demand for expiation on the one hand and the craving for stability and fixed order on the other. In society's, or our own, infliction of pain and punishment on others, the excuse is that we have to carry out such penalties, including maiming and hanging, in order to sustain or bring about the allegedly higher good of social order. This is why sacred cosmologies have often been construed on the model of, and for the sake of legitimating, a given social order.[24]

Although the idea of providence-as-design has been taken over, unconsciously perhaps, to justify expiatory visions of suffering, it is noteworthy that the Bible itself struggles to deliver suffering from a purely expiatory interpretation.[25] When Job objects to the unfairness of his suffering, his friends attempt to bolster his trust in a providential divine order or 'plan' by undertaking a relentless search for the hidden guilt in Job's life. Their assumption is that, once this guilt has been acknowledged, Job's suffering can make sense as expiation, and then the good order of his life and the cosmos will be restored. Yet, even as these expiatory arguments are exposed as empty, so also is the assumption that Job (or we) can here and now have a clear sense of any divine 'plan' (Job 38).

In spite of the Bible's own internal struggles to transcend it, the expiatory vision of redemption still wields great power over souls. The compulsive need to punish others or ourselves still gains legitimacy from the motif of expiation. This is deeply ironic from a Christian point of view, especially since Jesus' own life and preaching seek to take us beyond the expiatory vision towards the sense of a God whose love overtakes us while we are 'still in our sins', a love that shines indiscriminately on the evil and the good alike (Matthew 5:45). Instead of crushing the life out of sinners by demanding expiation, divine love offers new life unceasingly. Suffering may still persist, but it calls out for a theological setting that transcends or relativizes the role of expiation and education (divine pedagogy). Why so?

2. Evolution as Theological Opportunity

Evolution, it would appear, entails an account of God's creation in which the idea of a chronologically initial and integral created order is inconceivable. Consequently, a literal understanding of myths about an ancestral human disturbance of order, and hence the instinct to expiate such an imagined disturbance by way of suffering and punishment, must now have questionable applicability. Darwin's story of life's suffering challenges theology to ask in what sense, if at all, the symbiosis of expiation with the idea of providential order is any longer credible. Evolution invites Catholic theology to enrich its understanding of providential 'guidance' by uniting it to the more fundamental biblical understanding of providence-as-*promise*. Rather than simply governing what is, or restoring what once was, divine providence means God's constant 'providing' the creation with possibilities of becoming truly new.

Does this mean that a theology that takes evolution seriously requires a break with Catholic tradition, as my proposal may seem at first to be promoting? I suggest just the opposite. Making the theme of promise more central than 'guidance' or 'governance' in our quest to understand the meaning of providence after Darwin is radical only in the positive sense of returning to the biblical roots of Catholic faith. Evolution invites theology to connect the natural world no less than human history to the Abrahamic God who opens up a fresh future to all of creation, and 'who makes all things new'. The Bible, after all, belongs to Catholics too.

Of course, in opposition to this reconfiguration, intelligent design advocates, including some Catholics, still defend the idea of providential 'governance' by attempting to show that the evidence for Darwinian biology is scientifically weak or non-existent.[26] And it is no coincidence that the most fervent defenders of an expiatory theology, including not only evangelical Christians but some Catholics as well, are those for whom the idea of providence implies a fixed plan into which evolutionary information simply does not comfortably fit.[27] However, instead of being so defensive in the face of evolution, and instead of desperately arguing for 'intelligent design' and a providential 'plan', Darwin's new picture of life offers to Catholic thought a great opportunity to become more biblically grounded than ever.[28]

What I mean specifically is that after Darwin, theology may replace a spirituality based on nostalgia for a lost perfection with one based on hope for the coming of a new and unprecedented future in a creative process that is still far from finished. Expiation and education can now give way more deliberately than ever to *expectation* – that is, hope – as the fundamental setting for theology's response to the evil of suffering. Instead of asking why God permits the suffering of life, and rather than trying to find an *intelligible* place for suffering within either a religious or Darwinian understanding of the world, theology's proper stance is to identify itself with life's suffering in crying out for final redemption from all pain and death.

Of course, religious instruction and popular piety will continue understandably to use traditional expressions such as God's plan, guidance, design and governance to express confidence in a providential God. But Catholic theology, especially after Vatican II's document *Dei Verbum*, now has the responsibility of letting a more substantially biblical understanding of faith purify our ideas of providence from medieval and modern accretions that at least tacitly deny the openness of nature to indeterminate creative evolutionary outcomes. God's intimate care for creation is not exhausted in an original moment of magical, finished perfection, nor in maintaining the cosmic status quo, but in being the world's ever faithful Future. It is hard to conceive of a more intimate kind of Care than a divine presence that breathes into the world the promise: 'You will forever have a new Future and I will always be that Future!' In this promissory understanding of providence, the intelligibility and coherence of our still evolving world can be glimpsed not by pining for a primordial state of a perfection now lost in the past but only by our looking in hope towards what Karl Rahner calls the Absolute Future.[29]

In this promissory vision of nature and evolution, the high degree of contingency in Darwin's evolutionary recipe, which neither Kitcher nor his anti-evolutionist religious opponents can reconcile with their fixed assumption that providence must mean perfect design, is completely consistent with the idea of a providential care that keeps the universe open to a new future. After all, a completely ordered universe, one devoid of any accidents, would be frozen so stiff that there would be no room for life, freedom, or anything new to happen at all. Likewise, the alleged impersonality of natural selection is also compatible with a promissory sense of divine providence. Without predictable, recurrent, or 'lawful' routines, the natural world would lack the consistency and continuity that would allow it even to have a future connected to its present and past. And finally, the fact that evolution takes so long – at least when measured from our human calendrical point of view – is completely compatible with a providence that is caring enough to grant the world ample time to experiment with a rich array of possible forms of being, and in this way participate in its own creation.

By way of summary, then, after Darwin we may now speak in a more biblical way than ever of divine providential Care as operating characteristically in the mode of promise. God's providential activity is, before all else, that of providing a vision (a dream?) of how the world may become new, of keeping a space open for life and human freedom, and of inviting conscious and free beings to awaken to a life of hope, creative participation and joyful *waiting* for the fulfilment of all things. Our remembrance of the suffering of *all* of life can include the hope that this 'prelude' (to used Kitcher's term) is also subject to God's promise of new creation. A biblically informed Catholic theology after Darwin may think of God's fidelity as that of always giving the *whole* world a future, a future that will bring all things to fulfilment and an end to the suffering of *all* of life. If we can learn (again) to think of providence as promise, and not simply as guidance, order, design or plan, such an understanding would be wide enough to embrace and render more meaningful than ever the new scientific information about evolution.[30]

Notes

1 For a theologically appreciative study of this evidence see Wentzel van Huyssteen, *Alone in the World?: Human Uniqueness in Science and Theology* (Grand Rapids: Wm. B. Eerdmans Publishing Company, 2006).

2 *The Catechism of the Catholic Church* § 396–421, see http://www.catholic doors.com/catechis/. See also Joan Acker, H. M., 'Creation and Catholicism', *America* (16 Dec. 2000), 6–8; Daryl Domning, 'Evolution, Evil, and Original Sin', *America* (12 Nov. 2001) at https://www.americamagazine.org/content/article.cfm?article_id=1205.

3 On the struggle of modern Catholic popes and bishops to come to grips with science, see Don O'Leary, *Roman Catholicism and Modern Science* (New York: Continuum, 2006). A notable exception among Catholic bishops is Józef Życiński, author of *God and Evolution: Fundamental Questions of Christian Evolutionism*, trans. Kenneth W. Kemp and Zuzanna Maslanka (Washington, D.C.: Catholic University of America Press, 2006).

4 I can testify to this fact personally, and anecdotally, because of countless letters I have received over the years from many Catholic and other Christian scientists expressing gratitude that my own books have argued that faith and theology are completely consonant with science, including evolution.

5 However, *The Catechism of the Catholic Church* (§ 302) states that even though 'Creation has its own goodness and proper perfection', 'it did not spring forth complete from the hands of the Creator. The universe was created "in a state of journeying" *(in statu viae)* towards an ultimate perfection yet to be attained, to which God has destined it' (§ 303). The witness of Scripture is unanimous that the solicitude of divine providence is *concrete* and *immediate*; God cares for all, from the least things to the great events of the world and its history. The sacred books powerfully affirm God's absolute sovereignty over the course of events: 'Our God is in the heavens; he does whatever he pleases' (Ps 115:3). And so it is with Christ, 'who opens and no one shall shut, who shuts and no one opens' (Rev 3:7). As the book of Proverbs states: 'Many are the plans in the mind of a man, but it is the purpose of the Lord that will be established' (Prov 19:21). (See: *The Catechism* § 269).

6 Even John Thiel, who provides an otherwise sophisticated discussion of human suffering and the question of God, has little to say about the larger story of evolution and the innocent suffering of nonhuman life. See his *God, Evil, and Innocent Suffering: A Theological Reflection* (New York: Crossroad, 2002).

7 Pope Benedict XVI, *Encyclical Letter Spe Salvi*, § 5: http://www.vatican.va/holy_father/benedict_xvi/encyclicals/documents/hf_ben-xvi_enc_20071130_spe-salvi_en.html.

8 Philip Kitcher, *Living With Darwin: Evolution, Design, and the Future of Faith* (New York: Oxford University Press, 2006), 124.

9 Charles Coulston Gillispie, *Genesis and Geology: A Study in the Relations of Scientific Thought, Natural Theology, and Social Opinion in Great Britain, 1790–1850*, (Cambridge, Mass.: Harvard University Press, 1996), 18; 220.

10 Pope John Paul II, 'Address of Pope John Paul II to the Pontifical Academy of Sciences', (22 October 1996), in: *Origins, CNS Documentary Service* (5 December 1996).

11 'Communion and Stewardship: Human Persons Created in the Image of God', International Theological Commission (July, 2004), § 69. See: http://www.bringyou.to/apologetics/p80.htm

12 Kitcher, 73.

13 Kitcher, 73–116. Kitcher, like Richard Dawkins and other evolutionary materialists, apparently thinks that his critique of intelligent design is enough to have demonstrated that the only other realistic option is a world devoid of any providential influence.

14 Nora Barlow (ed.), *The Autobiography of Charles Darwin* (New York: Harcourt, 1958), 89.

15 Pierre Teilhard de Chardin, *Christianity and Evolution*, trans. René Hague (New York: Harcourt Brace & Co., 1969), 81.

16 See, for example, Eileen Flynn and Gloria Thomas, *Living Faith: An Introduction to Theology*, 2nd Edition (New York: Rowman and Littlefield, 1989), 246–56.

17 On 'divinization' and its meaning for Christians East and West, see Stephen Finlan and Vladimir Kharlamov (eds), *Theiosis, Deification in Christian Theology* (Eugene, Ore.: Pickwick Publications, 2006).

18 Pierre Teilhard de Chardin, *Activation of Energy*, trans. René Hague (New York: Harcourt Brace Jovanovich, Inc., 1970), 231–43; and Pierre Teilhard de Chardin, *How I Believe*, trans. René Hague (New York: Harper & Row, 1969), 42.

19 Imre Lakatos, *The Methodology of Scientific Research Programmes: Philosophical Papers Volume 1* (Cambridge: Cambridge University Press, 1978).

20 An expiatory theology may therefore reinforce the belief that God remains faithful, no matter how severe our suffering is. But unfortunately it may happen that expiation, with its inherent linkage to the need to maintain a divinely established order, may itself gradually become the inner core of a person's or community's religious understanding. Then, simultaneously, the idea of God or providence can begin in fact to function as an auxiliary hypothesis to support the order/expiation complex. Whenever providence is thought of solely in terms of guidance, plan, or design it may lend itself to such abuse. On the legitimating role that the idea of God can play with respect to human conceptions of societal order see Peter Berger, *The Sacred Canopy* (Garden City, N.Y.: Anchor Books, 1990).

21 John Hick, *Evil and the God of Love*, Revised edition (New York: Harper & Row, 1978).

22 Kitcher, 126–7.

23 See, for example, Terrence Tilley, *The Evils of Theodicy* (Washington, D.C.: Georgetown University Press, 1991).

24 See Paul Ricoeur. *The Conflict of Interpretations: Essays in Hermeneutics*, edited by Don Ihde (Evanston, IL: Northwestern University Press, 1974), 354–77. In an expiatory understanding of suffering, 'punishment only serves to preserve an already established order.' Paul Ricoeur, *History and Truth*, trans. Charles Kelbley (Evanston: Northwestern University Press, 1965), 125.

25 Ricoeur, *Conflict*, 354–77. As Gerd Theissen has argued, the central message of the Letter to the Hebrews is that expiation is now religiously obsolete. Christ entered the temple once and for all. Gerd Theissen *The Open Door*, trans. John Bowden (Minneapolis: Fortress Press, 1991), 161–7.

26 It is ultimately for this reason, it seems to me, that Christoph Cardinal Schönborn, at the incentive of American 'intelligent design' advocates, submitted an essay 'Finding Design in Nature' that was highly critical of 'neo-Darwinian' science to the *New York Times* (7 July 2005).

27 In general, the conservative Catholic journal *First Things* publishes articles that ignore the contingency of evolution. See, for example, the recent discussion of evolution by Christoph Cardinal Schönborn, 'The Designs of Science,' *First Things* (Jan. 2006): http://www.firstthings.com/article.php3?id_article=71)

28 I have developed this point in much more detail in *God After Darwin: A Theology of Evolution*, 2nd Edition (Boulder, Colo: Westview Press, 2007); and *Christianity and Science: Toward a Theology of Nature* (Maryknoll, New York: Orbis Press, 2007).

29 Karl Rahner, *Theological Investigation*, Vol. VI, trans. Karl and Boniface Kruger (Baltimore: Helicon, 1969), 59–68. See also Wolfhart Pannenberg,

Faith and Reality, trans. John Maxwell (Philadelphia: Westminster Press, 1977), 58–9; and Ted Peters, *God – The World's Future: Systematic Theology for a New Era*, 2nd Edition. Minneapolis: Fortress Press, 2000).

30 I do not have the space in this essay to deal with the many other relevant questions raised by my proposal to ground the doctrine of providence more firmly in the biblical theme of promise. For example, there is the great mystery of why the Creator would create an unfinished rather than a finished universe in the first place. For a small beginning to such a discussion I would refer the reader to my books *God After Darwin* and *Christianity and Science*.

GUIDE TO FURTHER READING

The following select bibliography offers a sample of recent work directly related to this volume's main line of inquiry, and published in the English language. The reader is reminded that many of the primary sources regarding Charles Darwin and regarding the official position of the Catholic Church are available online at:

http://darwin-online.org.uk/
http://www.vatican.va/archive/index.htm
http://www.vatican.va/offices/papal_docs_list.html

General

Häring, Hermann, 'The Theory of Evolution as a Megatheory of Western Thought', *Concilium* (2000), 23–34.

Haught, John F., *Is Nature Enough? Meaning and Truth in the Age of Science* (Cambridge: Cambridge University Press, 2006).

Ruse, Michael, *Darwinism and its Discontents* (Cambridge; New York: Cambridge University Press, 2006).

——, *Can a Darwinian be a Christian? The relationship between science and religion* (Cambridge: Cambridge University Press, 2001).

Russell, R. J., Stoeger, W. R., Ayala, F. J. (eds), *Evolutionary and Molecular Biology: Scientific Perspectives on Divine Action* (Vatican City State: Vatican Observatory Publications, 1998).

History

Artigas, Mariano, Glick, Thomas F., & Martínez, Rafael A., *Negotiating Darwin: The Vatican Confronts Evolution 1877–1902* (Baltimore: The Johns Hopkins University Press, 2006).

Brooke, John Hedley, ' "Laws Impressed on Matter by the Creator"? The Origin and the Question of Religion', in: Michael Ruse & Robert J. Richards, (eds), *The Cambridge Companion to the 'Origin of Species'* (Cambridge: Cambridge University Press, 2008).

Desmond, Andrew, & Moore, James, *Darwin. The Life of a Tormented Evolutionist* (New York/London: W. H. Norton & Company, 1994).

Dupré, Louis, *Religion and the Rise of Modern Culture* (Indiana: University of Notre Dame Press, 2008).

Hawkins, Mike, *Social Darwinism in European and American Thought, 1860–1945: Nature as Model and Nature as Threat* (Cambridge: Cambridge University Press, 1997).

Kelly, Alfred, *The Descent of Darwin: The Popularization of Darwinism in Germany, 1860–1914* (Chapel Hill: University of North Carolina Press, 1981).

Lindberg, David C., & Numbers, Ronald L. (eds), *God and Nature* (University of California Press, 1986).

Numbers, Ronald L., & Stenhouse, John (eds), *Disseminating Darwinism: The Role of Place, Race, Religion and Gender* (Cambridge: Cambridge University Press, 1999).

O'Leary, Don, *Roman Catholicism and Modern Science: A History* (New York: Continuum, 2006).

Paul, Harry W., *The Edge of Contingency: French Catholic Reaction to Scientific Change from Darwin to Duhem* (Gainesville: University Presses of Florida, 1979).

——, 'Religion and Darwinism: Varieties of Catholic Reaction', in: *The Comparative Reception of Darwinism*, edited by Thomas F. Glick (Austin: University of Texas Press, 1974), 403–36.

Schmitz-Moormann, Karl, 'Evolution in the Catholic Theological Tradition', in: S. Andersen & A. Peacocke (eds), *Evolution and Creation: A European Perspective* (Aarhus: Aarhus University Press, 1987); 121–31.

Philosophy

Ayala, Francisco, 'Biology Precedes, Culture Transcends: An Evolutionist's View of Human Nature', *Zygon* 33/4 (1998): 507–23.

Barrera, Albino, *Economic Compulsion and Christian Ethics* (Cambridge: Cambridge University Press, 2005).

Boyd, Craig A., 'Was Thomas Aquinas a Sociobiologist? Thomistic Natural Law, Rational Goods, and Sociobiology', *Zygon* 39 (2004): 659–80.

Dupré, John, *Human Nature and the Limits of Science* (Oxford: Oxford University Press, 2001).

Grygiel, Wojciech P., 'The Metaphysics of Chaos: A Thomistic View of Entropy and Evolution', *Thomist* 66 (2002): 251–66.

Maurer, Armand, 'Darwin, Thomists, and Secondary Causality,' *The Review of Metaphysics*, 57 (2004): 491–514.

McMullin, Ernan, 'Evolution and Special Creation,' in: David L. Hull & Michael Ruse (eds), *The Philosophy of Biology* (Oxford Readings in Philosophy) (Oxford: Oxford University Press, 1998), 698–733.

Miller, Kenneth R., *Finding Darwin's God* (New York: HarperCollins Publishers, 1999).

O'Hear, Anthony, *Beyond Evolution: Human Nature and the Limits of Evolutionary Explanation* (Oxford: Oxford University Press, 1997).

Pope, Stephen J., *The Evolution of Altruism and the Ordering of Love* (Washington, D.C.: Georgetown University Press, 1994).

Swindal, James C., & Gensler, Harry J. (eds), *The Sheed & Ward Anthology of Catholic Philosophy* (Lanham, MD: Rowman & Littlefield, 2005).

Trigg, Roger, *The Shaping of Man: Philosophical Aspects of Socio-Biology* (Oxford: Basil Blackwell, 1982).

van Inwagen, Peter, 'Genesis and Evolution', in: Peter van Inwagen, *God, Knowledge & Mystery: Essays in Philosophical Theology* (Ithaca, NY: Cornell University Press, 1995), 128–62.

Theology

Gregersen, Niels Henrik & Görman, Ulf (eds), *Design and Disorder: Perspectives from Science and Theology* (Edinburgh: T & T Clark, 2002).

Grumett, David, *Teilhard de Chardin. Theology, Humanity and Cosmos* (Leuven: Peeters, 2005).

Haught, John, *God after Darwin* (Oxford: Westview Press, 2007).

McGrath, Alister, *Dawkins' God: Genes, Memes, and the Meaning of Life* (Oxford: Blackwell, 2005).

Peacocke, Arthur, *God and the New Biology* (New York: HarperCollins, 1986).

Pope, Stephen J., *Human Evolution and Christian Ethics* (New York: Cambridge University Press, 2007).

Rahner, Karl, *Hominsation: the Evolutionary Origin of Man as a Theological Problem* (Freiburg: Herder, 1965).

Ratzinger, Joseph, *In the Beginning. A Catholic Understanding of Creation and the Fall*, trans. Boniface Ramsey (Grand Rapids: Eerdmans, 1995).

Stebbins, J. Michael, *The Divine Initiative: Grace, World Order, and Human Freedom in the Early Writings of Bernard Lonergan* (Toronto: University of Toronto Press, 1995).

van Huyssteen, Wentzel, *Alone in the World?: Human Uniqueness in Science and Theology* (Grand Rapids: Wm. B. Eerdmans Publishing Company, 2006).

Życiński, J., *God and Evolution: Fundamental Questions of Christian Evolutionism* (Washington, D.C.: Catholic Press of America, 2006).

INDEX